Community and Worldview among Paraiyars of South India

Bloomsbury Advances in Religious Studies

Series Editors: James Cox, Craig Martin and Steven Sutcliffe

This groundbreaking series offers original reflections on theory and method in the study of religions, and demonstrates new approaches to the way religious traditions are studied and presented.

Studies published under its auspices look to clarify the role and place of Religious Studies in the academy, but not in a purely theoretical manner. Each study will demonstrate its theoretical aspects by applying them to the actual study of religions, often in the form of frontier research.

Other titles available in the series:

Appropriation of Native American Spirituality, Suzanne Owen

Becoming Buddhist, Glenys Eddy

Conceptions of the Afterlife in Early Civilizations, Gregory Shushan

Contemporary Western Ethnography and the Definition of Religion, Martin D. Stringer

Cultural Blending In Korean Death Rites, Chang-Won Park

Globalization of Hesychasm and the Jesus Prayer, Christopher D. L. Johnson

Innateness of Myth, Ritske Rensma

Levinas, Messianism and Parody, Terence Holden

New Paradigm of Spirituality and Religion, MaryCatherine Burgess

Redefining Shamanisms, David Gordon Wilson

Reform, Identity and Narratives of Belonging, Arkotong Longkumer

Religion and the Discourse on Modernity, Paul-François Tremlett

Religion as a Conversation Starter, Ina Merdjanova

Religion, Material Culture and Archaeology, Julian Droogan

Spirit Possession and Trance, Patrice Brodeur

Spiritual Tourism, Alex Norman

Theology and Religious Studies in Higher Education, Edited by D. L. Bird and Simon G. Smith

Community and Worldview among Paraiyars of South India

‘Lived’ Religion

Anderson H. M. Jeremiah

BLOOMSBURY
NEW DELHI • LONDON • OXFORD • NEW YORK • SYDNEY

BLOOMSBURY INDIA
Bloomsbury Publishing India Pvt. Ltd
Second Floor, Building No. 4
DDA Complex LSC, Pocket C – 6 & 7
Vasant Kunj, New Delhi 110070
www.bloomsbury.com

BLOOMSBURY, Bloomsbury Academic India and the Diana logo are trademarks of Bloomsbury Publishing Plc

First published in India 2020
First published 2013
Paperback edition first published 2014

This edition published with permission from Bloomsbury Publishing Plc, 50 Bedford Square, London, WC1B3DP, UK

British Library Cataloguing-in-Publication Data
A catalogue record for this book is available from the British Library.

Library of Congress Cataloging-in-Publication Data
A catalog record for this book is available from the Library of Congress

ISBN: 978-93-89351-38-5

For sale in the Indian subcontinent only

Typeset by Deanta Global Publishing Services, Chennai, India
Digitally printed and bound in India by Replika Press Pvt. Ltd.

Contents

Preface

On a hot and humid summer Sunday morning in 2002, I travelled from my hometown of Vellore in South India to Palligramam, a remote village 60 kilometres away. I was sent there to conduct a communion service, on what happened to be 'Trinity Sunday' in the church calendar year. After having just completed my theological degree at the seminary, I felt equipped with sophisticated theological insights, and therefore ready for 'ministry'. Whenever I met someone from a rural congregation, I tried to communicate my 'theology' to them while turning a deaf ear to their own Christian experiences. On that particular Sunday, I found the congregation anxiously waiting for me to arrive, since they had not seen a priest for sometime. Without wasting time, I went and got into my white robes and stood in front of the congregation ready to confer my newly attained theological knowledge. When the time for the sermon arrived, I stepped into the pulpit and preached my well-prepared sermon, in which befitting of the Sunday, I explained my complex theological understandings of the 'Trinity' within the Christian tradition. Midway through the sermon, I began to see an uneasy calm and confusion on the faces of the congregation. Following my instinct, I asked them 'are you all with me? Do you understand what I am saying?' There was no reply for sometime, which only led to my unease and discomfort. After some time, an elderly person from the congregation hesitatingly raised his voice and said, *ayya, saptu rendu nalachu, neenga solrathu onnum puriayala!* ('It has been two days since we have had any food, so we cannot understand what you are saying'). That response came both as a shock and surprise to me. So I stopped my preaching and asked them why the Palligramam congregation had nothing to eat. They explained that because of the failure of the monsoon rains, the village lake had dried up and the crops withered, hence they did not have any work. Furthermore, the mango processing factory that offered daily labour to some of them had to be closed due to the lack of mangoes, also a consequence of the failure of the monsoon rains. With no work or money to buy food, most of the villagers, especially the Christian congregation, began using their food reserves, which eventually ran out. There they were, hungry and starving, yet they made a point to come to the church to worship the God they knew.

As a new assistant priest, my job was to visit the congregation of Palligramam along with 17 similar ones and conduct communion, preach a sermon on the designated passage and then return to my comfortable home. This profound encounter with the reality of rural Dalit Christians confronted me and questioned me at various levels. I began to wonder what the relevance of being a priest was, if he is unaware of the lived reality of his parishioners. Had I known about the drought, I certainly hope that I would not have been preaching about the complex relationship between the Father, Son and the Holy Spirit!

This encounter also exposed the gaps in my own theological limitations. There I was, educated in one of the most prominent Indian theological colleges in the country, including intensive studies on Dalit Christians and Dalit Theology, standing in the pulpit realizing my ignorance. I was indeed using some of the ideas that were taught to me in the seminary as 'Theology from the people', only to find myself preaching theology *at* the people. Some of the fundamental questions which are raised in this book stem from this encounter on that summer day. The lived reality of impoverished Dalit Christians, their sufferings and struggles for life, came to occupy my thinking for many months, and thus began this journey to understand one such excluded Paraiyar Christian community.

The experience also triggered a different process to unfold in my own self-understanding. As an urban-educated son of a priest and as a priest myself, I began to gather how my parents escaped the difficult lives from their home villages. Before I began questioning my parents, I had no idea that they too came from similar Dalit Christian rural congregations. From them, and others I met during my seminary days, I came to the realization that *I* was a Dalit Christian. Understandably, because of their education and financial security, my parents made the choice to raise us not as Dalits, but as 'Christians'.

Adding to my own quest to understand Paraiyar Christians, my current research interest also stems from the following observation by Sathianathan

Clarke, which supports the idea of the 'continuity' of local practices within rural Christian communities, largely ignored by the local church. He says,

> My experience of living with the Paraiyar Christian has convinced me that elements of Dalit religion are still operative in Dalit Christian communities. However, even while the Paraiyar Christian practices Dalit religious rites and practices at various occasions, they are reluctant to admit it openly let alone claim it as their own.[1]

Clarke's suggestion implies that elements of Dalit religion are still functional within the religio-cultural realm of rural Dalit Christian communities, which are too readily brushed aside as superstitious practices by church authorities. Bearing this in mind, in this book I first wish to examine how the different realms of Paraiyar religious practice and Christianity have been integrated and functionalized within the everyday life of rural Paraiyar Christians. I aim to negotiate their space within the village community without necessarily using dichotomies like Christians and non-Christians. Second, I intend to observe the incorporation of Paraiyar worldviews in processing their understanding of the Christian message which is often glossed over.

I approach the present research from a personal perspective. As a Paraiyar Christian myself, I have attempted to understand my own identity, its social construction and consequences. I also traced my own past from which my parents protectively distanced me raising me up under the shadow of Christianity. This process gave me a unique understanding of the dilemma and complexities faced by Dalit Christians in rural India. It is also important to keep in mind that I am observing religion in its broadest sense in the lives of Paraiyar Christians through the lens of social anthropology.

This research stems from the experience of Dalit Christians and the continual tension between being a Dalit and being a Christian within a community fragmented by caste ideology. Expressions of the Christian faith in South India vary from one community to another and are not uniform even within culturally and linguistically similar groups. Dalit Christians are generally comfortable to view God and follow Christian principles within their localized and traditional ways, even though the church may see 'Christians' as different from their non-Christian counterparts. This diversity in religious experience has prompted me to raise questions pertaining to their *lived local expressions of religion*,[2] principally in rural Dalit Christian communities, where it is particularly visible. Hence, the focus of this book is to understand or at least to scratch the surface of the Dalit Christian worldview and the meaning-making system within which it is present and operative, not necessarily conflicting with, but also mutually complementing their situatedness.

In order to understand the complex workings of religion among Dalits, I decided to focus on one Dalit Christian community in particular for clarity: the Paraiyar Christian community in Thulasigramam.[3] Gleaning the ethnographic accounts from my research, I will pursue the following aspects:

1. Historically locating the experience of Dalit Christians within the church in South India through the study of missionary responses to the 'Caste' system.
2. The importance of understanding the various processes that shape the individual, communal and social identities within Dalit Communities. It also argues how dynamic and fluid the concept of identity is while facilitating multiple belongings.
3. Identifying and describing the religious and social worldviews operative in Dalit communities in order to argue that they are very much context-bound and locally conceptualized.
4. Explore the notion of power and the replication of social hierarchies within the Dalit community.
5. Examine the utilization of religious space and spiritual artefacts within a particular Dalit community which bears the subtle, yet subversive process of negotiating its social and religious status.
6. My final attempt is to think beyond the boundaries of Paraiyar Christians and weave other similar works in order to develop a contextual approach to the study of religion in local communities.

There are a few limitations of this work that need to be kept in mind. This book neither strives to provide a comprehensive ethnography of the Paraiyar Christian community in South India nor extensively theorize their lived religious life on an abstract level. Rather descriptively analyze it, allowing the research subjects from one particular rural community to articulate their own perspectives and opinions regarding what it means to be simultaneously Christians and Paraiyars, which will thereby, provide a representative view. What is attempted in this volume is to engage critically with the limitations of boxed understandings of religion.

Acknowledgements

My initial interest in researching Dalit communities was sparked during my seminary days at the United Theological College with colleagues and friends drawn from across India who helped me to think practically and responsibly about the country and religion I call my own. This study would not have been possible without the cooperation, patience and openness of the people of Thulasigramam, to whom I am greatly indebted. I was honoured to share in their lives and struggles, and though I came as a stranger, I left feeling like a member of the community.

Moreover, the Centre for the Study of World Christianity at Edinburgh University opened my eyes to the realities of Christian experience around the world. It was an honour to have worked with people like Duncan Forrester, Jack Thompson, Afe Adogame and the late Marcella Althaus-Reid. A special word of gratitude to Elizabeth Koepping, whose encouragement, guidance and support during the entire process of my research enabled me to stretch my own assumptions and conclusions. I am delighted to have been welcomed into the vibrant academic environment of the Politics, Philosophy and Religion department at Lancaster University.

This research also brought to light the struggles and sacrifices made by my parents on behalf of siblings and myself. Therefore, I thank my Dad, Jeremiah, my Mom, Lilly Manoharam, and my wonderful family, Ida and Job, Evelyn and Annie, Anbu and Mercy, and also my Canadian parents, Barbara and Horst Aechtner.

Finally, the completion of this book has only been made possible through the meticulous work, constant encouragement and unflinching support of Rebecca Aechtner, my best friend, my love and my wife. As my beloved companion, you have academically challenged me and pushed me to think outside of the box, making this journey a great joy. As I write this the arrival of Sundiya has brought us both inconceivable joy. Above all, I thank God for giving us all of these blessings and the life to experience them.

1

Introducing the Dalit Context

Dalits in India

Similar to the geographical diversity in India, the country is also divided on the lines of language, culture and most importantly caste, constructing a distinct system for the oppressive social stratification in the subcontinent. The caste system forms the backbone of the Hindu[1] social order in India. Interestingly, the term *Caste* is Portuguese in origin derived from the Latin *castus* (chaste, the unadulterated, pure breed) used to designate the complex social system, as it did not fit into the early classifications of the European anthropologists.[2] Over the years it has evolved and become synonymous with the *Varna* system and is also considered identical to various social classifications in Indian society. This word needs to be used with caution as it carries various meanings, and modern understanding of the caste system tends to be very complicated. The social structure and ideology of the caste system is provided by the Hindu Dharma as outlined in the best-known *Manusmriti* or *Laws of Manu*, the law code of Manu.[3] Various studies point to the fact that there is a possible merger of two social structures, the *Varna* (colour/vocation) class divisions and the *Jati* (birth) divisions.[4] There are further divisions on the basis of *purity* and *pollution*,[5] primarily at the religious ritual level and its implied social consequences as well as occupational.[6] *Varna* literally means colour and is not a social group, but a classificatory unit that can be used for people as well as gods, animals, plants or other things. Within the Hindu society, owing to its religious origin, the Varna system facilitates a sense of order among people and prevents the society from disintegrating into chaos. With reference to society, it is essentially an order of birth class, *varnashramadharma*,[7] and a division of social functions, but not a caste system. There are five different levels of the system: Brahman (Priest), Kshatriya (Warrior and Landowners),

Vaishya (Merchants), Shudra (Agriculturalists) and Outcastes (polluted Untouchables).[8] Within each of these categories are the actual castes, or *jatis*, within which people are born, marry and die. Jati derives its root from the word *jan* (to be born), which is partially synonymous with Varna. It has many meanings: descent, birth, race, family, genre, species, type, clan, state, nation, etc. and is more commonly used as *subcastes* by the social scientist. The Varna system has been in use for many years. Even today, the values of the Varna system are strongly held. In the Vedic Hindu system, the Untouchables are the Outcastes, primarily due to the nature of their traditionally prescribed professions involving polluted things, making them polluted people and pollutants in turn.[9] There are various theories explaining the emergence and function of the caste system in the Indian sociocultural system.[10] The caste system has far-reaching impact and consequences in Indian society as Nagaraj succinctly states, 'the caste system in India is not only a structure of cultural values but also a certain pattern of inequitable distribution of power and wealth of different kinds along the lines of caste hierarchy'.[11] The significant aspect emerging from the discussions on the caste system is that a large section of people are left outside of the caste system and are designated as 'Untouchables'. Either they belonged to a different Varna or 'god' simply created them to be lesser.[12] This social stratification and exclusion of outcaste is ordained, pursued and perpetuated by dominant religio-political and sociocultural forces.

The Outcastes were marginalized and pushed to the peripheries of Indian society. Against this background, various Self-Respect movements in India during the freedom struggle under leaders like Joythirao Pule and B. R. Ambedkar encouraged the Outcaste communities to rename themselves from 'Untouchables' or 'harijans'[13] to the affirmative 'Dalits', meaning 'broken', 'split-open' and 'oppressed', which connotes their wretchedness of life.[14] As James Massey accurately describes, 'Dalit is not a Caste. Dalit is a symbol of change and revolution'.[15] The term 'Dalit' is also an overarching and mobilizing term to represent more than 450 'Untouchable' communities in India. While it may initially seem counterintuitive to appropriate such bleak terminology, it did and does continue to raise awareness and to potentially empower those living in such a repressive system. The distinction and classification based on caste and occupation continues even today in most aspects of Indian society. Explaining the existential situation of Dalits in India, M. E. Prabhakar opines,

> The Dalit condition is that of destitution and dehumanisation, Dalits have been the most degraded, downtrodden, exploited and least educated in our society. They have been socially and culturally, economically and politically subjugated and marginalized through three thousand years of our history and remain so, even after half a century of 'protective discrimination', under the aegis of the Government of India.[16]

According to the 2001 India census, the Dalit population constitutes about 16.2 per cent of the total Indian population, that is, 170 million people experience different kinds of discrimination in their life every day, the majority of whom work as daily labourers and landless agricultural workers in the unorganized sectors of Indian society.[17] A majority of Dalits experience extreme poverty within the contemporary market-driven liberalized Indian economy.[18] Further, Dalit communities are the most violated, both physically and mentally, within the Indian society.[19] Dalits are considered ritually impure and physically polluting in the religious realm, which has serious implications for sociocultural relations. Dalits in general are not allowed to enter many Hindu temples, nor are they permitted to eat in or even enter the houses of non-Dalits. This attitude and perception of 'untouchability', physically and mentally, still prevails in most parts of the country in devious and explicit ways, even though untouchability is constitutionally outlawed.[20] The late K. R. Narayanan, former president of India, and the first Dalit to occupy the highest office in the country, recollected on the golden jubilee celebration of the Indian Republic thusly,

> Untouchability has been abolished by law but shades of it remain in the ingrained attitudes nurtured by the caste system. Though the constitutional provision of reservation in educational institutions and public services flow from our constitution, these provisions remain unfulfilled though bureaucratic and administrative deformation or by narrow interpretations of these special provision.[21]

As mentioned earlier, Dalits in India are not a homogeneous category, but a collective of numerous sub-castes resulting in further internal fragmentation and alienation. Adding to the external discrimination by the higher castes, internal conflict within Dalit communities contributes to furthering their misery. Many researchers have shown that the immediate adversaries of a Dalit community are perhaps ironically another Dalit community, which is fighting for the same resources.[22] In such a context it was hoped by the Dalit leaders that the creation of a collective Dalit Identity must heal those inner squabbles and mobilize Untouchable communities towards transformation of their lowly cultural, socio-economic and religio-political status.

Dalit Christians

Dalit Christians constitute about 10 per cent of the total Dalit population but make up 70 per cent of Christians in India, yet their situation is no better than that of non Christian Dalits.[23] Rather, discrimination merely assumes a different dimension and manifests itself in many patterns. Along with the burden of being a Dalit, Dalit Christians have to endure multifold discrimination, at the hands of the state, the society *and* of the institutionalized church. Within the Indian church, caste manifests the worst form of discrimination.[24] Non-Dalit high-caste Christians are often biased and they discriminate against Dalits at all levels of institutional, communal and administrative bodies. Being Christians, Dalits are also deprived of the educational and employment benefits from the Indian Government for the Scheduled Caste category. In most of the cases within the church, Dalit Christians are not even given the option to express their voices against exploitation, because the sermons and official teachings encourage them to be passive and submissive towards authority figure since their situation is due to the consequence of the Original Sin (the fall of Adam) and they need forgiveness for their sins, not social liberation.[25]

In the process of uncritical inculturation the Indian churches have incorporated the hegemonic Vedic system of segregation, and have thereby become a place for further discrimination.[26] Even though Dalit Christians constitute the majority of the Indian Christian population they continue to be denied educational opportunities and social responsibilities, both within the church and outside of it. The Indian church is a blatant example of division on the basis of caste, with each Christian denomination identifying with a particular caste group and some churches even having separate Eucharist services for Dalits and non-Dalits. This situation partially mirrors the state of Dalit Christians in India today.[27] Dalit Christians face unfair treatment in both subtle and very explicit ways. This discrimination has become an enculturated habit resulting in segregation and ostracism.[28] According to many studies, the dominant caste communities continue to hold authority within the church,[29] and as Monikaraj comments, 'Unfortunately the evil of caste identity crept into the Church. Dalits, who longed for human dignity and worth, were shocked to see the same discrimination making inroads in to the church premises'.[30]

It is this context of the marginalization of Dalit Christians that gave birth to Dalit Theology, which emerged in the early 1980s as a critique of the dominant Indian Christian theology espoused within the mainstream high-caste-dominated churches. The context of discrimination within the church and society is the foundation for theological reflection by Dalits.[31] Along with being critical about traditional Indian Christian Theology, Dalit Theology expresses the aspirations and reflections of Dalits from their own situatedness of marginalization. The process of theologizing in Dalit Theology primarily stems from the pain-pathos experience of the Dalits. A. P. Nirmal, a pioneer in Dalit Theology, observes that Dalit Theology is 'about Dalits, from the Dalits and by the Dalits',[32] which expresses the faith of the depressed classes. From the perspective of this research, it is helpful to introduce a general view of the religio-cultural worldview of Dalit communities. As this book focuses on Paraiyars, a Dalit community in Tamil Nadu, a brief introduction may be helpful.

Paraiyars

Paraiyars are a Dalit community with a significant presence in South India.[33] Paraiyars are predominately agricultural labourers living in the rural parts of the country; however, according to the Hindu social order, they occupy a low status due to their traditional occupation of dealing with dead animals, which in turn makes them ritually impure and socially polluting resulting in their untouchable status. Thus, the Paraiyar 'outcaste' status operates at both religious and social stratums. Unlike other theories regarding the origin of caste system in India, Paraiyars have their own myths of origin. The common understanding is that Paraiyars descended from a relatively equal position or even superior status to Brahman.[34] Some of the myths suggest that actually the

Paraiyar is the elder brother and the Brahmin is the younger brother, through such interpretation Paraiyars claim precedence over Brahmins.[35] Robert Deliege suggests that,

> if the Paraiyars are poor, suffering and hard working, it is not because of their deeds in a previous life or because of some congenital defect, but because of a misunderstanding about their mythical ancestor. Consequently, the low status of the Paraiyars as a whole is largely underserved.[36]

The important observation is that Paraiyars were once in an equal social status and succumbed to lower status. Sathianathan Clarke provides another theoretical view point that, 'the Paraiyars are not Dalits because of their low and menial occupations. Rather, they are condemned to these occupations as a punishment for breaching caste laws established and enforced by the caste communities'.[37] He also accounts for Paraiyars' association with the *parai* (drum), which provides them with their vocation and identity; however, not all Paraiyars engage in the drum beating profession.[38] On the contrary, Michael Bergunder traces a more recent nineteenth-century understanding of Paraiyars 'origin' through the work of Ayotti Tasa who claims them to be the 'disinherited children of the soil'.[39] These differing preceding observations capture the difficulty of defining and pinpointing the origin of Pariyars, whether Christian or Hindu. Various researches conducted among Paraiyars conclude that in spite of their historical substantiation, they hold a culturally unique place in South Indian society.[40] Moreover, with a significant population they have come to represent other outcaste communities in contemporary Tamil Nadu. Even though Paraiyars have been the subject of many research projects, this work considers often glossed over areas residing in the crossroads of culture and religion.

Dalit religio-cultural worldview

The diversity and complexity of religious beliefs and rituals in India itself is a pointer to the presence of multiple religio-cultural worldviews. In India, religion and culture are not two exclusive areas, but mutually influence each other and are arguably one and the same. According to some Dalit scholars, historically the religious and cultural practices of Dalits were distinct from that of the dominant Hindu worldview.[41] Thus we now briefly take a detour to get a glimpse of the Hindu worldview.

The dominant Hindu worldview is informed by the Vedas and assumes an integral part in all the scriptural philosophical writings that developed afterwards.[42] The creation of human beings as outlined by *Manusmriti* or *the Laws of Manu* describes in detail the status of all four Varnas within the world and their duties, the *varnashramadharma*.[43] Hierarchy on the basis of one's birth and work was at the core of this system with Brahmin as the supreme, pure creation and the Shudra as the lowly servant.[44] The Shudras were not allowed even to hear the Vedas let alone read it[45] and the Dalits or Chandalas are considered inferior to the Shudras. As one Dalit historian writes,

> A householder is exhorted to throw some food for them and they are supposed to eat along with the crows and dogs outside the house, after all members of the household have taken their meals. The Chandala is to enter a village for sweeping, etc., in the first half of the day, carrying a broom under his armpit and a small pot hanging around his neck.[46]

Such a graded worldview found its way into various aspects of Hindu religious belief instilling a structural understanding of society upheld by other important religious scriptures, epics and the Upanishads.[47] To summarize the modern Hindu belief we may draw upon Gandhi's views, who stated that,

> I believe in the Vedas, the Upanishads, the Puranas and all that goes by the name of Hindu scriptures, and therefore in avatars and rebirth. I believe in the *Varnashramdharma* in a sense in my opinion strictly Vedic, but not in its present popular and crude sense. I do not disbelieve in idol-worship.[48]

Further reflecting on Hindu religion and culture, Gandhi makes it obvious that he followed the ashrama theory as providing universal governance and order.[49] Adding to this worldview it may also be helpful to have a brief understanding of the 'ultimate' and the 'self' within Hindu philosophy. For the sake of contextuality, I will outline *Advaita* school of thought, particularly Sankara's concept, as it is very influential and prevalent within the South Indian Hindu worldview. It is well documented that Sankara was a revolutionary in the field of philosophy but remained a conservative in his social thinking,[50] because Advaita Vedanta's foundation was in the sacred scriptures and the Upanishads of the Vedic corpus.[51] Sankara is also credited with the revival of Vedic

Hinduism, a task he was able to achieve through numerous commentaries that he wrote on the Vedas and Upanishads. In Advaita Vedanta *brahman* is clearly mentioned as the ultimate consciousness that holds everything in it, existence outside of it is meaningless, *atman* (self) is a manifestation of it which is partly represented by the *jiva* (ego).[52] The *brahman* cannot be an object of knowledge and is not a personal God.[53] Vensus George explains this concept further,

> Thus, *brahman* is one: It is not a 'He', a personal being; nor is it an 'It', an impersonal concept. It is that state which comes about when all subject-object distinctions are obliterated. Ultimately, *brahman* is a name for the experience of the timeless plentitude of being.[54]

As mentioned earlier, even the understanding of *atman* is unique to Advaitic thought. *Atman* is part of the absolute reality and has no relevance outside of it. This is the centrality of Sankara's thought, the non-duality of *brahman* and *atman,* in other words,

> The atman, as the self-existent reality, pure and eternal consciousness, birthless and deathless supreme Being, that is the source and foundation of all that exist which essentially means one and the same reality.[55]

Sankara very strongly holds the view that *brahman* is absolutely real and the external world is *maya,* often translated as illusion or unreality. In other words, Sankara denied the existence of the external world outside the absolute being *brahman.* According to him, the *atman* continues to live in this *maya* (the world) until it realizes its ignorance and becomes part of the absolute being (*Brahmaanubhava).*[56] For Sankara this experience is possible only through the path of knowledge (*Jnaanayoga*). He proposed that it is possible to remove the veil of ignorance through rigorous physical, moral and intellectual preparation which opens up the *atman* for self-realization, *Aham brahmasmi* (I am brahman).[57] For the advaitic *brahman* the phenomenal world is an illusion, *maya,* within which the *atman* is lost in ignorance and needs to go through the path of self-realization and become one with the supreme being or consciousness. In *Brahmaanubhava,* Sankara does not talk about the notion of God, a deity to be worshipped or to be devoted to, but rather realized in pure consciousness.

In Advaita Vedanta the whole process of self-realization is a personal effort, which even after attained, the individual does not need to have any relationship with the other or to a community of others, because all such associations would be irrelevant and unreal to the *Brahmajnaani*. Thus, Sankara's path to self-realization does not give any significance to I and Thou relationship that is genuine and inter-subjective communion of hearts between human persons. Sankara's path to realization is a *Jnanamarga* of calmness, self-control, self-settledness, forbearance, faith and complete concentration and the hunger for the liberation of the *atman* from *avidya,* ignorance. The intellectual preparation includes the three stages of hearing, reflection and meditation, a path of complete renunciation. The Vedic concept of the endless cycle of birth and death is considered a bondage from which one must attain liberation that is *moksha* or *mukti*. Though this is a brief observation into the complex Hindu worldview, we shall see in the course of this book how this perception finds its way into both the popular level and academic discourse.

Unlike the scripture-based understanding of the world, Dalits developed their perception from the orality of their culture. The understanding of the concept of gods, deities, spirit, soul and human life within Dalit communities were developed from their lived reality, but does bear the impact of Hindu religious worldview.[58] Through a detailed analysis of the differences between the Hindu and Dalit conceptions of goddesses, Sathianathan Clarke concludes that there are definite differences in content and approaches.[59] Other scholars also point at that Dalit religious practices are a response to the local condition within specific local communities, rather than being part of a universal belief system.[60] Due to the oral nature of these practices, they are relegated as inferior to that of written and word-based religious traditions within India. Often designated as superstitious and unreligious activities by the high-caste Christians and enlightened Hindus these beliefs need to be changed within civilized religion.[61]

Theophilus Appavoo, a Dalit scholar, argues for the distinctiveness of Dalit religion as opposed to Hindu religion.[62] According to him, there is place for protest and dissent within the religious sphere, since it is participatory, community centred and liberative in nature emphasizing corporate worship and not personal holiness.[63] Because there is no priestly class within the community, it assumes equality exists among the worshipers. He expounds,

> The Dalit religion is a religion of equality. There is no priest-class or caste in this religion. In most of the places the priestly office is rotated. Women

> are treated equally. They are allowed to do priestly work. In fact, they have precedence over men in some rituals . . . In Dalit religion, all the worshippers have equal and active participation . . . There is no special or sacred ritual which is earmarked for a particular section of the believers.[64]

He further adds that one of the hidden reasons for Dalit worship is to gather as a community and celebrate, which frequently assumes festive proportions.[65] Felix Wilfred also argues that the subaltern religious experience has a strong cultural basis and stems from the experience of being subjugated and marginalized. He also highlights the place of spirits in the material life of Dalits, stating,

> The subaltern religious experience is wrapped in the world of spirits with whom people are in communication. These spirits are present in the most ordinary things of daily life-in groves, on trees, in the pot of water at home, in the cremation grounds, and so on.[66]

Another important observation by Wilfred is with regard to the nature of subaltern deities, which usually emanates from a conflict situation and were localized, thus,

> it is interesting to note that most of the gods and goddesses of the subalterns emerge from concrete social contexts. As a matter of fact, the story of many of these deities is connected with some or other historical events and persons. In other words, the subaltern gods do not descend from above but ascend, as it were, from beneath the feet of society. The deities are often historical persons who were in conflict with the unjust system of casteist and feudal society and its laws and injunctions. They are persons who transgressed, for example, caste norms, or fought against injustice, or defended their community against the onslaught of the upper castes and dominant classes.[67]

He further observes the 'non-mediated' religious experience and decentralized religiosity of the subalterns which characterizes their communal life.[68] However, it is important to recognize the danger of an exclusivistic approach towards understanding the cultural universe of Dalits, which might undermine its extremely rich and multi-layered nature.[69] Sathianathan Clarke suggests that it is crucial to understand the 'particularity and universality, geographical locatedness and boundlessness; fixity and fluidity; determinedness and openness; resistance and assimilation'[70] that characterizes the Dalit worldview.

This perspective moves away from merely emphasizing the distinctiveness of Dalit religion and culture, and seeking instead to understand its universality. Paraiyars are no exception as they share in the wider Dalit worldview. Many of the aforementioned researches conducted among Paraiyars, which suggests that irrespective of their religious belonging (Christian or Hindu), there is a shared worldview that informs their social existence.[71] Joe Arun also expresses a similar view with reference to Paraiyar Christians;

> despite their conversion to Christianity, Hindu customs continued to exercise a strong influence on Paraiyar practices. From my field study, it appeared that the Paraiyars were still essentially Hindu in terms of their approach to and practice of the Christian religion.[72]

The preceding brief observations from the literature on Dalit religion may not only paint an idealistic portrayal of the Dalit religious worldview, but they were also able to exemplify its complexity. At this juncture, it is safe to suggest that there are aspects of continuity as well as distinctiveness in the Paraiyar perceptions of religion and worldview.

Thulasigramam and methodology

Thulasigramam is a village situated 120 km west of Chennai, the capital city of the state of Tamil Nadu. It is a small agricultural village with a population of about 150 families. The village conforms to traditional demarcations and divisions in its geographical space on the basis of the caste system and Hindu worldview described earlier. A large church with a tall bell tower surrounded by thatched roof houses forms the entrance of the Paraiyar *Cherie* (the Untouchable settlement, also known as Colony) in the village. The road further leads to the *Oor* (the high caste village), composed of concrete houses, were the *Reddyars*[73] live. They own the agricultural lands and are the employers of the Paraiyars and the other caste communities in that village. A temple devoted to various Hindu gods is situated at the centre of the village populated by the Hindu Reddyars. The Paraiyars, both Hindus and Christians, 70 families in total, live in the Cherie. Paraiyars belong to the untouchable community but consider themselves to be high within the Dalit sub-structure. With the exception of one family, the rest of the Christians in this village come from the Paraiyar community and live in the Cherie. The Paraiyar Christian families live mostly around the church premises, the church building itself being enclosed by a wall, and the church has a membership of 32 families. The Paraiyars are mostly landless agricultural labourers working for meagre daily wages in the fields of the Reddyars, with the exception of a few who have joined the Indian army and returned after service. Unlike other Paraiyar communities in Tamil Nadu, there seems to be no further organizational divisions within their community.[74] The Paraiyars rely wholly upon the Reddyars for their work, if there is any for them, which clearly shows their utter economic dependency on the Reddyars. Some still work as drumbeaters, their caste-designated occupation, and thus earn a living (both in cash and in kind), even though some, particularly Christians, consider it as a disrespectful 'polluting' profession. A few younger Paraiyars try out new jobs such as working as labourers in factories and private companies. Since the literacy level among Paraiyars is considerably low, there is very little hope of the younger generation leaving the village for better-paying jobs. To the west of the Paraiyar Christian settlement are the Hindu Paraiyar hamlets with a Ganesha temple (one of the Hindu gods) forming the end of the street, where most of their Hindu religious festivities take place. Apart from these communities there is also another Dalit community, the *Arunthathier*,[75] who are considered to be inferior by and to the Paraiyars; they live on the northern edge of the village. Only one family from the Arunthathier community converted to Christianity in 1994 and since then there have been no other conversions in this village. Interestingly, as it emerged during the fieldwork, even Paraiyar Christians consider the Arunthathier convert as inferior to themselves and avoid frequent or unnecessary interaction.

In terms of the literacy rate, the vast majority of Paraiyar adults are illiterate, and due to the presence of a malfunctioning government school, less than 35 per cent of the young people are able to read and write. Those who can afford to go to school in the nearby town where there is the hope for educational advancement. Agriculture and brick making are the major sources of employment for the entire village, all owned by Reddyars creating an economic dependency of the landless people on the landowners for their livelihood. Thulasigramam has a strong history of inter-caste conflicts, which continues to influence the present caste community relationship. Except for the Reddyars there is no public display of political affiliations other than at election times. It was recounted by the Paraiyars that there were few attempts by political parties supporting Dalit causes to organize representation within the village but the Reddyars thwarted such endeavours.

Although Thulasigramam is situated near a big town, life in the village still follows a traditional pattern. Hinduism and Christianity are the two religions practised. Irrespective of religious affiliation, most of the villagers join in celebrating the common village festivals, fulfilling their roles laid down by the traditional practices. The Paraiyars, both Hindus and Christians, continue to intermarry. The Christian community is very much a part of this sociocultural setting, making it necessary to examine the above-mentioned aspects during the research process. Thulasigramam was selected as the research location due to its composition, as it represents at micro level the complexity of caste system in India. It should be noted that the name of the village and the peoples' names have been changed due to confidentiality and will be used in the book without any further explanations.

My research in Thulasigramam began in 2005 on a bumpy note, as the people in the village did not know what to do with me, a stranger from the town. On top of it some of them knew my father as a priest and knew that I was also a priest. In the beginning I was treated like a clergyman with respect and people kept their distance from me, giving me the usual 'Priest' treatment. In the beginning of my research my 'priest' status was rather a hindrance than a help in relating with them. Things began to change only after I repeatedly communicated that I was there in their midst as a student, seeking to understand their lifestyle and perceptions of religious practices. There were also issues related to my staying in the village as there was a sense of apprehension as how to accommodate me in their houses, with limited space designated only for their families. So I decided to keep my bags and sleep on the church veranda, which seemed to me neutral ground, so that everybody in the village could relate with me. Despite my attempts at neutrality I was perceived as being related to one particular family, who are related to the local church leader. I had requested that they provide food for me by paying them in advance, since it was not possible for me to cook for myself. It was only after two months, when I shared meals with other families that I was able to remove this demarcation and be accepted into their families.

I was also largely seen as an outsider, even though I spoke their language and looked like them, because I was not born in the village. Such an attitude did not change until I began to take the initiative to visit them in their homes without any assistance from people trying to 'help' me. It took couple of months for me to begin to comprehend the power dynamics operative within the Christian community in Thulasigramam. A couple of families attempted to direct and control my interaction among the community, seeing my unfamiliarity with the context of Thulasigramam. All these people tended to have clear links to the institutional church. However, after consistent efforts I was able to move beyond that association and was welcomed into households within the Christian community. However, my biggest breakthrough came when some people in the village found some genealogical details about my family background, which led them to find instantly links between individuals in the village and my relatives. It was during that time when I began to interact and deeply engage with the lived reality of the Paraiyars in Thulasigramam.[76]

As mentioned earlier, I was unable to delve deeply into the different levels of meanings of the said views of the community members for the first couple of months. Disclosing personal details about myself that enabled the community members to 'place' me as a relative was vital in gaining access to the community. Regardless of the trust I gained through perceived familial relationships I still had to strive to develop a conversation on any particular topic. This meant that I had to go along with each informant and participant during his daily life and wait for him to touch upon something important. Sometimes I had to wait for more than six months to get their intimate views and opinions on certain issues. Thus most of my conversations took the format of 'small talks', informal, unstructured and random conversations, which I had to later bring together under various themes and headings. Despite being accepted into the community, the fact that I am a male and a priest made women extremely hesitant to speak with me and share some of their intimate thoughts; hence, unfortunately, there is a large disparity between conversations with women and men.

My year-long stay in Thulasigramam had exciting moments and very mundane dull periods. But in retrospect, it was those mundane moments that taught me the patience to wait for the people in the community to share their lives with me, at their own pace rather than I interfering with their flow of life. It actually took me awhile to realize that they had accepted me into their community long before I saw myself as a community member. Once during the summer, due to a heat wave, I decided to take a break from my fieldwork and go away to the safety and comfort of my family's air conditioned home. During that time in my correspondence with my academic mentor, I mailed, '*we* have been asked to go to cooler places to avoid dehydration, so I am staying away from the village'. I got a quick reply from her, asking 'where did the villagers go?' At that moment I realized, even after few weeks of staying in the village, that I did not think of myself as part of them, considering myself as an outsider, even though I wanted to be an insider; a realization that taught me that it is the researcher who also needs to be 'open minded'. As a researcher I carried heavy baggage of preconceived ideas about the community than they had about me. I believe that participant observation in research is a mutually disclosing process, which is effective only to the extent that both the community and the researcher share with each other. The experience in Thulasigramam has taught me that without opening myself to the community, I may never have succeeded in establishing the relationship that I did and continue to have with them. Having said that, it is also important to be aware of my own position in the community, abiding by the practices and respecting the local custom, lest I jeopardize such a relationship.

From the beginning of my field research, the community was made aware of my identity as a priest, despite the fact that I came as a researcher attempting to learn and observe the Paraiyar Christian lifestyle. I often had to struggle between their perception of me as a member of clergy and my aim as an academic observer. In Thulasigramam, there was no memory of priests staying overnight in the village, and were I to hazard a guess, I would say that more than 65 per cent of priests from the local diocese live in cities and towns, whereas their parishes are located in rural areas. Very often they 'visit' their pastorates and never actually live in the villages themselves. In such a context my stay in the village had an interesting impact on the community; initially it resulted in their hesitation to relate with me, but changed after their curiosity about me subsided.

Following the examination and evaluation of the archival and written materials, participant observation in the form of informal random unstructured interviews and interaction with the subjects of this research provides the core content of this book.[77] This ethnographic and anthropological approach stresses the importance of Dalits being the subjects as well as the objects of the research.[78] A rural Dalit Christian congregation in the village of Thulasigramam is the locale of this participant observation in which I lived for a year interviewing them in their own life situatedness.

During my stay in the village I engaged in informal conversations with most of the Thulasigramam Paraiyar Christian, meeting mostly near their houses or at their places of work. Patience proved to be a great virtue when even after hours and days spent with a single person, frustratingly no useful information for my research was provided. Very often I had to employ indirect questioning methods to tease out important information from the subjects, such as their opinion on someone else's opinion instead of asking them direct questions. This method proved to be strategic and effective on many occasions during my fieldwork.

As mentioned earlier, my basic research assumptions also stem from my subjective experience as a Dalit Christian and do not simply mirror reflections of the social world of the Paraiyars in Thulasigramam. Hence, there is an element of subjectivity involved in this research as in my life, which is unavoidable in ethnographic research. While explaining reflexive ethnography Harry F. Walcott recognizes the inevitability of the causal relationship between the researcher and the researched.[79] Rosanna Hertz has also observed the fact that 'the respondents' voice is almost always filtered through the authors account',[80] which suggests the inevitability of reflexivity. Further, the presence of symbolic social interaction and understanding of other people and societies in the research field enables one to transcend and transform the ethnographer's subjective ideas. Charlotte A. Davies clarifies that

> The purpose of research is to mediate between different constructions of reality, and doing research means increasing understanding of these varying constructions, among which is included the anthropologists' own constructions. Ideally the research is a conduit that allows interpretations and influences to pass in both directions.[81]

Thus, this book is a product of engaging with my personal experience as a Dalit Christian with the experience of living among the Paraiyar Christians in Thulasigramam. Such an approach also raises questions regarding the insider and outsider divide. As I suggested earlier, as a Dalit Christian, I am an *insider* yet in Thulasigramam I am an *outsider*, because I was not born and raised there. But, during my fieldwork I learnt that such perceptions are negotiated and become opportunities for better understanding, since it is the community that decides the status of the researcher.[82] Moreover, as Isabelle Baszanger and Nicolas Dodier argue, it is necessary for the researcher to remain open and engage with the experiences he is faced with in order to have a grounded knowledge of the context being observed and studied.[83] My fieldwork in Thulasigramam not only opened my understanding about the lives of Paraiyars in Thulasigramam, but in the process also provided a context for my different world knowledge.

Finally I agree with the views of Judy Miller and Barry Glassner, who suggest that importance should be given to the 'honest and intelligent use' of people's stories and the context in which they are conceived in order to understand the larger social world in which we live.[84] In this light, as a researcher living among research subjects, one cannot help but encounter serious ethical dilemmas. The main ethical issue I faced was in my role as a researcher, as I was both an outsider and an ordained priest in the Church of South India. When I encountered obvious abuses of power, I was tempted to take the side of the person at the receiving end. However, since it was frequently within the church structure that such social transactions were taking place, I found myself in a difficult moral situation. Numerous times I had to fight against my own self-righteous urge to advocate against such injustices or to convey them to members of the Church hierarchy. Moreover, this empathic outlook can be found in many of my written accounts of the incidents as well. Ethnographic and anthropological approaches are employed in this research as a means to understand the nature of Christianity as a religion experienced and lived by Paraiyar Christians in Thulasigramam. By observing the relationship between the lives of people and their belief systems, one can better understand the local religious practices.

To date, the Paraiyar Christians of Tamil Nadu have been the subjects of many anthropological research projects. Therefore, I will restrict my discussion to earlier works on Paraiyar culture and religion by Robert Deliege,[85] David Mosse,[86] Lynn Vincentnathan,[87] Hugo Gorringe,[88] J. C. Arun[89] and Sathianathan Clarke. I will reference these anthropological and theological works throughout the remainder of this book. While each of these is concerned with presenting a general view of Paraiyars in Tamil Nadu, my research further develops some of their observations and contributes few new insights. Nevertheless, I shall make references to these works as and when required, either to underline their arguments or to further their ideas through my fieldwork experience.

Foundational literature and resources on the lives and status of Dalits in India were predominantly drawn from the libraries in New College (Edinburgh), United Theological College (Bangalore), Gurukul Lutheran Theological College (Chennai) and Tamil Nadu Theological College (Madurai). Dalit Resource Centres in Chennai and Madurai that house vast collections published in vernaculars have also been extensively used. In order to maximize the impact of this research, the fieldwork observations from Thulasigramam will be analyzed, using the sociological theories of Richard Jenkins, Pierre Bourdieu and Anthony P. Cohen, and anthropological views of religion by Emil Durkheim, Clifford Geertz, Talal Asad, Victor Turner, Michel Foucault and Catherine Bell, as well as theories of power by Gianfranco Poggi and Steven Lukes. However, many more theoretical and philosophical claims have been left implicit in order to stick to my intention of presenting a descriptive ethnographic account of the Paraiyar Christian community inviting the reader to take it further. I would consider this volume as a work in religious anthropology, an effort to understand the complex ways in which human communities believe in, express and utilize religion.

The rest of the book

This book concentrates on the ethnographic information gathered from extensive fieldwork in South India and analysed under four different themes: understanding the Paraiyar identity, the religious worldview of Paraiyar Christians, the reproduction of social hierarchies among Paraiyar Christians and the utilization of religious symbols and performances by Paraiyars to advance social change.

Following on from this introduction, which historically located Dalits within the social, religious and cultural arena in India, Chapter 2 historically traces the missionary attitudes towards the caste system and the initiation of caste-based discriminatory practices within the South Indian churches. This chapter tries to explore the link between denominational identity and caste identity which are the factors behind the current fragmented state of churches in South India. The deprived status of Dalit Christians within the church can be understood only in the light of the various dominant forces that are operative within the church. The following four chapters will capture what goes on in Paraiyar life, under the umbrella of 'religious experience', thus problematizing the simplistic categorization of religion.

Through some of the basic sociological theories of identity, Chapter 3 attempts to understand the identity markers of Paraiyars in Thulasigramam. Various elements contributing towards the construction of Paraiyar identity are identified and discussed. Because the Paraiyars are still rooted and located within the caste-dominated village society, this chapter argues that the multiple and discursive process of self-conceptualization and identification can be understood only in its communal context framed by religious belonging.

Chapter 4 is concerned with understanding the conceptualization of the visible and less visible worlds of Paraiyars, particularly the Christians in Thulasigramam. The relationship between their lives and notions of *Yesusami* (the local Paraiyar expression of Jesus Christ), and how he is rooted within their local notions are articulated through the voices of Paraiyar Christians. This chapter further argues that their Christian faith is couched within their local religious belief and that there is no evidence for any sense of discontinuity. Instead there is an indication for the blurring of boundaries and confluence of worldviews.

Chapter 5 has the specific task of comprehending the place and role of the local church in the lives of Paraiyar Christians in Thulasigramam. Aspects such as the replication of hierarchy within the church, the implications of local political disengagement and its impact on the lives of Paraiyar Christians, which leaves them vulnerable, are discussed at length. It also argues that some of the policies of the local church leave their members uprooted and displaced within their village community.

The focus of Chapter 6 is the Paraiyar religious rituals and social practices, which are central to the Paraiyar community in Thulasigramam, and through which they contest their inferior status within the village society. With the knowledge of the political nature of temple ritual processions in South India, this chapter seeks to understand similar processes within the Paraiyar Christian community. Along with observing the loaded ritual process, the utilization of religion itself by Paraiyar Christians towards negotiating a new social status will be interrogated.

The concluding seventh chapter draws various strands of the previous chapters and weaves them together to develop a clearer understanding of *religion* among the Paraiyars in Thulasigramam. Employing the collage of Paraiyar experiences as a prism and gathering other similar accounts, while engaging with previously discussed anthropological and sociological approaches to religion, this chapter makes a case for a broader perception of what constitutes religion and the need to move beyond syncretic approaches of religion among Paraiyars and beyond.

2

Caste in Contemporary South Indian Churches and its Historical Roots

The history of Christianity in South India dates back to the first century, when St Thomas, a disciple of Jesus Christ, is said to have landed on the shores of Kerala, the southernmost state in India. He established a Christian community, which remains a significant part of Indian Christianity even today.[1] In the south-western corner of India, these Christians, known as Thomas Christians, continue to grow into distinct and vibrant communities until the arrival of the Catholic and Protestant missionaries fourteen centuries later.[2] Most of the Catholic and Protestant missionary organizations from Europe and America established their missionary fields in various parts of South India.[3] As a result of such intensive missionary activity, the majority of the Indian Christian population is located in the South Indian states.

The encounter between the missionaries and the indigenous peoples of South India was and continues to be largely dominated by the contentious issue of caste, widely practised among Indians, set out in the Hindu religious scriptures. Missionaries struggled to address this aspect, which was the backbone of Indian society, and consequently adopted various measures to deal with it. Very often efforts made to address the caste system differed according to each missionary organization and these practices eventually became part of their church hierarchy and Christian practice. This is still the case and the preservation of Christians own distinct identities and caste in their local traditions and practices conflicts with the growing presence of an ecumenical spirit.

Through careful observation, this chapter explores initial attitudes of the missionaries towards the caste system and any past associations between the denominational and regional identities within the caste-dominated South

Indian churches. Were such links to be identified, their significance would lie in current causes for division within the Christian community of South India associated with sociocultural factors. The link between the practice of the caste system within the church today and its historical roots is basic to any understanding of the present condition of Dalit Christians within the South Indian churches, who are the subjects of this research and too often seen as a somewhat essentialized mass.

It is also important to note that the social practices of discrimination within the Christian communities are inadequately documented. This has two results. Either 'rural Dalit Christians' are used to exemplify whatever the urban commentator wishes or they are not brought into the discussion 'as they are' because they are simply not known.[4] Given these lacunae, this chapter remains exploratory in nature. One point that needs no explanation is the fact that the situation of Dalit Christians has not changed much within the church, becoming an accepted reality. That this has and will continue to have an adverse effect on the church in the future, the purpose for which the institution exists, makes the issue one of considerable interest.

The 'mission' and 'caste' in South India

The advent of colonial 'missionary' Christianity in India resulted in an interesting interaction between the message of Jesus Christ as brought by the Western missionaries and the socioculturally polarized setting of South India. As described earlier, this part of India was the hub of much Christian missionary activity and proved to be a great field of experimentation. The existence of an Orthodox Christian community in the tradition of St Thomas, with membership mostly from the 'caste' community, did very little towards the expansion of Christianity.[5] As Stephen Neill records the reason for such a practice,

> The community of the Thomas Christians became almost hermetically sealed off from the Hindu world around it. Marriage was always within the community. Conversion from the non-Christian to the Christian world was so rare as hardly to enter into consideration. The status of the Christian world was roughly the same as that of the Nayars, the great land holding Hindu caste.[6]

Since St Thomas Christians are mostly from the high-caste community, the newer missionary movement found successful new converts from the 'outcaste' community through mass movements into Christianity. The Catholic missionaries were the first ones to come to the shores of South India to begin their missionary work. These Catholic missionaries were instantly confronted by the caste reality and its deep-rootedness in Indian society.

After some initial hesitation, the European missionaries attempted to convert all the 'pagans' to Christianity without getting embroiled in the caste conflict, taking the 'safer' method of avoiding confrontation. This accommodative approach is exemplified in the life and work of Robert De Nobili.[7] Even though he was hailed as the first missionary to think seriously of utilizing Indian cultural aspects for the presentation of the gospel, later known as contextualization, his decision to have separate priests for the 'upper' and 'lower' castes resulted in a fragmented Christian community.[8] Summarizing the attitude of the Catholic missionaries Duncan Forrester observes,

> Roman Catholic mission (aries) . . . from the beginning appear to have regarded the caste system as the given and religiously neutral structure of Indian society within which evangelization, understood as the conversion of individuals without detaching them from their social context, and also the conversion of the whole caste group, might proceed. Christianity, in other words was seen as neither threatening nor undermining the caste system, but rather working within it and accommodating western social standards to the norms of caste.[9]

The resourceful missionaries also thought that if they succeeded in getting the 'high caste' converts then it would trickle down to the low caste, making their mission work easier. However, the high-caste converts objected to sharing their places of worship with low caste people, being accustomed to separation in their Hindu practices.[10] Fearing that the negative attitude to the caste system would adversely affect their prospect of getting more Christian converts, priests decided to tread carefully by adhering to caste distinctions. The result brought the caste system into the church, arguably rather contrary to the Gospel teaching.

The Protestant missionaries arrived two centuries later, but by then the Catholic Church had made progress in terms of establishing itself. Ziegenbalg and Plutschau were the first Protestant missionaries to arrive on the South

Indian coast of Tranquebar from Halle, Germany in 1706. With their strongly Pietistic background,[11] they took the missionizing of the 'heathens' seriously by teaching and educating the local people from various caste communities. But when it came to establishing a worshiping Christian community, the division between the 'upper' and 'lower' castes again became a stumbling block. The missionaries cleverly worked out a plan to accommodate Christians from different caste groups by designating specific spaces in places of worship, so that there would be no inter-caste interactions which could potentially cause tension. The first church designed by Ziegenbalg, the New Jerusalem Church in Tranquebar, bears witness to the fact that the 'Untouchable' Christians sat in the wings of the cross-shaped church and the 'upper' caste Christians occupied the main body of the church. As historians record, there was no interaction during the Eucharist, as the caste groups were offered communion separately.[12] Other Protestant Missionaries like Christian David, Christian Schwartz and the Anglican Bishop Heber also promoted such an 'accommodating' attitude towards caste in the community of Christians, which is still experienced in various ways today.[13]

As the nineteenth century developed, South India appeared animated with various missionary organizations working vigorously to Christianize the 'heathens'. Interestingly, the Protestant missionaries had a contrasting point of view from that of their Catholic predecessors, as they considered that 'caste within the church was an unmitigated evil'[14] and did make genuine efforts to ward it off. But the policy of the East Indian Company, which was not to disturb the local customary practice, worked against them.[15] Since they found the caste system to be too complicated to manage, they eventually yielded to social religious pressure. When each caste group converted in large numbers, they also brought along with them the cultural baggage of specific caste practices. Regardless of the missionaries' concerted efforts, Webster mentions, the impact of 'the missionary dilemma', their decision to take up a conciliatory approach towards caste and its significance in the history of the South Indian church.[16] Holding a similar view, Ayub Daniel concludes that the missionaries' attitudes towards caste system over the past centuries were of three kinds, 'accommodation, rejection and compromise', all of them pursued with an intention of preserving their mission of Christianizing rather than emancipating the lives of Outcastes.[17]

Caste and denomination: An associational view

Unlike the doctrinal and class struggles manifested in the denominational division in Europe, the fertile mission fields of South India provided a different model for the development of denominational identities. As an outcome of the inner missionary struggle to dominate and control, missionaries belonging to various churches and mission bodies during the late nineteenth and early twentieth centuries agreed to work within particular territories and communities in order to avoid conflicts and confusion. Highlighting this development, Sister Carol Graham records in her work,

> Since the great missionary conference held in Edinburgh in 1910 almost all the reformed churches and mission bodies have agreed to work within clearly defined geographical limits . . . this has at least to some extent lessened the confusion and decreased the Babel of many voices proclaiming the one Gospel, but it has also created a situation among Indian Christians in which their church affiliation depends entirely upon the area in which they are born.[18]

This pattern of exclusive mission fields gave impetus to each denominational missionary organization and churches assuming distinct geographical identities.[19] But unfortunately it had an adverse side effect, in that the geographical boundaries came to signify certain caste groups from which the majority of Christian converts were drawn. Underlining this development, Forrester records,

> The L. M. S (London Missionary Society) in Travancore and some of the C. M. S (Church Missionary Society) and S. P. G (Society for the Propagation of the Gospel) stations in Tinnevelly became known as 'Nadar churches' and converts from other castes were not encouraged. In Travancore the vast majority of Christians were L. M. S Christians. Thus relations between denominations could have a caste dimension. It was also the case that congregations in a particular area might be composed virtually entirely of converts from one caste, forming a kind of caste-sect within the larger church organization . . . the Nadars in the south were able virtually to take over the church and use it in part as an expression of their caste identity.[20]

This period saw the emergence of a confused identity as a result of such denominational restrictions and the caste system. It is also crucial to note that this method of accommodating and working within the caste framework brought the missionaries rich dividends in terms of the number of converts to Christianity. Yet they had to be very shrewd so as to not squander their chances of getting high-caste converts, for it was *their* conversion, and theirs alone that was perceived as contributing to social legitimacy for Christianity. In some cases they even had to take special measures to keep them coming, efforts that had a negative impact on the emancipation of the Dalit communities, particularly Dalit Christians.

Though the missionaries provided various avenues of hope and progress for the Dalit communities, some of their efforts to safeguard the mission hampered the development and transformation of Dalit Christians. In an extremely well-researched article, Dayanandan deconstructs the myth that the missionaries completely reformed Dalit life, arguing that they followed discreet methods to accommodate the high caste in the church. He also describes the denial of educational opportunities for the Paraiyar community in the northern Tamil Nadu region. He observes that even though the Free Church of Scotland mission opened up educational avenues, they denied opportunities for Dalit students, thereby hampering community's progress.[21] According to the missionaries, if the Christians were drawn from one particular caste community, it meant that there would not be room for inner and inter-caste conflicts within the church. Since they felt that such a situation would distract them from their Christianizing aim, they further strengthened the distinct caste identities for different Christian communities. Having set out these key issues, let us now consider some specific examples from the South Indian churches in order to understand the issue under discussion.

The prevalence of caste in South Indian churches

The Church of South India (CSI) offers a good example of the dynamics of caste reality. The CSI is a union of churches from Anglican, Presbyterian, Wesleyan Methodist and Congregational missionary backgrounds. These missionary movements each found members from various caste communities, with an especially large number from the 'Outcastes'.[22] Even though the CSI was formed as an organic unity in principle, the groups involved in the union continued to preserve their own denominational missionary heritage, and by extension, caste-leanings in the lives and ministry of the local congregations, thereby safeguarding caste identity. A Church Missionary Society (CMS) pamphlet published in the early days of the CSI depicts a clear picture,

> No thought was given to unity on the mission field: Anglicans, Presbyterians, Methodists, Lutherans and a score of others busied themselves building separate churches. Now all thoughts turns to unity and sees its longing coming to realization in the church of south India, formed in 1947 by the union of Anglicans, Presbyterians, Methodist and congregational churches. Amid much change and upheavals, fundamentals are permanent.[23]

During the CSI's formative years after India attained independence, for practical administrative reasons dioceses were formed based on these denominational mission boundaries.[24] This process has left an indelible mark on the current life of the CSI and its members.

It may be helpful to observe some more facts about South Indian churches. In his pioneering work, Ninan Koshey exposes the wide gap between various Christian groups and enumerates the harsh realities experienced by the Dalit Christians within the churches in the South Indian state of Kerala.[25] The subtle manner in which caste distinctions are accepted as the norm among Christian communities, allowing segregation and subjugation, is well documented in his works. Koshey also observes the 'elitism' associated with the Syrian St Thomas Christian identity and their patronizing attitude, irrespective of church affiliation, which points to the deep rootedness of the caste issue.[26] In an article titled *Christian Missionaries and Caste in Kerala*, Gladstone (the former CSI bishop of the South Kerala diocese) traces the roots of the caste conflict between Syrian Christians and Dalit converts from the days of CMS and London Missionary Society (LMS) missionaries, which laid the foundation for the corrupt caste segregation that exists without any Eucharistic communion.[27] In a recent historical study, the church historian George Oomen observes the complexity involving caste identity in spite of the presumed mobility in social status after converting to Christianity. The Pulayas (a Dalit community) are accepted in some areas of life if they imitate Syrian Christians but rejected if they continued to live according to their Dalit cultural practices.[28]

Godwin Shiri records that widespread segregation among Christians in the Karnataka region was superficially expressed through their mission allegiance, but essentially reflected caste demarcation. For example, if a person is from the German Basel mission background in the Mangalore region (of South Karnataka), it is almost sure that he hails from the 'Billava' caste, since most of the converts exclusively belong to Sudhra Caste with few Brahmin converts.[29] Dalit conversion in this region was negligible. Highlighting the high-caste Christians attitude he says, 'It is true that the Mangalore Christians for long, perhaps even now to some extent, carry a bias against Christians of interior Karnataka who happen to come mostly from Dalit origin'.[30]

The southernmost diocese of Tamil Nadu, which was under the Anglican missionary society's spiritual dispensation, was dominated by converts from the Nadar community who preserve their Anglican tradition even today.[31] They tend to look down upon other dioceses, dioceses which draw their members from Dalit communities as in north Tamil Nadu, which were either once Scottish or American mission fields. It is also observed that there is very little social interaction between these Christian Dalit and non-Dalit communities and inter-caste marriages are a rarity. Some Dalit priests are able to take services in some of the non-Dalit congregations but separate cemeteries are kept for Dalits and non-Dalits. M. Azariah, a former bishop of CSI, expresses his anguish at the prevalence of segregation and oppression on the basis of caste remarking that the 'the attitudes of caste division among Christians seem to be not at all different from those of the orthodox Hindus'.[32] Explaining further he writes,

> even after coming into the Christian church the different segments of the population continue to carry not only in their mind and consciences, but deep in their soul and spirit the different caste and outcaste identities. These identities or stampings leave different types of markings on their souls within different segments of the population.[33]

In the state of Andhra Pradesh in South India, the Lutheran and Baptist Churches bear further testimony to this exploitative system of caste within the Christian and practice hierarchy. In Andhra Pradesh, Mala and Madiga are two Dalit caste communities who are constantly in conflict with each other due to the historical rivalry between them. Lutheran missionaries predominantly worked among Dalit communities, and inevitably the Lutheran churches bear a Dalit identity. For example, the members of the Andhra Evangelical Lutheran Church are predominantly drawn from the 'Mala' community and as such it is invariably known as the 'Mala' church. Similarly, the Baptist missionaries along with Catholic predominately worked among the 'Madiga' communities[34] in Andhra Pradesh and continue to have a distinct caste identity known as 'Madiga'.[35] The historical denominationally based rivalry between these caste groups not only results in a strained relationship between the churches concerned but also further complicates its associations with some of the Christians institutions with a distinct high-caste leadership (such as 'Reddyars').[36] Given the CSI with its prevailing caste identities, it is clear that there is presently little scope for an ecumenical relationship between these churches. Furthermore, the 'Syrian Orthodox Christian' churches look down upon all the non-Orthodox, Catholic and Protestant churches as 'churches with no tradition' and therefore unworthy of any degree of association.

Comprehensively analysing the situation in South Indian churches, Webster records the associational view between caste and denomination within the segregated Christian communities and the ensuing conflicts, which continue to play a significant role in the current church polity.[37] The situation of Dalit Christians in the Roman Catholic Churches in South India bears further testimony to the prevalence of caste practices. As Webster succinctly observes,

> In South Caste played a lesser role in protestant than in Catholic church, where separate seating for caste and Dalit Catholics still continues. There are also separate burial places in Catholic cemeteries as well. Dalits have been assigned inferior roles in Catholic mass, in Catholic funerals and in the celebration of Christian festivals.[38]

Such historical observations are supported by S. M. Michael who provides detailed accounts of discrimination from the Catholic Church in Tamil Nadu.[39] More recently, in two ethnographic studies on the Kerala Catholic churches (who account for the majority of Catholics in South India), Sunil George Kurian brings out the divisions on the basis of their colonial patronage as well as the plight of the Dalit Christians at the hands of a few powerful high-Caste Christians dominating church administration and life.[40] From these and other insights into the historical and contemporary experience of Dalit Christians in the churches in South India, it is possible to conclude that the role and influence of the caste system in the life of the Church, regardless of denomination, is still alive and active, excluding Dalit Christians full participation within the Church at large.

Continuing exclusions

> Clearly, different groups, while drawing on regional traditions and patterns, constituted their identity in unique and complex ways. Processes of continuity and discontinuity are discernible everywhere and appear to be constructed out of several elements.[41]

This concluding remark by Rowena Robinson, discusses the interaction of Catholic and Protestant missionaries within the caste system and its related denominational identity. These tightly meshed identities of caste and denomination have far-reaching consequences in terms of socio-economic status and therefore education, creating a hierarchy that smoothly paves the way for justifying the biased leadership, domination, marginalization and subordination of Dalit Christians within the Church. To clarify this pattern, two broad areas that manifest such discriminatory practices will be briefly outlined in order to show the impact of the caste system on the lives of Dalit Christians. We will conclude by looking at the impact of such processes on the formation of Dalit Christian identity and its drawbacks.

Social ramifications

Within the South Indian context, the Catholic and Protestant churches run a significant number of educational and health institutions, acting as a significant educator and employer. With the preceding discussion it is obvious that educational and employment opportunities are usually decided on the basis of caste and since most institutions are controlled by people from the non-Dalit communities, Dalit Christians are often denied access to such opportunities. One of the strongest critical observations of this process comes from Chandran Devanesan, an important educator and church figure:

> There are Christian institutions today that look as if they are the private property of particular castes that have been converted in the past. Anybody

> who does not belong to that caste cannot hope to be appointed as a teacher in that institution. So the appointments are no longer in terms of who is most qualified or in terms of academic merit. You have to belong to the right caste to get in![42]

What was observed two decades ago is not only history but also a continuing living reality in the lives of South Indian Dalit Christians who remain uneducated and unemployed within such institutions. Commenting on the wider Dalit Christian situation, Lancy Lobo observes that Dalit Christians,

> experience social discrimination in education and employment. Socially, in the larger society of non- Christians, they are still treated as untouchables by the caste Hindus, especially in the rural areas. They also suffer alienation from their own fellow 'untouchables', the Hindu Dalits, because of the religious differences. Moreover the Hindu Dalits frown upon Christian Dalits as potential competitors for a share of the reservations. Within the wider regional Christian community, Dalit Christians continue to be considered 'untouchables' or 'Neo-Christians', in some places they used to be segregated inside the church during worship.[43]

What is implied here is that as long as the majority of Dalit communities remain illiterate and out of work, their dependence continues on the 'high caste' Christians, who control the resources and access to training, furthering the vicious cycle of exploitation and marginalization. Later on it will be illustrated in this book how such exclusions and dependencies are daily realities in the lives of Dalit Christians.

The administration of the churches in South India provides a glaring example of caste discrimination as the domination of particular caste groups within the power structure of the church hierarchy can be perceived from the grass-roots level to the highest echelons.[44] For a long time in the Church of South India (CSI), the leaders and officials were always elected from the high-caste communities, who consequently benefited from their leadership were people from the same communities. During the election for the church administrative bodies, one could recognize the various political alignments based on the region/diocese. Reflecting on this situation, Webster notes,

> Caste has certainly played its role in this struggle for power within the churches, at least in the south where caste provides the basis for informal

> political alliance from the congregational level on up. The basic division has been between Dalits and non Dalits, except among Andhra Pradesh Protestants, where the rivalry between Madigas and Malas has been even more serious. The politics of caste affects not only election to position of leadership and power, but also appointments and promotion in Christian institutions.[45]

This painful history has left an often-times inflexible hierarchy controlled largely by non-Dalits or by some economically powerful Dalit communities, thereby incorporating and continuing the unfair structures. In his work, Godwin Shiri critically records the gross negligence regarding Dalits within the Church, which amounts to a betrayal of their hopes and aspirations.[46] While half of the CSI bishops are Dalits, the situation has superficially changed; this is so because the new bishops represent the economically powerful urban Dalit communities. The larger Dalit communities, tending to live in the rural parts of South India, continue to be neglected, and are thus marginalized by every power holder involved.

Though on the surface level the reason for disunity among Christians in South India is attributed to distinct doctrinal and missionary heritages, a judicious observation reveals that caste divisions become a significant factor keeping the different groups from realizing an ecclesial communion. What are the results of such a continuation? The churches in South India have become best examples of fragmentation, infighting and litigation, embodying social injustice, moral corruption, bankruptcy and deep-seated failure of its leadership. Most of these issues are fuelled by strong socio-economic factors since the fact that the Church being one of the largest land and property owners invariably leads to bitter internal and external relationships among various groups. Additionally, it is uncommon at the community level to witness inter-caste marriage and the 'Eucharist' shared among various denominational groups. Because of these inner divisive dynamics, the churches in South India find themselves wrestling with the issue of ecumenism and as such fail to work cooperatively for the benefit of its marginalized members.

Constricted 'Indian Christian Theology'

Theologizing remains a task of the privileged and educated, because the 'illiterate' Christians are considered unable to contribute towards it and their views irrelevant. Christian doctrine and theological precepts therefore reflect the worldview of those educated in missionary schools and thus mirror the corresponding dominant scriptural tradition. Hence, theological reflection on the life and ministry of the church in South India embodies the exclusivist attitude of the caste-dominated society. Furthermore, theological articulations tend not to address the needs and realities of the majority Christians living on the margins of the 'church' and outcaste by the dominant society. Theological preoccupations have tended to be intellectual and transcendental in nature, emphasizing the otherworldly and benefits promised in the world to come undermining the relevance of Christianity and Christian struggles in this life.

What came to be known as 'Indian Christian Theology' in the early twentieth century clearly replicates such a process. Since theologians during this period were predominantly from the dominant 'high' castes, they advocated theological notions that accommodated Vedic ideas outlined earlier. Commenting on this development, Sugirtharaja observes,

> In the name of indigenization/inculturation, Christian themes such as Incarnation, Atonement and the Trinity were superimposed on to Hebraic and Hellenistic concepts, in an attempt to force a spurious theological validation, which does not easily emerge organically.[47]

As a consequence, theology almost became the given privilege of the high-caste minority, reproducing the nature of the caste system itself, in which Brahmins are regarded as the rightful owners of Hindu theology, and the 'illiterate' Dalits became the passive recipients. The metaphysical and transcendental domination of Indian Christian Theology also contributed towards the maintenance of church hierarchy, which in turn replicated the caste structure of society.

With the background knowledge of Hindu worldview provided in the last chapter, let me highlight some fundamental ideas of Indian Christian Theology, which are problematic from a Dalit Christian perspective. As a high-caste Hindu Keshub Chunder Sen, a pioneer in Indian Christian Theology, trained in Hindu scriptures and a leader of Brahmo Samaj of India (a Hindu reform movement founded in 1828), contributed to some of the seminal ideas of what later came to be known as Indian Christian Theology, as carly as the mid-nineteenth century.[48] K. C. Sen suggested that in Christianity the Trinity is strikingly similar to the threefold Hindu concept of *Sachidananda*, the conglomerate of 'Sat', 'Chit' and 'Ananda'.[49] Sen describes *Sachidananda* as states of consciousness, essentially 'three conditions, three manifestations of Divinity'.[50] While comparing the Christ of Christianity to Brahma in Hinduism, Sen suggests that 'the Supreme Brahma of the Veda and the Vedanta dwells hid in Himself (Christ)', a central idea that still continues in the tradition of Indian Christian Theology.[51] In the twentieth century, Sen's theology was continued by Brahmabandhab Upadhyaya, a Bengali Brahmin Christian,[52] who comments,

> in customs and manners, in observing caste or social distinctions, in eating and drinking, in our life and living, we are genuine Hindus . . . Our thought and thinking is emphatically Hindu. We are more speculative than practical, more given to synthesis than analysis, more contemplative than active.[53]

This emphatic affirmation of adherence to Hindu ways of thinking and living by Upadhyaya forms the framework of his theology. Commenting on Upadhyaya's theological arguments, Robin Boyd explains that 'the highest possible Hindu conception of God, that of *Brahman* or *Parabrahman* or *nirguna Brahaman*', as found in the *Advaita* philosophy of Sankara, articulates the God of Christianity.[54] As a Roman Catholic, Upadhyaya claims that such Vedic philosophy corresponds to Natural Theology's Trinitarian understanding of the divine Sonship of Christ. He writes,

> in the Vedas are found a very sublime conception of one Supreme Being, the idea of divine generation somewhat resembling the Christian doctrine of divine Sonship, and an account of the sacrifice of the first-begotten of God the virtue of which supreme act is far reaching.[55]

Such an observation suggests the impact of Vedic philosophy on Indian Christian theology,[56] which arguably continues to the present day. Indian theologians like K. P. Aleaz frequently imbue the exclusive Vedic caste ideology, present in Indian society, into their theological systems.[57] In his apt analysis of Indian Christian Theology, Robin Boyd clearly shows the continuing impact of Vedic philosophy in the long tradition of doing Indian Christian Theology. He notes how Sanskritic terms were simply substituted with English terms in order to express Christian doctrines, and therefore Indian Christian Theology became an intellectual and contemplative enterprise, which excluded the majority of Indian Christians most of whom are uneducated Dalits.[58] This

Sanskritization of Indian Christian Theology consequently served to alienate doubly Outcaste Christians from doing and understanding theology, as they could not read Sanskrit in the Vedas, let alone Biblical concepts laden with Sanskritic terms.

As it is found in the Hindu tradition where the caste system is validated by the Hindu scriptures, Indian Christian Theology, by neglecting the lives of Dalit Christians as the theological focus, indirectly legitimizes caste practices in the church and also contributes towards the perpetuation of the otherworldly and transcendental nature of Christianity in India. In other words, 'Indian Christian Theology' epitomizes the extreme form of uncritical inculturation resulting in compromise and conciliatory incorporation of discriminatory power structures within the church.

Indian Christian Theology following in the footsteps of the missionaries felt that the majority of the Dalit Christians had no valid religious knowledge and needed to be educated in Christian faith by Christianizing the ignorant illiterate. The dominant pattern of theologizing in India had no place for the life and experiences of the majority of Dalit Christians. Such theological attitudes continued to displace Dalit Christians even within their own communities. It was this situation that gave birth to 'Dalit Theology', theology from the perspective of Dalit Christians.

The preceding discussion showcases that even though decades have gone by since the arrival of 'missionary' Christianity, caste continues to dictate terms in the subsistence of the churches in South India. The re-reading of this history is significant because a great deal of attitudes and activities found within the church are based on them. Moreover, in order to maintain the status quo and run the institution of the church, this approach becomes important. Not only can this be seen as a failure on the part of the church to live out the promises made by the missionaries, but it has also preserved various discriminatory practices within the institutional framework. As most of the Dalit thinkers observe this is nothing but the rejection of the Christian message in its entirety in the process of controlling and dominating, which is reflected at the core of the caste system.[59] In its broadest understanding, caste ideology is the *modus operandi* employed to channel power relations within a community through subjugation and domination. With the continuation of caste practices, the churches in South India continue to struggle with the issue of caste discrimination. This is the very constitution of Dalit Christian identity, issues such as the imposition of a very particular Christian identity onto Dalit identity and the resulting aspects of power and representation need to be critically observed.

Problematizing Dalit Christian identity

In the process of resisting caste-dominated Christianity, Dalit thinkers began to develop the notion of a Dalit Christian identity. Dalit identity has tended to be essentialized, ignoring their religio-cultural frameworks of meanings, which have effectively intermingled with their 'converted' Christian lives. Even 'Dalit Theology' by Christianizing the Dalit worldview falls into the same trap as the missionaries did in the past, considering everything in India as Hindu and reduces the complexity of spiritual worldviews and experiences in India.[60] As Devasahayam succinctly states, 'the Bible, as the point which provides the Christian identity and continuity with our Christian tradition needs to be brought back to the centre stage of theological reflection'.[61] In this method of theologizing and reflecting, there seems to be an imposition of a biblical world onto the Dalit historical-cultural world.[62]

Furthermore, it can be asked as to whether the theological conceptions of God, Jesus Christ and other aspects of the Christian faith reflect the way in which the spiritual realm is conceived within the Dalit world. Or is it just the theological constructions of academic theologians conceptualizing in their own terms? What is the similarity between the God of Christian faith and the Dalit spirituality?

The romantic notion of Dalit culture and community also needs to be critically appraised. As outlined earlier, Dalit Christian thinkers have asserted in the past and in the present that the Dalit worldview is the epitome of unity and embodies the values of justice and equality in every aspect.[63] The issues concerning hierarchy, inequality and abuse of power within the Dalit community were brushed aside as insignificant in comparison with caste oppression. It should also be noted that 'Dalit' as a category was constructed and utilized as a homogeneous category collapsing all the differences and diversity within the Dalit communities into one homogeneous whole.

Such an approach poses serious challenges in addressing the core issues of community formation and fails to recognize the discursive processes of negotiation within a particular community. On the back of this analysis and through the ethnographic study conducted among the Paraiyar Christians in Thulasigramam, one of the Dalit communities in South India, I shall seek to understand four aspects in the following chapters: first, the complex Paraiyar identity formation, second, the multi-layered worldview of Paraiyar Christians, third, the issues of power within the Christian community and finally the various processes of social negotiations.

3

Identity and Community among Paraiyars

> *Ideological glosses of humanity and academic glosses on ideology, leave out too much of what men and women themselves find most meaningful: their aspirations and discontents, much of their suffering, the texture of their lives and the flow of their experience. We need to explore such experience and not just the ideology of Caste.*[1]

This observation by Steven M. Parish holds true especially in the Dalit context. Within Dalit studies, often the ideological impact of the caste system and its sociological consequences assumes importance over the mundane and ordinary things in Dalit communities. Most importantly, the complex socio-religious landscape in which Dalits actually reside is glossed over in favour of broad categories unrelated to the actual negotiations of lives. It is against this background that the ethnography of one particular Dalit Christian community, the Paraiyar Christian community in Thulasigramam, becomes a significant means to understand the various processes and complex texture of their lives. Religion, as I explained earlier, is not just a narrow aspect of human life; it rather permeates into the entire social fabric of a community.[2] Thus, the focus of the four following chapters will be, first, the social construction of Paraiyar Christian identity and its complexity, second, the socio-religious worldviews prevalent among the community, third, the negotiations and contestations of socio-religious boundaries and finally, the experience of the church among the Paraiyar Christian community. This section will also explore how all the above-mentioned aspects are interconnected and contribute to the lived expression of religion within the Paraiyar Christian community in Thulasigramam.

Self-conceptualization and identity of both individuals and communities are context bound, demanding localized perception in order to be understood.[3] Any examination of (Christian) *Paraiyar* identity inevitably becomes context specific. The conception of communal or personal identity arguably emerges as a collective (but not uniform) expression of localized cultural and traditional consciousness, which is variously disseminated and negotiated within a particular community. Previous discussions on Paraiyar identity have contributed towards understanding the complexity of the rural Paraiyar community in Tamil Nadu.[4] In addition, this chapter proposes to develop a representational, nuanced understanding of identity markers that contribute towards the formation of Paraiyar social identity in Thulasigramam.[5] Here, issues such as kinship, community and the self-perception of the Paraiyars in opposition to the Reddyars will be addressed. Furthermore, the impact of the physical location and ensuing socio-psychological domination in identity formation will be looked at. The presence of stereotyping, name calling, role reversals among Paraiyar women and the multi-layered perception of being Paraiyars and Christians will be discussed in the light of contemporary views on social identity discourse. In doing so, it also introduces the subjects of my fieldwork and their own self-understanding within their community.

Contemporary discussions on social identity

Identity as a subject matter has been at the centre of sociological studies for some decades, producing diverse material on identity discourse. For the purpose of expounding a non-essentialist perspective on the identity of Paraiyars within the context of an essentialist caste understanding of Indian history, it is important to gain a basic understanding of the current discussion on 'social identity'. The following analysis will touch upon three important aspects raised by social theorists when expounding social construction of identity. They are: (1) the importance of the mundane, everyday facts of life, (2) belonging, locatedness and relational nature of identity and (3) the dynamic and complex nature of identity formation.

According to Richard Jenkins, identity is about the simple facts of people's lives and how they distinguish themselves from others through the various activities that comprise the fundamentals of identity formation.[6] Complementing that idea Jeffrey Weeks explains further,

> Identity is about belonging, about what you have in common with some people and what differentiates you from others. At its most basic it gives you a sense of personal location, the stable core to your individuality. It's also about your social relationships, your complex involvement with others.[7]

The preceding explanation lays the emphasis on the distinct and specific particulars of an individual or community in their everyday lives or 'habitus'[8] as Bourdieu suggests, which is often glossed over by generalized analytical approaches.[9] In the light of Paraiyar Christian identity formation, the notion of belonging and locatedness is expressed in their mundane lives through routine transactions within the community.

Exploring some of the conceptual aspects of identity, Jenkins observes that similarity and difference are the two overarching and dynamic principles of identity. When a person says something about others, she is often saying something about herself. In Jenkins words, 'in social terms, similarity and difference are always functions of a point of view, our similarity is their difference'.[10] Moreover, identity that stems from such principles cannot be neutral since the values behind them are often conflictual in nature.

Furthermore, as Jeffrey Weeks observes, 'by saying who we are, we are also striving to express what we are, what we believe and what we desire'.[11] If we have to understand this thesis by its antithesis, by expressing who we are *not* and how *we* are different from the *others* and how *they* are different from *us*, we also implicitly strive to express who we are, what we believe and what we desire. Kathryn Woodward sheds additional light by observing that 'difference' defines identity as well as establishing distinction between one identity and another.[12] She further suggests that 'difference' should not be understood as rigid binary oppositions of *us* and *them* but as deferred meaning, which creates space for the fluidity of identity.[13] Thus, within the sphere of perceived dissimilarities, it becomes important to recognize the dynamic nature of identity formation.

However, this chapter stresses how differences are highlighted and furthered by the process of *othering* and creating *otherness* out of the *other*. Identities are constituted in relation to that *otherness* internal to Paraiyar Christian meaning-making system through articulating incommensurable difference. Alienation and objectification in relationship to the *other* in substance and essence provides the variance and similarity necessary for the conceptualization of self and communal identity. Often objectified as untouchables, through social conditioning and learning, a person from the *Paraiyar* Christian community gathers around the idea of not being a *Reddyar*, who is known to be higher than him by birth. This process generates respect for the Reddyars and self-pity for those non-Reddyars. By contrast, the same person learns through social observation that he should be happy not to be an *Arunthathier*, who are perceived to be lower than Paraiyar by birth and occupation within the caste system.

Let us return to Richard Jenkins' view that the, 'self as each individual's reflexive sense of her or his own particular identity, constituted vis-à-vis others in terms of similarity and difference, without which we would not know who we are and hence would not be able to act'.[14] Advancing the relational nature of identity, Jenkins remarks that self-identification is an ongoing process of internal and external dialectic, as individuals negotiate their identities within the interaction and relational social order.[15] Stuart Hall, further explaining such a process, suggests,

> Identity is not as transparent and unproblematic as we think. Perhaps instead of thinking of identity as an already accomplished fact, which the new cultural practices then represent, we should think instead, of identity as a production, which is never complete, always in process, and always constituted within, not outside, representation.[16]

In other words, identity has to be understood as an outcome of a combination of processes that underlines the complexity of identity as well as the tension between individual and society where the self cannot be considered as a given.[17] Individual and communal identity is a product of its context and derives its meaning from it. Thus, individual identity is a social construction and does not have significance in isolation from its social location since the subject or 'the selfhood is thoroughly socially constructed'.[18] Richard Jenkins clarifies that people actually,

> collectively identify themselves and others and they conduct their everyday lives in terms of those identities which therefore have practical consequences, . . . collective identities are generated in transaction and interaction and are at least potentially flexible, situational and negotiable, . . . identity is a matter of ascription: by individuals of themselves, and of individuals by others.[19]

Such constructive processes create 'new negotiated space' of contested and negotiated individual identities through subversion and transgression.[20] Similarly, Paul du Gay rightly explicates the Weberian idea,

> We have no essence waiting to unfold itself but are instead remarkably malleable creatures whose capacities and dispositions are formed and reformed in the various spheres of life in which we are placed and place ourselves.[21]

Homi Bhabha broadens this idea by suggesting that the socio-cultural milieu constitutes selfhood, providing the framework of meaning for an individual and the community through 'interpellative practices'.[22] To summarize, an individual identity is dynamically constructed as *different* from the *other*, providing the power to make one experience their *self* as the *other* within a community. This process is crucial to understand the Paraiyar identity, which is socially constructed and prescribed by caste ideology and internalized by Paraiyars to fulfil their roles in the community.

The similarities and differences, contrasts and negations of the *other* and the subject's relation to his locatedness and multi-layered consciousness, are some of the most prevalent modes of constituting an individual identity within a community. Using the preceding discussion on social identity, I would like briefly to examine some observations of individuals in their context and the communal aspects of how the Paraiyar Christians in Thulasigramam perceive themselves and construct their identity in a marginalized situation. It is in this process of weaving various strands together that we might be able to develop a plausible understanding of Paraiyar Christian notions of the individual and community. At this juncture it is also important to recognize the contextual differences and ideological trappings of the contemporary identity discourses in social-anthropology discussed earlier.

Kinship, food and community

According to many Indian social theorists, individuals construct their identity as members of a particular community.[23] The fluid and dynamic nature of individual identity is possible because an individual's identity is acquired and relates to a specific community. Hence there is no 'one' identity but several reference points provided by the community, which are dynamic in nature, since a person is in multiple relationships and roles. Furthermore, it is the community that provides the individual with his referential base, which therefore needs to be understood as much as if not more than the terms of its meaning and content rather than its forms and structure.[24] Through his studies on peripheral communities Anthony Cohen argues that 'community exists in the mind of its members' and not just in geographical space.[25] Drawing upon Cohen's explication, Richard Jenkins suggests,

> Emphasising the symbolic construction of community, Cohen advances three arguments; first, he says that symbols generate a sense of shared belonging, secondly, community is itself a symbolic construct upon which people draw, rhetorically and strategically, thirdly community membership means sharing with other community members a similar sense of things participating in a common symbolic domain.[26]

In this light, community expresses a relational idea and provides the individual with a sense of belonging and meaning for existence, which would not be otherwise available.[27] It is the social relationships and networks through which an individual experiences his community that provides his social identity. Furthermore, observing the significance and interplay of communal and individual identity within the Paraiyar social worldview will yield valuable insights into self-identification. In this section, two aspects will be explored: first, the contribution of kinship relationships towards identity formation and second, how a practice such as excommunication functions to maintain communal identity.

It is clear that an individual by himself does not have an identity in isolation, and this is naturally also true for the members of the Paraiyar community of Thulasigramam. In the village, individuals are known as somebody's daughter, son, wife, husband, brother, sister, uncle and aunt and by more complex patrilineal and matrilineal relationships like *Mama* (maternal uncle), *Periyappa* (father's elder brother), *Chithappa* (father's younger brother), *Athai* (father's sister), *Chithhi* (mother's younger sister), *Mami* (maternal uncle's wife), *Anni* (elder brother's wife), *Thatha* (grandfather) and *Patti* (grandmother). The above-mentioned descriptive terms were just some of the identities that emerged during conversations within the community. The prevalence of such recognized relatedness underplays the perception of an individual as the bearer of a particular familial lineage. It is this consciousness of belonging to somebody that facilitates individual and communal identity, all being interwoven.[28] This process gets reinforced time and again through the verbal interaction of individuals. While attempting to get the attention of someone in the street or in a public place, people call the person as the daughter or the son of someone, mentioning their father's or mother's name. The individual is never just a sole individual. This becomes important to understand such a process through which an individual conceives and understands himself/herself as somebody's son, daughter, grandson, granddaughter, brother, sister, niece, nephew, wife, husband, uncle and/or aunt. Individual identity is always formulated in relation to others within the community through which the collective is realized and upheld.

Continuances of familial links through paternal and maternal relationships are also products of this process as Paraiyars emphasize the continuation of kinship ties through intermarriage within the community, further strengthening communal relationships.[29] Significantly, previous research on similar communities does not relate this naming process to the contribution of self-understanding, which stems from the group and only finally reaches the individual. When asked to describe themselves, most individuals in Thulasigramam first explained their position in the community through parents and relatives, eventually arriving at themselves. Often there would be very little left to explain about themselves after they had narrated their family trees and located themselves on one branch or another. This process, known in the parent-child aspect as teknonymy,[30] facilitates dynamic and multiple identity matrixes within a community. It is also important to note that such a matrix provides various reference points from which each individual can function and evolve within a given community eluding the concept of a fixed identity. Clearly in an endogamous community multiple links are inevitable; here they are mentally mapped and used.

Food plays a vital role in the communal lives of Paraiyars in Thulasigramam. While living in Thulasigramam it came to light that even their everyday greeting, *Saptiya?* (Did you eat or have food?), is used to determine the well-being of a person. Much of the Paraiyar social activity and festivity seems to be centred on food and most relationships are based on the sharing of food. After a few weeks into my stay in the village, when sitting on the church veranda, someone from one of the houses brought me some food to eat. If I accepted this food then it confirms that I accept them, if I refuse, then it is not only a degrading but a humiliating gesture. In the first few days, one particular family was providing me with food, but within the village, it sent interesting message that I was a guest of that particular family and as such the rest of the community had no business with me. Not only that, but they also branded me as belonging to 'their' particular group. After a few conscious attempts on my part others began to invite me to their homes and share their food with me. Only after that news spread within the community and I was welcomed in other households and the community at large.

The sign of me becoming adequately accepted as a person to talk to within the Paraiyar Christians in Thulasigramam was when I was invited into their homes to dine with them. In this caste-aware context, food becomes a means to determine the nature of a person, his status in the community and the relationship one shares with him. Among the Christians, the most keenly awaited times are the annual Christmas and Easter festivals when the whole community slaughters a bull or cow, makes a meal and shares this with each other (including the Hindus). This pattern of celebration draws its strength from the essential concepts of sharing, participation and solidarity among the community with commensality as the focus of that gathering in which 'God' is experienced. An important religious dimension in the sharing of food among Paraiyars is that when a person offers food to another, he is offering the meal to God and the person receives it as if God is giving it himself. Hence, while eating in her home, Poovamma from the Paraiyar community once mentioned, 'it is like God is having food in my house', which actually explained this spiritual transaction through commensality. On a different level, it could also mean that as a priest, for Poovamma I might have represented God, as the local priest has never visited her home, let alone ate with her. It also reflects the local Hindu practice where the priest is the representative of god and meals offered to him amounts to offering food to god. One of the characteristics of the Paraiyar Christian community is the shared commensality: even though there might be bickering, no accepted member goes hungry for it would shame the community. This dynamic determines the importance of food as well as the one who offers and receives it as god is perceived as the giver and receiver of it through human beings. This strengthens the communal relationships and establishes a commensurable fellowship.

In order to sustain such a collective communal identity, excommunication is effectively used as a disciplining and teaching tool. As Arul explained his own experience of being excommunicated for his anti-community activity, by supporting a young man from the Paraiyar community who eloped with a Reddyar young woman, and accepted back after he sought forgiveness from the community,

> the worst punishment given to a person in our community is to exclude or excommunicate him from the life and activities of the community. This is more painful than being stoned to death, because you will see everybody, but nobody will talk to you or entertain you.

Excommunication is the process by which all forms of communication and relationship are severed, leaving the individual or even families on their own to deal with their issues. In some cases, they are even physically removed and sent away from the village and prohibited from all communal activities and festivities. In extreme instances, the excommunicated cannot even make use of basic village amenities, such as the water well or the grocery shop. Other members of the community will not talk or even smile at them if they walk by, effectively removing or severing off communal links and thus the identity of the individual.

Within the Christian community, excommunication additionally means the forbidding of participating in church activities and special occasions. The excommunicated family/person will be ignored and the priest will be discouraged from visiting them or allow them to participate in the Eucharist, lest he face the resentment of the community. Anybody who entertains the excommunicated individual or family will first be reprimanded and then given a stern warning of dire consequences if such an action is repeated. This form of communal organization, with clear rules and regulations, ensures that every member of the community subscribes and adheres to the collective, sometimes sacrificing their individual interests.

For example, on the occasion of a young man or young woman eloping and is marrying against the wishes of their families, the families are expected to disown them and never to entertain or welcome the disobedient couple again in their households. Such incidents are seen as disrupting the continuance of familial or kinship relationships, which essentially destabilize the collective communal identity. The culprits are severely punished and those who do not support that ruling are ridiculed and later excommunicated. There are mechanisms in place to rectify such disruptions, if the concerned individual/family is willing to seek forgiveness and if all the members of the community are willing to forgive them and accept them in their midst. Within the Christian community in the case of such a 'rogue' couple, they are brought to the church and led through a 'regularizing' process by the priest. It is my contention that these factors of kinship and commensal relationships, and excommunication, act as symbolic tools of the community, which contributes considerably towards the formulation of collective consciousness from which the individual shares and draws his/her identity.

Self-perception in opposition

> Many high-caste Hindus have certain ideas in mind about people belonging to the lower orders: ideas that they are dirty, lazy, quarrelsome, not reliable, that the women enjoy much more freedom than rural high-caste women and above all that 'they (the women) have no morals and therefore deserve to be raped'.[31]

This key observation by Pillai-Vetschera while studying the Mahar women in Maharashtra captures the general perception of Dalit communities, which holds true in Thulasigramam. It is in such a context of understanding the conceptualization of an individual's identity within the situatedness of a particular community that is the focus of this chapter. Such a process happens simultaneously at various levels, eventually contributing towards one's own self-perception. Even as Pillai-Vetschera found in her own fieldwork among the Mahar in Maharashtra, such general perceptions about the Dalits are often contrary to the reality of the community. During fieldwork I also observed the dynamics of community formation through: differentiation (us and them), the impact of spatial relations on subjective conceptualization and the physical and mental framework within which these processes take place. Within this analysis different issues pertaining to pollution,[32] chastity, bravery and morality and their contribution to the 'self' understanding of Paraiyar Christians will be expounded in the light of the foregoing discussion on social production of identity. Following are five specific examples to illustrate the above mentioned context in Thulasigramam.

'We are not as dirty as they are'

Dayama, the middle-aged wife of Raju, a farmhand, born and brought up in Thulasigramam, described her experiences of living as a Paraiyar Christian in the village. She recalled the changes that had happened within her community and in its relationship to the high-caste Reddyars. She vividly remembered her childhood days, of not being allowed into Reddyar households, even to clean or get a glass of drinking water while working in their field. Although such rigid attitudes have changed, she explained that

> the Reddyars still think that we are dirty, polluting and very unclean but on the contrary they are the unclean and dirty people. We at least bathe often, but they only dress up and look clean but if you go to their houses it will be stinky and worse than our houses.

In principle, Dayama is convinced that the Paraiyars are not as dirty as the Reddyars perceive and treat them as being, even though they claim a higher status because according to the caste system they are 'purer' and 'cleaner'. By comparing and contrasting herself to the Reddyars, Dayama thinks of her community as far better in terms of cleanliness, thus reversing the social prejudice. Her own self-understanding of being a Paraiyar woman is derived from the fact of her not being the Reddyar. This insight is very vital, as the 'polluting' Paraiyar identity is constructed on the basis of their physical dirtiness and moral filthiness, which becomes the central cause for their exclusion from mainstream social life within the caste-dominated society. Dayama's idea sheds light onto one of the most important elements of the Paraiyars' self-conception that in fact it is actually the Reddyars who are dirty and not them.

'They are cowards'

The local popular Reddyar perception in Thulasigramam is that Paraiyars are cowards, but Prabu corrected that notion by saying, 'they (the Reddyars) are cowards'. Prabu thinks that if somebody fails to listen to Paraiyars' problems then violent means of achieving solutions are acceptable. As a middle-aged man growing up in Thulasigramam, he vividly remembers the violence meted out to the Paraiyar Christians on different occasions by the Reddyars. Interestingly, he thinks that it is out of fear as a means to safeguard themselves that Reddyars act violently since, as he claims, Paraiyars are *Veeramanavanga* ('brave and strong'). Whenever there is an opportunity, according to Prabu, Paraiyars would attack and 'teach the Reddyars a lesson!' His favourite story to recount is the violent clashes that happened between the Reddyars and Paraiyars a few years ago, as a result of conflict surrounding the organization of the local village temple festival. It became such a serious issue that the district police had to intervene in order to resolve and broker peace between both communities. But according to Prabu's account, during these series of attacks the Paraiyars were the ones who carried out violent acts on the Reddyars, which escalated the tension between the two groups. Prabu observed that the Paraiyars were able to do this because 'the Reddyars are cowards' and make use of various systems to exploit Paraiyars. In Prabu's opinion, the 'strong and brave' Paraiyars have become victims because of the cunning and manipulative nature of the Reddyars rather than through physical weakness on their part. This self-image of the Paraiyars being physically stronger than the Reddyars who hide behind caste rights and the police is important for understanding the Paraiyar identity, and negates the caste ideology which sees them as weak and vulnerable.[33] The Paraiyars are neither inherently violent nor aggressive, but as Prabu claims they are also not 'pushovers' but able to retaliate and teach the 'cowardly' Reddyars a lesson as and when required. This attitude was actually shared by other young men and women, enabling them to become very assertive in the past few years, resulting in tilting the balance of power in favour of the Paraiyars who are perhaps more reactionary as their subordinate position gives them more to fight against.

'They are not as sutham (chaste) as we are'

Jeyakodi, a woman belonging to the older generation, touches upon the most common misconception about *Paraiyar* women that they are very 'loose' in their character and sexual morals. Rather, she argues that it was 'them', the Reddyars who are promiscuous because their men have sexual relations with every other women in the village, be it Paraiyar or otherwise. This 'fact' is of course not spoken about openly in public and is ignored by the Reddyar women as Jeyakodi explains,

> they cover themselves so much and give a false impression that they are very good, which is not actually true. We may not respect certain public rules, but we are much more faithful to our men than the Reddyar women! They are not as chaste (*Karpu*) as we are.

This insight into the context of Paraiyar women who are often treated with disdain and sexually exploited shows how instead of internalizing such a degrading reality, they insist that in contrast it is the Reddyar women who have no 'chastity' (*Karpu*) and demonstrate sexual promiscuity by sleeping with men other than their husbands. Jeyakodi's idea of herself consists of the comparative freedom that she enjoys within her community as well as her comparative chastity, rather than the virtuousness depicted by the Reddyars. She constructs her identity essentially by rejecting the dominant notion and contrasting herself with the Reddyar women. In the same breath she added that the 'chekli' (Arunthathier) women would do 'anything', and that is why they are lower than Paraiyars, placing herself as purer than both the Arunthathier and Reddyars, and thus chastity relates to *us* and promiscuity to *them*. Such attitudes seem to be extremely affirmative and significantly change the way in which Paraiyar women understand themselves and their marriages. Additionally, it helps them to claim their place in the community as well as strengthening their communal identity in relation to other castes. Again, this image of Paraiyar women as creative and not passive victims totally escapes Dalit studies.

'They always do wrong and illegal things'

The opinion of the young men who represent the new generation of Paraiyars in Thulasigramam is well informed, and Simon, an economics undergraduate student in the nearby town, is their unofficial spokesman. Apart from being an active member in the church, he asserts to know some inside details about the accumulated wealth and properties of the Reddyars. His claim was that most of the Reddyars have a hand in the illicit liquor business based in the nearby hills and make most of their money illegally. In order to run such unlawful businesses, they bribe the police and other authorities not to pay any attention to their involvement. Not only that, Simon explains that most of their land and other properties have been accumulated through equally exploitative methods. Simon believes that most of the agricultural land owned by the Reddyars once actually belonged to the Paraiyars, but through unscrupulous means their elders were duped and made to pledge their lands for meagre amounts to the Reddyars. With this theory Simon expressed his anguish, 'I would be surprised if Reddyars do anything good at all, because they always do wrong and illegal things'. He added that very often Paraiyars had become victims in these illegal transactions due to their ignorance and lower status. Moreover, he conceded that Paraiyars should also take responsibility for part of the blame, for they spend money foolishly, a weakness, which was exploited by the Reddyars. He stressed that by nature the Paraiyars are 'good', in contrast to the devious lifestyle of Reddyars. This notion is contrary to the popular perception that Paraiyars are the people who commit all the offenses in the village: during my fieldwork whenever there was a problem in the village it is usually somebody from the Paraiyar settlement who is taken into police custody and interrogated. Simon's opinion draws attention to the consciousness of victimization within the Paraiyars community, which at one level results in the internalization of inferiority within their self-understanding. As he and others insisted, there are other ways of defining their situations and root causes.

'We always beat them up'

Thulasigramam has a long history of inter-caste conflicts and Dass sheds light on some aspects of it. Dass was the most entertaining character within the Paraiyar Christian community. He was a school dropout with a quick intellect who struggled with a very short temper. He was beaten up many times by the Reddyars for infuriating them, picking fights with them and teasing their girls. I was told that he almost died in one such encounter with some Reddyars and the matter had become so serious that he had to go away to work in a factory in another state, but had recently returned. While conversing with him, I assembled a different image as he recounted all the heroic deeds he and others made on the Reddyars and their properties. According to Dass, it was him who had attacked 'those' (Reddyars) more often than the other way around.

His stories have gained so much popularity that most of the young Parariyar children and adults, both Christian and Hindu kept repeating that he would do anything to pick a fight and irritate the Reddyars. Most of the stories narrated by Dass ended with the Reddyars being beaten up and humiliated, which in many cases was contrary to the truth. What needs to be understood here is that Dass's identity is constructed and consistently shaped by his stories of violent encounters with the Reddyars and his enjoyment in inflicting humiliation on them. These stories are in turn appropriated by the younger generation of Paraiyars who develop their own idea of who they are in opposition to the 'always beaten up' Reddyars. These dynamics are very interesting and although the stories recounted are often imaginative, they reflect changes in the attitudes of youths in the Paraiyar community.

In the light of the early discussion on identity formation, the aforementioned examples represent a cross section of the Paraiyar community and their self-conceptualization.[34] These cases exemplify how the Paraiyar Christians are aware of their own identities by differentiating, contrasting and juxtaposing themselves with the Reddyars on crucial issues such as chastity, bravery, legitimacy and honesty, which shape individual and communal identity. Very often, Paraiyars distance themselves from the accepted and popular perceptions of themselves by actually projecting the prejudices onto 'others' the Reddyars or Arunthathier communities. It is in this regard that one need to keep in mind that the Paraiyars, as suggested by Vincentnathan[35] and Deliege,[36] do not subscribe to the dominant understanding of their lower status due to their ritual pollution (internal) and social exploitation (external). Further, by re-projecting these socially imposed discriminations, of purity and pollution upon the Reddyar community, the Paraiyar community have reinterpreted their identity. This process of knowing oneself in opposition or through difference to the Reddyars within the Paraiyar community also functions to discredit the high-caste community as well as developing far more complicated and nuanced non-subordinate identities for themselves.

Physical location and social hierarchy

In Thulasigramam, spatial representation or geographical locatedness in the village has a direct impact on an individual's conception of self-identity.

In other words, the physical location, whether one lives in the *Cherie* (the Untouchable settlement, also known as the Colony) or in the *Oor* (the high-caste village), determines who that person is and what his or her status is in the village.[37] Even within the Cherie, if a person's house is situated on a particular side of the main street, it is clear as to whether that household is Christian or Hindu; if the house happens to be near the church building or the Hindu temple it has its own understood status within that groups ranking system.

Oor and Cherie

The oldest member of the Paraiyar Christian community in Thulasigramam, Deva, recollected a statement made by one of the Reddyars, 'As long as you live in the Cherie you should know your place in the village', to explain the fact that where he lived significantly contributed to the understanding of who he was. The demarcations existing within the village define the nature and status of its inhabitants. Different settlements for all of the different Caste and Outcaste communities are situated well away from each other, avoiding physical interaction between individuals and possible cross-pollution. Each caste group is obliged to respect their prescribed boundaries and abide by the rules laid down by the Reddyars, who are the land owners and high-caste group in Thulasigramam. The very idea of the Cherie represents the physical alienation, exclusion and isolation of the Untouchable communities from the hub of village life. The location of the *Cherie* and its dependence on the *Oor* (village) contributes to their self-understanding. The statement highlighted by Deva clearly explains this fact; the Paraiyars are forced to keep to their spatial and moral place.

From the location of a person's household within the village boundary one can identify his caste affiliation and place within the village hierarchy. Any move to challenge or alter this aspect by the Paraiyars or other 'low' caste communities would be met with violent reactions: as one Reddyar reportedly said 'they would be taught a lesson or two about who they are'. The geographical locatedness of homes contributes to the way in which a person conceives his own identity in relation to the *others* in the same village and to the outside world. To interpret the statement recollected by Deva further, a person knows about their selfhood on the basis of their physical locatedness, which in turn informs their expected functions and place within the village community, a vicious circle of inequality in thatched roof and mud floor.

This pattern of social reproduction and learning is undoubtedly crucial to Paraiyar identity formation. When a child grows up in the Cherie, he learns the prevailing norms of the village community and incorporates them within the process of knowing who he is and how he is to live within the caste-perpetuated social norms. During conversations, youth and children recollected the instructions given to them about doing 'certain things' and which 'forbidden places' to avoid in order to prevent confrontation with the Reddyars and other 'low' caste communities living in the village. It is vital to note the fact that the existing spatial boundaries in Thulasigramam are inflexible and rigid, making it seemingly impossible to change one's location in a caste group and property as a means to move to a different place without totally leaving the village. In other words, Paraiyars are bound to their place within the village and cannot escape, and moreover, most do not have the option to do so.

Social hierarchy

Understanding the internal dynamics pertaining to location within the Paraiyar community yields interesting insights into the way in which an individual conceives of himself. The central and most prominent place in the Paraiyar Cherie is occupied by the huge concrete church building with its tall bell tower visible from far away. The church is considered to be a sacred and holy place, and a Christian priest, as a representative of God and by virtue of being associated with this 'holy' place, occupies the highest position in the Christian hierarchy. In the Paraiyar Christian community, one common perception is that the closer one lives to the church building, the 'holier' one is. Two prominent families in the Paraiyar Christian community, Yesurajam, the church elder and Nathan, the church secretary, are interesting examples of this facet.[38] Their houses are located nearest to the church building and apart from being key figures in the church; Nathan's family holds the 'key' to the church (both literally and figuratively). He was given this job, more than just a symbolic task, of acting as the gatekeeper in the absence of the catechist, who used to live in the house next to the church until he moved to the nearby city. During many conversations, Nathan pointed out that those living a little farther away from the church, even if only by a degree, are not 'good people; they pick fights all the time and the men and women drink most of the time. So in a way it is good that they are living far away from the church'. In other words, he implied that those people who live farther away from the church were 'sinful, weak and socially insignificant' within the Paraiyar Christian community, which reflects the perception of Paraiyars by the Reddyars. It should also be mentioned that those living at a distance from the church hardly have any role to play in church or Christian community life and are often considered to be the trouble makers and sources of conflict. One can notice the subtle replication of hierarchy taking place in this situation.

It is interesting to note that the same view was held by the Paraiyar Christians people themselves as they prefer to live farther from the church because they consider themselves to be 'not good enough' or unworthy of living closer to the sacred space. As Mano says, 'it is better to stay away from all those "holy people" than getting blamed for everything'. This phenomenon needs to be understood on two levels: First, the consequence of associating the area immediately around the church and those who occupy it as holy and powerful, proximity to which symbolizes power and superiority; second, due to the church's location it comes to represent the core of the Cherie, thereby creating a centre and a periphery, as well as paving the way for an internal hierarchy within those real and imagined structures.

Additionally, there is a clear demarcation between the Christian and Hindu Paraiyar houses, located on opposite sides of the same road, clearly marking a division among the communities on the lines of religious affiliation, a division that is seldom reflected in their familial relationships, where intermarriages are still common. Another important observation is that none of the 'non-core' or less important Christian households were located adjacent to the church building: all of them being at some distance on the opposite side. There was a general consensus among the Paraiyar Christian community that they should keep a healthy distance from the church building, a belief that could be due to their past experience of religious marginalization and relegation, or it could be argued that it gives them freedom to act in ways (drinking alcohol/doing local rituals) to which the priest or the church elder might object. The style and construction of houses also conveys vital information about the people who inhabit them. Concrete and brick houses usually mean that their occupants are comparatively better off and not totally dependent on the Reddyars for their living. While a family living in a house made of straw suggests that they are economically poor and labour in the Reddyar fields. These details have further specific meanings about status within the functional hierarchy of the Paraiyar Christian community.

An individual's proximity to the 'sacred' space of the church is paralleled by his taking the 'moral high ground' seeing those who live farther away from the church as 'sinful and unholy'. This perception is accepted, and becomes increasingly internalized with age. Notably, the same hierarchy is reproduced when members from the Paraiyar Christian community came into the church building for worship. Excluding the children and the youth, the men and women have specific places inside the church and occupy seats according to the hierarchy and gender. The higher one's status, one gets to sit in the front row of chairs; while those of lower status sit on the back bench or on the floor. The women do not even get to sit in chairs and are expected to sit on mats on the floor. Holiness (and comfort) through proximity to the sacred is thus a male prerogative, which does not include women.

It can be concluded that geographical locatedness within the village, proximity to the church's 'sacred' space and the assigned place during worship significantly contributes to and defines individual and communal identity among the Thulasigramam Paraiyar Christians. This social organization clearly feeds into and demonstrates a hierarchical order, and provides a framework for the people to relate to one another, consciously aware of their status and position in the community.

Alienation from resources

Physical alienation and distancing of an individual from his livelihood impacts self-conceptions within a community.[39] Some 'means of alienation' experienced by the Paraiyar Christians in Thulasigramam include the denial of access to resources, landlessness, lack of public amenities and the perpetuation of dependency. All of these significant aspects affect Paraiyar Christian self-perceptions.

On both sides of the road leading through the Thulasigramam village, the government planted tamarind trees to give fruit and shade during the summer for the villagers. Even though they are public property, the Reddyar landowners have usurped the right to decide what becomes of the fruit crop. Most of the Paraiyar houses are built along this road under the tamarind trees. The Reddyars by virtue of their caste status have unilaterally passed a decree that the village (represented by them) would lease the trees and their fruit to the highest bidder. Obviously, Paraiyars cannot even think of affording to make a bid, and even though they live right under the trees they cannot even eat the fruit that they themselves harvest for the Reddyars. There are numerous street fights when a Paraiyar has been found taking tamarind fruit without permission. The Reddyars drag the 'guilty' person onto the road and humiliate them through verbal abuse and in some cases hit them and warn them not to repeat their offence. In spite of such violence, as I have witnessed, some Paraiyars secretly climb in the dead of night to gather a few tamarinds for their households. This situation is one of obvious alienation of the Paraiyars from a public resource which is right in front of and above their homes, intended for all, but denied to them due to their social status. Paraiyars can only see the tamarind trees and can never legitimately participate in their fruits (quite literally). As mentioned earlier, those tamarind trees are public property and no one community legally can lay claim to them, but evidently this is not the case in Thulasigramam; and a law case would be laughable.

Within the Paraiyar Christian community, only two families own cultivable lands: the church elder who served in the Indian army, and the local church leader who worked in the local mission hospital. Most of the other Paraiyars work as agricultural labourers on the Reddyars lands around their settlement. As soon as one enters the village, the fertile nature of the soil, the abundant coconut groves, banana plantations and rice paddies and peanut fields are evident. Ironically, it is the Paraiyars who toil in the fields but can barely manage to have a decent daily meal. While they work to cultivate the land and crops, they never reap the fruits of their labour, living at the mercy of the Reddyars. Painful alienation of this type has a deep impact on Paraiyar self-understanding as many expressed their helplessness and a sense of wretchedness over their inability to provide a decent meal for their families and their frustration at producing food for the Reddyars. Such a situation results in low self-esteem, which over time accentuates their existence in a domineering system leading to a pessimistic view of life for the Paraiyar Christians (and Hindus) in Thulasigramam.

The fact that the public amenities and governmental resources are all located in the Oor (the main village) where the Reddyars reside, and not in the Paraiyar Cherie, adds an increasingly complex dimension to the situation of Paraiyars. This means that the school, post office and ration shops were until recently off-limits for the Paraiyar community who were not allowed to enter and 'pollute' the Oor. Although the situation has changed considerably, hesitation on the part of Paraiyars in terms of utilizing them still exists. When I requested to make use of the public phone booth in the Oor, there was clear reluctance among the Paraiyars to take me there.[40] Moreover, the only middle grade school in the village is in the Oor, so most of the Paraiyar Christians send their children to another village several miles away where they feel more welcomed. When I enquired about this, a common explanation given by parents was of their own painful memories of being ill-treated by the teachers and Reddyar students in the past and the continuance of such behaviour for their children. Instead of putting their children through similar unforgettable experiences, they choose to send them to a different school in a farther village, where they actually have to pay fees for education. The government school is supposed to provide free education for the entire village, but the Paraiyars cannot access it or choose not to access it, not because of any rule but because of the fear and hostility towards them from the Reddyars. Although they incur a financial debt, the Paraiyars see schooling their children elsewhere as a socially liberating act. Again this development highlights that Paraiyars are merely observers of the 'communal' facilities and not receivers of them.

Alienation from basic resources results in the perpetual dependency of the Paraiyars on the Reddyars for their daily sustenance, which leaves a significant impression on their self-perception. As Mosse suggests while outlining the cultural construction of subordination that the Dalit 'identity itself is principally defined by dependence and service',[41] a statement that rings true in the case of Paraiyar Christians in Thulasigramam. The examples explained above show that most of the Paraiyars have large financial debts to the Reddyars, who can consequently demand work from Paraiyars as a means of repayment at whatever wages they set. And since there are no other jobs available for the majority of the Paraiyars, they must work in the fields as farm hands. Therefore, due to debt and the lack of labour options for Paraiyars, the Reddyars are able to offer low wages, which the Paraiyars have little choice but to accept. In fact, the Paraiyars *must* accept the Reddyars' conditions in order to survive. Only a small few within the Paraiyar Christian community are able to break away from this vicious cycle, by finding factory work in nearby towns. When a family tries to break free from this dependency, as in the case of the Christian Paraiyar Rathnam and his wife Esther, they were met with public ridicule from the Reddyars for failing to pay their debts, and no doubt for their guts in thinking they could break loose. Eventually due to economic uncertainties they were forced to continue working for the Reddyars. A common saying in the Paraiyar community is, 'a known devil is better than an unknown god', capturing their helplessness in some cases. Such Paraiyar views of life create their own set of propositions in terms of their self-understanding, their relationship with others and the rest of the world.

Psycho-social assemblage

Two crucial human feelings of *fear* and *shame* are used extensively by the dominant caste groups to subvert and subjugate the formation of communal and individual identity. They have become psycho-social tools of the oppressive system to perpetuate hierarchical systems within the realms of religion, society, economics and gender relations further marginalizing individuals and communities, particularly within Outcaste communities. This manifests itself both externally and internally in rural Dalit Christian communities. These emotional ties find root in the traditional Hindu understanding of purity and pollution, which has direct impact on the psycho-social world of Paraiyars, as elsewhere in South Indian society. Pertaining to their own status as Untouchables and Outcastes, Paraiyars in the village are bound by purity and pollution notions constantly reinforced in their daily life. Due to centuries of adherence to the caste norms of religious pollution expressed in social life, Paraiyars continue to abide by them, despite changes in their social demographics. As mentioned earlier, fear and shame are crucial psychological elements used to regulate purity and pollution processes as well as physical violence and sexual abuses. Let us now observe two incidents as a means of understanding this issue within the context of relationship between the Paraiyars and Reddyars, and within the Paraiyar Christian community itself.

Until recently, the Paraiyars of Thulasigramam lived under the constant threat of being attacked and violated in their own Cherie, whenever they did not follow instructions of the Reddyars. Men and women in the Paraiyar community were routinely physically attacked and verbally abused in the Cherie, and sometimes even inside their houses for non-payment of their debt or failing to turn up for work. As mentioned earlier, Rathnam and Esther, a couple in the Paraiyar Christian community, have been victims of constant ill-treatment by the Reddyars. If either of them failed to turn up for work in the fields of Raju Reddy, his sons would go into their houses and create a public spectacle of abuse known to the whole village. Rathnam and Esther confided that they live in constant fear of 'them' (the Reddyars) and are often ashamed to face the rest of the people in the colony because of the insults hurled at them by the Reddyars.

Sathyamma, an elderly lady in the Christian settlement, adds another dimension to this tendency for Paraiyar Christians to feel fear and shame. She worked as an agricultural labourer, and one day when she was very ill and unable to get up, the landlord barged into her home and literally dragged her to work, saying, 'Who will pay all your debts?' The following day, even though she was not physically well, she forced herself to go and work in the field. When I enquired about this incident, she said, 'I am ashamed and afraid, so I would rather go and work instead of facing more humiliation and harassment'. Such occurrences were performed in public places so that the message quickly gets out loud and clear to others in the Cherie where most of the agricultural labourers live. Their 'drama', as the Reddyars call it, is not tolerated and leads to inevitable consequences and punishments. Most of the Paraiyars in Thulasigramam share in this experience and have undergone similar insulting and humiliating incidents in the past. Because of their perpetual social dependency on the Reddyars due to their caste-prescribed 'religiously impure' status and poverty, they continuously live in a state of fear and terror. This routine strongly influences the way they think of themselves and relate with others in the colony as well outside of it. Furthermore, these psycho-sociological effects give rise to a sense of worthlessness in the subjective understanding of the Paraiyars.

The place of the Paraiyar community within Thulasigramam is defined by their religious 'impurity and bastardry', since they are 'outcastes and untouchables'.[42] Until recently, Hindu and Christian Paraiyars were not even allowed into Hindu temples and were denied participation in religious festivities. They were forced to stand far off and could only be spectators, not active participants. Even now the 'deity visitation' performed by taking the Hindu idol out of the temple and which was then carried around the village but not entering the Paraiyar Cherie. The notion of religious uncleanness is systematically reinforced by such rigid exclusion in the village life. Although Paraiyar Christians are not directly affected, they still share in the religiously impure nature of Paraiyars.

Interestingly, the Paraiyar Christians bring similar concepts of purity into their Christian practices. The church building is associated as the 'holy sacred place', and many Paraiyars prefer to stand outside of the church when they feel unclean or if they were drunk the previous day. One Sunday, Paul a regular harmonium player in the church, did not come into the sanctuary during the worship service and preferred to stay outside on the veranda. Later when I asked about this, he replied, 'I drank too much last night and did not feel "clean" enough to come into the church today, so I decided to stay outside'. Similarly, menstruating women or those who have just given birth are not encouraged to come into the church building. This idea of staying away from the 'sacred' due to impurity, in this case, can clearly be traced back to their local Hindu religious practices.[43] Feeling impure and worthless in the religious realm impacts and reflects in the Paraiyar life and creates a sense of fear of the 'sacred and dominant' and shame in front of others. These aspects contribute to the internalizing of imposed categories of worthlessness, which negatively impacts their self-identity.

Stereotyping and name calling

Name calling is a common feature in human societies and assumes additional importance within structurally organized societies. Pierre Bourdieu explains that attributed names come to represent structural hierarchy and control, access to social existence and social identity, which is reinforced every time they are mentioned.[44] This process paves the way for the formation of stereotypes, and in the words of Richard Jenkins, 'stereotypes are extremely condensed symbols of collective identification'.[45] Exploring some of the social interactions in Thulasigramam through this prism, I observed that the Reddyars used insulting names for the Paraiyars in order to assert their dominance. They are frequently called *Sombayri* (lazy bums), *Paranai* (untouchable dogs), *Mollamari* (unscrupulous fellows) and *Thiruda* (thieves). Women are given particular degrading treatment being called frequently *Thevdiya* (prostitutes and bastards). Apart from the last example, most of the other names are casually used and it was curious to observe that many Paraiyars from the older generation respond without protest. It might seem that they do not actually carry any deep-seated hatred or aversion to such name-calling that stems from stereotypes about the Paraiyar community fostered by the Reddyars. True to the earlier observation by Pillai-Vetschera, in general the dominant caste group portrays the Paraiyars of Thulasigramam as lazy, quarrelsome dogs who eat filth and steal anything possible.[46]

Calling a woman a 'prostitute' remains one of the worst forms of humiliation in village society and is employed to inflict psychological pain upon the woman in question, her family and the Paraiyar community in general. As detailed earlier, Paraiyar women were often suspected to be 'loose', promiscuous and questionable in character. Due to their upright body posture, carefree attitude and 'big mouths', Paraiyar women are often stereotyped as immoral and unfaithful to their husbands. This view helps the Reddyars, when they sexually assault, abuse and harass Paraiyar women as a means to justify their acts of violence claiming that the women were already promiscuous. This is one form of Reddyar power that is not publicly paraded or discussed, but remains a private matter of humiliation. It is not only Reddyar men who do this as Paraiyar men also exploit and rape Paraiyar women. This name calling results in real, physical abuse of Paraiyar women, an abuse that unfortunately validates and perpetuates further name calling.

To gain a nuanced understanding of name calling, it is important to recognize the fact it becomes the means through which stereotypes are reinforced and perpetuated by the dominant communities. What happens during this process is that these terms are internalized and accepted by the Paraiyars (at least by the older generation) as legitimate, so that they do not even protest about such pejorative labelling. By instilling a false notion of inferiority and helplessness in the Paraiyars, they are left with nothing but apathy and self-pity for themselves. As Bourdieu observes, by reinforcing these names, the dominant community perpetuates an oppressive system, as well as an exploitative worldview in which Paraiyars become subservient and apathetic.

Another example is the common refrain that 'Paraiyars are all alcoholics and drunkards'. No doubt, alcoholism was and is a serious problem in the Paraiyar community of Thulasigramam, heightened by the Cherie's location near to the hub of an illicit liquor brewery owned by the Reddyars. Many of the men in the Paraiyar Cherie justify spending most of their earnings on alcohol 'to overcome the pain of toiling in the fields all day'. The implications of alcoholism is felt and experienced by every family in the Cherie, but branding and stereotyping the Paraiyar community as a whole as 'alcoholics and drunkards' by the Reddyars is farfetched. The Catechist, a Paraiyar, again subscribing to such a view, warned me not to visit any homes after dark, since 'most of them would be drunk'. I found this to be largely incorrect. Such notions work both internally and externally in the Paraiyar community, as it leads individuals to believe they cannot help but drink. However, I came to discover that the Reddyars were actually involved in running many of the illegal brewing places, selling unlicensed liquor to the Paraiyars making a substantial profit. Certainly some men were feckless drunks, liable to hit their wives and not provide food for the children, yet the continued reiteration of such stereotypes about the Paraiyar community in general perpetuates negative impression, further victimizing the community by manipulating their subjective understanding. This pattern of providing alcohol for despised groups, raping the women and blaming the entire group for being drunken and immoral is not unique to South India as white Australian interaction with rural Aboriginal communities has been precisely the same.[47]

Role reversals

Hugo Gorringe captures the general perception on the status of women among the Dalit communities in Tamil Nadu, where women are generally seen as confined to do the domestic work and men are the breadwinners and protectors of the family stating, 'the Patriarchal nature of Tamil households dictates that the women do the cooking, fetch water and collect fuel'.[48] But, both Gorringe and Vetschera further argue that a judicious observation of the daily lives of Dalit women proves otherwise.[49] We need to separate what is said and what actually *happens*.

In Thulasigramam, I observed that Paraiyar women often work much harder and longer than the men bringing more money into the family. Most of the women in the Paraiyar community including the Christians toil in the fields, while only a few go to the nearby town to be a factory labourer. Comparatively, more men than women have the freedom to go out into the factories for occasional employment.

Raju, a middle-aged man in the Paraiyar Christian community, once mentioned that he did not want to send his wife Dayama to the shoe factory as there was a stigma of 'suspicion' attached to the women there. Although factory labour is slightly less physically demanding than farming, Raju preferred to see Dayama in the field and not in the factory. Many of the men also work as labourers in the nearby brickyard or in the poultry farms, but are often paid weekly or fortnightly. In such situations, it was the daily earnings of women that kept the family running and met their basic needs. Adding to that, the problem of alcoholism and debts incurred by men further strains family budgets. During my interactions it became evident that most of the Paraiyar Christian families, including the men, divulged that they survive due to the hard work of their women, a fact not mentioned in public. This reversal from the ideologized norm is an important aspect in the formation of Paraiyar women's identity within the community.

Mala is a good example of this process. Prabu, Mala's husband, works occasionally in the brickyard and earns a meagre income, which was insufficient for the family of four. They had to pay for the education of their two children, along with taking care of their elderly parents. In this situation, it was the daily wages Mala earned by working in the fields that sustained the family. This reality is reflected in the family dynamics as Mala controls and makes most of the decisions regarding family finances. But to the outside world, it was Prabu, 'the head of the house', who is the main breadwinner and provider. Considering the tough life of the Paraiyar community, the women go to extremes to provide for their families, mostly of which goes unnoticed.

A simple thing like collecting firewood essential for cooking is done only by women, walking miles into the forest in the hills. Yet they continue to do it for the sake of the family, while the men often sit around and chat in the village. Grace and Lakshmi offer good examples; they both go to forest every day after providing breakfast and sending their husbands for work, leaving the little ones in the care of Periyamma, an elderly neighbour. They very often shared their stories of being attacked by wild animals, snakes and being bitten by poisonous creatures, yet tirelessly go day after day to provide for their family.

Amutha, an elderly widow, plays a very active role in the lives of Paraiyar in the community. She works as a child care teacher in the village and demonstrates strong leadership qualities. Against all odds and disdain from the community for her widowhood, she provides hope for many women in the community. From her experience of working in the child care centre and the awareness of the government and non-governmental organization (NGO) schemes, Amutha was able to organize the women in the Paraiyar community to meet once in a week in the evening and share their family problems. This effort has paid rich dividends in different ways, informing them of governmental benefits and encouraging them to save some of their earnings that can be used during times of need. Amutha brought this quality into the Christian community as well, as she was a regular churchgoer and her strong leadership qualities posed a serious threat to the male leadership of the Paraiyar Christian community. The Catechist very often spoke about her using suspicious language, calling her names and questioning her motives for doing community work. He also became uncomfortable with the fact that she enabled a few women to ask questions with regard to the maintenance of the church, which until this point had been unheard of. This process led to an open conflict when Amutha's son Charles got married to a Hindu girl from a different village and the Catechist refused to accept and regularize their marriage, citing various legal reasons. But many of the women expressed the view that she and her family were being penalized for taking a leadership role.

It is important to recognize the dynamics involved in this process. Contrary to the popular notion that Paraiyar women do not contribute much to the community life, Amutha proved that she could provide valuable leadership and inspire other women to follow suit. Significantly for the first time in the history of Thulasigramam, they were able to elect a woman president from the Hindu

Paraiyar community for the village *panchayat* (administration).[50] Interacting with many women in the Christian and Hindu Paraiyar community as she did, it is not unreasonable to suggest that her work bolstered their sense of self worth and identity. Paraiyar women in Thulasigramam showed that they constantly reverse the social roles given by the 'norm' and play a vital part in contributing to the family and the community.[51]

Multi-layerity: Being Paraiyars and Christians

In the Thulasigramam Paraiyar Christian community, conversion to Christianity, which began nearly a century ago, has facilitated a process of reconstituting and reclaiming a new identity. In the South Indian Paraiyar context, the process of conversion to Christianity was often perceived as a rejection or negation of one's cultural and religious heritage, in favour of a 'new' and arguably 'foreign' religious identity. This resulted in deep cultural implications as individuals and communities do not erase their past but accommodate their new identities with the historically grounded present. However, the important interplay between different socio-religious systems and its impact on individuals and communities are frequently underestimated. Judicious observation of the Christian community in Thulasigramam and their meaning-making systems sheds light on such processes of multi-layered consciousness.

Differentiating

A common response I received when asking people directly about their history in the Thulasigramam Paraiyar Christian community was that they had little knowledge of their past. On one level, this is a perfectly common response, given those social discriminatory practices, including the religious, knowledge of the past is legitimized precisely by being 'eternalized' in light of the present. Yet there are other or additional ways of seeing this. In the view of Frantz Fanon, a post-colonial theorist, who observed colonization's distorting and disfiguring effect on the colonized people's consciousness,[52] it could be stated that Christianity was a colonial process that flourished through supplanting existing religious practices in its mission fields. In Thulasigramam, questions concerning Paraiyar cultural and religious heritage were often met with hesitation or simply evaded. Even though this was often frustrating for me as a researcher, persistent efforts suggested that this dilly-dallying can be understood as an effective mechanism to avoid answering questions regarding their past and thereby avoid shaming themselves before me, an urban priest, as well as avoiding being 'defined'. 'I don't know what happened then' was the usual reply given by Paraiyars to any questions about their history. After meandering through various topics, they would come back to the issue of their life before becoming Christians, but change topics quickly. The general response was, 'our grandparents lived similar lives to us, working tirelessly for the Reddyars, and making them wealthier'. The focus here is not on the details of history itself, but their hesitation, indeed refusal, to narrate it. During a conversation with Deva, the oldest man in the village, I quickly realized to what extent he had internalized the Christian story as his own story. Deva's answers to my questions regarding how long caste oppression had gone on were interesting, and reminded me of Paraiyar origin myths discussed in introduction. He replied 'from the time of Adam and Eve we are like this!' Two important points need to be underlined here; first, by adding Christianity to their origin myth, their history has been given a new meaning and direction. Second, by returning to their past, Paraiyar Christians may be utilizing the Christian element to avoid dwelling on what is remembered as too dreadful to discuss.

Further, being a Christian, as understood by Paraiyar Christians in Thulasigramam, is also associated with being modern, wearing 'foreign' clothes, carrying electronic gadgets and smoking cigarettes rather than *beedies* (locally rolled tobacco leaves). This change in self-identification, associating themselves with modern external standards, has drastically altered their self-perception. To comprehend this process one has to take into account the way Christianity was originally presented by the missionaries as an alternative for Paraiyars to their existing oppressed lifestyle. This declaration of Christianity as something 'new' and liberating continues to hold resonance with the local church. 'All of you should be different from them, the Reddyars and the Hindus' were statements by both the Catechist and the Priest in their sermons, emphasizing the importance of Paraiyars being 'different' from 'them'. This call for difference and separation from non-Christians should not be reduced to a merely theological undertaking. Paraiyar Christian identity means vastly more than abstract theological and doctrinal self-conceptualization, and is rather embedded in practical and observable differences from the dominant Hindu religious tradition and its social system.

The ways such distinctions are manifested is evident in all aspects of daily Christian Paraiyar life. While they may only have one pair of pants and a shirt, they will wear them whenever possible to be '*olunkum*' (decent) rather than running the risk of being called an 'indecent' person. When they attend church, Paraiyars make a special effort to look 'nice and decent' with 'proper' clothes, and those who do not are ridiculed for not dressing 'decently'. The youth go to great lengths to get contemporary stone-washed jeans, t-shirts, shirts and dresses wanting to be fashionable at church, which also helps in finding a potential partner. Women seem to bother less in this regard although some of them wear 'white' sarees for church, signifying 'purity', a conceptual legacy from the missionary times. These mundane observations offer interesting insights into Paraiyar Christian attitudes towards the 'externality' of proper dress as until two decades ago the Reddyars did not allow Paraiyars to wear clothing on their upper bodies, modern clothing being totally prohibited. A few years ago a young Pariayar man was beaten up and his clothes torn apart by the Reddyars for wearing what they considered to be offensive modern clothing.

With changing times and due to the availability of cheaper clothes, the men in particular tend to show off their new wardrobe in public. This act has an affirmative and almost defiant nature as the men in the Paraiyar Christian community dress noticeably more formal than the Hindu Paraiyars and even the Reddyars. Along with adopting Western fashion, young Christian Paraiyar men are known to possess fancy gadgets, like mobile phones, watches and music systems. Very often these were purchased in the 'Burma bazaar' a cheap Chinese market in the nearby town. Daniel for instance replaced his cheap mobile phone with an expensive model and became the village's main attraction for a few days. Smoking 'foreign' cigarettes instead of beedies seems to be another way of contesting one's identity within this context. Among the youth in the Paraiyar community, smoking beedies is almost regarded as degrading. They would go to any length to get a pack of 'foreign' cigarettes and make fun of the beedie smokers, who are predominantly their own elders. Furthermore, these youths smoke in front of the Reddyars as a sign of outward defiance. While these illustrations were in some cases particular to the Paraiyar Christian community they also existed in the Hindu Paraiyar community as well, but to a lesser extent. Interpreting these observations in the light of Paraiyar Christian identity formation in Thulasigramam, one can conclude that Christianity offers a new means to assert their identity in the face of exclusion and marginalization. Dressing up in foreign clothing, displaying modern gadgets and smoking cigarettes contributes to the way young people in the Paraiyar Christian community conceive of themselves and also seems to change their position in the village community. Ironically, it is through such external expressions that the young Paraiyar Christians show their dissent towards their own elders and also express their difference from the Hindu Paraiyars as well as Reddyars.

Multi-layered belonging

The complexity of the individual and communal spirituality that prevails in the Paraiyar Christian community can be understood through examining Prabu's statement:

> It is not a problem for me to go for *Madu viduthal* (Bull Race) or *Koil thiruvizha* (Temple festival) just after attending the communion service at the church. I enjoy the excitement and happiness that I get while attending those festivals. From childhood *Madu viduthal* is my passion and being a Christian does not stop me from going for one.

This comment was just one among many from a variety of Paraiyar Christians, exemplifying that for Paraiyars there are no rigid and strict boundaries defining and restricting their spirituality, nor does their Christianity negate observing other religious traditions. Rather, as I will argue, they have multi-layered spiritual reference points. Prabu feels no guilt over attending the Hindu festival of *Madu viduthal*, a bull race festival devoted to lord *Murugan* and a *Koil thiruvizha* (temple festival) in honour of the goddess *Kaliamma* after taking part in the church communion service. While he may be shifting from a 'Christian' spiritual setting to a 'non-Christian Hindu' spiritual location and ritual practice, there was no internal spiritual conflict for Prabu as there might be for onlookers or observers, such as myself. Moreover, he may participate in both religious arenas with no internal conflict. It is important to recognize that this is not an isolated incident but something that prevails in the whole Paraiyar Christian community. Spirituality is locally based and Christianity is part of it and is in no way exclusivistic. Even though religious affiliation is an important aspect, one is not confined in terms of strict adherence to one specific religion. In the village context there are many occasions and gatherings that are performed within a particular religio-spiritual arena, yet people participate irrespective of their own religious affiliation. Involvement in events rooted in Hinduism means participating in the fullness of *village life* and does not necessarily affirm the validity of Hinduism or negate their Christian identity. Even though the group performing the ritual may have a specific religious belief, the participating individuals do not need to believe and subscribe to the same system of belief, but rather partakes in the event out of communal obligation and celebration. Communal village action takes precedence over rather irrelevant religious divides. Prabu exemplifies such a process: in the morning he participated in the communion service at the church and then proceeded to the village Hindu festival. Prabu had no dilemma or inner conflict in attending both religious events, even though the Catechist expressed his disapproval. The prevalence of such attitudes among the Paraiyar Christian community underlines the coexistence of different religious spheres, spheres that are not necessarily seen as conflicting within individuals or the community. During Christmas, New Year and Easter celebrations, the Paraiyar Christians organize various activities in which many of the Hindu Paraiyars freely take part. Nathan, the church secretary, recollects that once one of the Reddyars, who was a Hindu, donated money to the church for decorating during Christmas festivities to fulfil a vow he had made earlier. It can also be observed that when Hindus pass by the church or Christians pass by the Hindu temple, they often pay their respects and say a little prayer to the gods residing in those holy places.

The story of Amos adds another dimension to this facet of multi-layered spirituality. Samuel is Amos' six-year-old son and was recently diagnosed with a serious case of heart disease. Unless Samuel was operated on immediately he would not survive for long, but the surgical procedure required a large amount of money, which Amos as a poor agricultural labourer did not have. He sought the help of many people in the village, including the bishop of the local diocese; but no one was able to help him or his son. Eventually he was taken to the local Hindu god-man, *Shakti Amma*, by another Hindu Paraiyar from the village whom Amos had opposed in a temple dispute earlier that year. Amos went to the Hindu god-man's temple ashram, prostrated in front of him and pleaded for help and the *Shakti amma* (Hindu god-man) gave 75 per cent of the medical expenses in order to carry out the surgery. This act of Amos seeking help from a Hindu god-man was greatly deplored by the Catechist and the Priest; however, it meant that Samuel's surgery was done successfully, and Amos, despite being a Christian, remains a very faithful supporter of this *Shakti Amma* and his Hindu charity works. This could very simply be brushed aside as an opportunistic event, but a nuanced interrogation reveals that he was operating at different levels of self-identity. His Christian identity did not stop him from seeking help from a non-Christian, Hindu spiritual figure whom he had opposed earlier. In fact, this incident has fostered a better relationship between the Christians and Hindus in Thulasigramam.

The above-discussed lived reality highlight the interface between Christians and Hindus, and the prevalence of coexisting multiple religious reference points from which people operate in their daily lives. In such a context, belonging to specific castes, religious and village communities function as different identity forming locations. Members within the Christian Paraiyar community pick and choose their points of belonging and operate from different positions without necessarily having any internal conflict. This can be best summarized by the words of Swami Kannu, an elderly person in the village, who wisely declared: 'whatever happens, blood and village relationship is thicker than the religious divisions'.

The preceding observation of the Paraiyar Christian community illustrated the dynamic and discursive nature of self-conceptualization and identification in the community. In conjuncture with the contemporary discourse on identity, several aspects that define and redefine local identity and community were highlighted. It also provides an understanding of the dialectic and strategic nature of identity formation not assuming that structure creates an identity.[53] One significant aspect of this process shows that discourses on identity cannot be essentialized, but rather understood in their dynamic, contextual reality. Nevertheless, it is important to grasp the polyvalence of cognitive conceptualizations of the self, which may not be always explicable in fixed terms. The differentiation of *us* and *them* are by no means strict marks of categories, but possible or pragmatic points of view, understood within a given communal matrix and liable to switching. These aspects are further intricately knotted within the religious and cultural consciousness firmly tied to the realities of location.

Individuals and communities operate and shape their world primarily by belonging to a system, which is often directed by dominant notions, yet internalized and potentially also subverted. To a great extent, lived realities determine the nature of self-conceptualization, which in turn informs and contributes to the way individuals and communities relate with one another. Aspects discussed earlier offer some of the possible ways through which individuals and communities come to understand and represent themselves within their lived contexts. It also shows that the Paraiyars, irrespective of their religious affiliation, share a collective worldview within the village community through a multi-layered belonging. There were enough indicators to explain that the process of being a Christian in a caste-dominated village has contributed to and complicated the formation of self-identity. While observing the religious practices in a context like the Thulasigramam Paraiyar Christian community, one has to be aware of the difficulty of Western-oriented studies of religion as a separate and even an exclusive system may pose. It is also important to recognize the fact that none of these processes function in a vacuum or isolation, but constantly interface and interpellate with each other, contributing to the construction of social identity.

4

Yesusami and the Less Visible World: The Worldview of Paraiyar Christians

> *When Dalits become Christians they leave behind everything and embrace Christianity in its totality, Christian history becomes their history and they no longer belong to their past, the God of Abraham is their God.*[1]

The above comment by Azariah, a former bishop in South India summarizes the dominant outlook among Dalit theologians about Dalit Christians in India. Such a view downplays the possibility of Dalit Christians to continue their pre-Christian worldview after their conversion. My fieldwork observations show that certain aspects of the local Dalit worldview go through a process of negotiation and continuity, even after they have embraced Christianity. The Paraiyar Christians in Thulasigramam demonstrate that the practical necessities of life also shape and constitute concepts of the visible and less visible worlds.[2] This conceptual framework suggests that there is a necessity to overcome the traditional Christian dualistic perception of the universe as either matter or spirit. By using 'visible' and 'less visible' world as mutually interacting categories, I argue that from the Paraiyar worldview, a holistic non-dualistic perception is possible.[3] This chapter sets out to explore the dynamics of the above-mentioned views and also attempts to lay bare the influence of local notions regarding the less visible world. This will be done by examining the process of absorption, adaptation and appropriation of the Christian worldview within the Paraiyar Christians' existing religious space. This chapter also endeavours to explain how these Christian converts have not 'embraced' Christianity in its totality, as claimed by Dalit theologians, such as Azariah, but rather that their Christian belief systems are couched within their continuing local understandings.

Anthropologically observing religion

One cannot examine the religious arena of Dalit communities without acknowledging the prevailing sociocultural systems in which they exist. Religion cannot be confined to one aspect as it touches upon many facets and is inextricably entangled in human life. Many of the contemporary anthropological approaches to the study of religion build upon the pioneering work of Emile Durkheim and his successors. The framework of study established by Dalit religious scholars also employs a similar approach; hence in the following section, I will provide a brief overview of an anthropological approach to religion in order to understand and problematize contemporary approaches while observing Paraiyar Christian religious experience.

From a socio-anthropological perspective, Durkheim defines religion as 'a unified system of beliefs and practices relative to sacred things'.[4] In other words, religion observes the sacred and the supernatural within society. Durkheim functioned within a dualistic perception of human life.[5] But there are limitations to this approach as Malinowski contend, claiming that Durkheim's theory that 'collective is religious', or mechanical solidarity, has to be critically examined due to its narrow and dualistic understanding of human life.[6] Contrary to popular perception as presented by Durkheim, religion is neither exclusively individual nor exclusively communal but is a combination of both.[7] Regardless of Malinowski's contributions, Clifford Geertz raises some important epistemological issues to his approach, particularly regarding the individual and his complexity.[8] Geertz succinctly summarizes the idea of religion as the experiences of an individual within a community, as 'it is not in solitude that faith is made'.[9] In a similar vein, Jack David Eller, through a systematic analysis, suggests,

> religion is part of lived human existence. How we define and conceptualize religion will affect what we accept as religion, along with what aspects of it we particularly attend to . . . what we find in the end is that religion is a profoundly human and social phenomenon-arising from and addressing intellectual, emotional and social sources-in which the nonhuman and "supernatural" are seen as profoundly human and social.[10]

However, it is important to acknowledge that many anthropologists tend to argue that religion in human communities has specific historical roots and cannot be understood without tracing the discursive sociocultural process that stems from.[11] According to Talal Asad, religious belief and its corresponding symbols are intimately linked to the worldly conditions within which they are experienced. Therefore, Asad calls for the abandonment of dualistic approaches to the study of religion, and instead proposes that scholars should study the intertwined and complex process of religious experience in human communities.[12] Andrew Dawson echoes a similar view on the back of Maduro Otto's observation on religion explaining that 'sociology engages the situated reality of religion by identifying, exploring and seeking to explain its relationship with overarching societal structures and process which both impact upon and are influenced by it'.[13] Furthering this sociological idea and embracing the environment, Tim Ingold suggests that human beings learn and conceptualize within 'the relational context of (their) practical engagement within the lived-in-environments'.[14] Tim Ingold explains further,

> We recognise that the mind and its properties are not given in advance of the individual's entry into the social world, but are rather fashioned through a lifelong history of involvement in relationships with others. And we know that it is through the activities of the embodied mind (or enminded body) that social relationships are formed and reformed.[15]

Theoretically, Bourdieu proposes that such an understanding is a process of 'internalisation of externality'.[16] Thus, it is impossible to understand religious actions and thoughts in abstraction from the context in which they are conceived and lived.[17] In other words, our knowledge as human beings is mediated and conditioned by our relationships with others and the environment in which they are located.[18] Stressing this dynamic Tim Ingold argues that human communities cannot be understood in isolation from their environment, and therefore must acknowledge the locatedness of it in all its diversity by having an inclusive and non-dualistic approach.[19] Basically, as Timothy Jenkins suggests, 'the religious sphere has to be considered in and as part of the wider context of human activity'.[20] Put differently, we need to understand how human beings see the world or what shapes their perception of the reality in which they live. The world as they see it in which they live. The *Weltanschauung*, the inescapable reality of human life, the knowledge about life and consequent action.[21] To summarize the notion of worldview in the words of Geertz,

> Worldview is their picture of the way things in sheer actuality are, their concept of nature, of self, of society. It contains their most comprehensive ideas of order . . . the worldview is made emotionally acceptable by being presented as an image of an actual state of affairs of which such a way of life is an authentic expression.[22]

Further, I will argue that the knowledge of the less visible evolves from the situatedness of an individual or community, rather than being externally imposed. This sheds light on the fact that human beings are not neutral observers, but are rather active participants in shaping their notions of the less visible. The religious world is not separate from the everyday 'profane' world, but it is affected, influenced and transformed by experiences in the 'commonsense' world.[23] This approach to the study of religion suggests that it is impossible to collapse all that happens within the religious space into an incomprehensible whole, rather observe the interwovenness of the whole. Interface between the visible and less visible aspects of the world is a fluid, dynamic and constantly creative space, where the individual and the collective realize their interconnectedness. With this background, I shall return to Thulasigramam.

Tangibility of Yesusami

Yesusami, the Tamil name that translates to 'God Jesus', comes to signify the collective experience of God in the Paraiyar Christian community of Thulasigramam. Insights from peoples' experiences show that such a collective idea emerges from their daily social interactions, combined with the knowledge received from traditional religious instructions. The local nature of such conceptions assumes significance in this context. Closely observing a few cases from my fieldwork I will examine the prevalence of such notions of Yesusami in Thulasigramam.

Protecting, providing and healing Yesusami

> Whenever I go into the forest to collect firewood and return in the late evening, unable to carry my bundle, I pray to Yesusami and he comes and lifts the bundle for me and walks me home safely, protecting from wild insects and animals.

Amutha explains her regular encounter with Jesus in such simple experiential terms that it seems almost impossible for a non-community member to conceive and understand such an occurrence. But the experience is very real to her and has a great influence on her relationship to Yesusami, as the source of help and support to her. Here, some observations are notable: first, the presence of Yesusami is assured for Amutha even in the middle of the forest, for whenever she calls on his name he will come to her aid. Second, it also reflects the immediate response of Yesusami to her, as if it is Amutha who controls Yesusami. In other words, the less visible divine is directed by the necessities of the human being, even during a mundane task. Third, the presence of Yesusami becomes real because of his participation in the life and struggles of Amutha so she in turn strengthens her belief in him. The reciprocal nature of the relationship between the human and the divine and its influence on the formation of faith is crucial in Amutha's experience.

The prevalence of such conceptualization of Yesusami is widespread in the communal lives of the Paraiyar Christians in Thulasigramam. The idea of the immediate and realistic presence of Yesusami at the instance of calling him for help is part of the local understanding of gods and goddesses, who are protectors and helpers in times of need. It can also be observed that these qualities are associated with the female Dalit goddesses and deities like Mariyamma and Ellaiamma[24]; hence, through Amutha's experience, Yesusami takes on the nature of a female goddess. In other words, Amutha connects with Yesusami through her familiar local channel of experiencing the divine. In addition, as a woman doing heavy domestic work, the necessity for Amutha to seek help in doing her routine work also shapes her religious observances. It is also important to note that Amutha's faith in Yesusami is real for her not only because he comes to her aid, but also her faith stems from and is shaped by such incidents, which in turn makes the encounter with Yesusami more real. Amutha demonstrates the Paraiyar Christian's relation with the less visible through these simple daily life occurrences, in which the divine is experienced and encountered. Amutha's lived religious experience can not only be traced back to the local Paraiyar experience, but more generally to biblical stories, such as Hagar and Ruth in the Old Testament, encounters which has been narrated and preached often among the Christian community. These different perceptions effectively combine with the already existing notions of the less visible, providing space for individual and collective experience. Amutha's encounters sheds light on the process of drawing from various cultural reference points to construct and validate new religious encounters.

Another facet of Yesusami is presented by Sathyamma, an elderly widow and Christian convert from the Arunthathier caste.[25] For her, Yesusami is the source of *nimmadhi* and *adaravu* (solace and succour) in this world of strife and sorrow. As a widow with five children, Sathyamma has undergone great difficulties during which Yesusami has become her source of strength. In fact, this prompted her to become a Christian against the wishes of her family and extended relatives. Sathyamma claimed that it is the motherly nature of god as expressed through Yesusami and experienced by her, which has given her the ability to face the world and carry on with her life. Yesusami provides her motherly care, as she explains, so that she can cry to him with all her of problems and be consoled by him.

> When I was a Hindu I used to go to the Mariyamma temple and pour out all my sorrows at her feet. Now that I have become a Christian, I go to Yesusami in the church and pour out all my troubles and he takes care of it. He is like a father to my fatherless children. Yesusami is the reason for the well-being of my children. I have cried and prayed to him everyday for them.

Sathyamma's observations clearly express the mode through which she and other women experience Yesusami. Yesusami is perceived by Sathyamma as a male, who can protect her family, yet is also strongly feminine in nature – the perfect comforting companion.

Furthermore, it is interesting to note that according to Arul, the local Christian Priest, there is hardly anything 'Christian' about this conception of Jesus in the understanding of Sathyamma. He claims that such views are rather 'superstitious beliefs and a product of ignorance', and that Sathyamma had constructed the idea of Yesusami from her previous Hindu gods and goddesses, adding to her limited knowledge of Jesus Christ that she had heard from others. Yet crucially, her image of Yesusami is very meaningful to herself, and from it she is able to draw the hope necessary for everyday life. Being an elderly widow and a daily labourer also substantially contributes to the way she conceives of Yesusami, so far as she is concerned the less visible becomes significant because she is able to experience the comfort and support he provides when she prays to him. In the context of being treated indifferently and disdainfully by the rest of the Paraiyar Christians because of her caste affiliation, her understanding of Yesusami assumes even greater significance. She refers to the Paraiyar Christians as 'these people who don't treat me respectfully and don't even consider me as a person, but Yesusami accepts me and becomes my comforter'. Even though her immediate experience of Christians is characterized by painful rejection, she is able to visualize and to believe in the caring Yesusami.

For a more passionate and caring understanding of Yesusami as a mother, let us observe the story of Jeba, a middle-aged woman who faced numerous hardships in her life. She suffered violent abuses from her husband, who is an alcoholic and an important member of the church. He has another wife and family in the neighbouring village and frequently neglects Jeba and her family. Because of the hardships at the hands of her husband and the humiliation from the community, she attempted to commit suicide many times but failed, a failure she looks upon regretfully. The church and the Christian community are places of judgement and condemnation, in which she finds no compassion or support. In fact, the Priest advised that she be avoided because she is a bad influence on the community, while her husband remains a legitimate member of society. Nevertheless, she was able to encounter the *Kirubai* (Grace) of Yesusami, who rescued and sustained her. Her image of Yesusami is also like that of a caring mother, who helps her in times of trouble. Jeba continues to lead a painful life due to her husband, who lives in both villages, and she has no choice but to accept this lifestyle for the sake of her children. Jeba looks at Yesusami not as an abusive male but a graceful and loving person, who like her also suffered at the hands of society, so he understands her sufferings.

Joshua, an elderly man, brings another dimension to the conception of Yesusami through his experiences. He used to be a self-professed 'hardcore' alcoholic and drunkard, never caring for his wife and three children, until one day he encountered Yesusami due to the relentless prayers of his wife, Annamma. She used to pray every *Ammavasai* night (the new moon day, which is auspicious in the Hindu calendar as a new beginning) to Yesusami for the healing of her husband. During one of those prayers, she claims that Yesusami revealed to her that Joshua is an alcoholic because, out of jealousy, someone in the community placed witchcraft on them and her husband will only get better if she gets rid of it. Joshua believed that his wife was able to remove the forces of witchcraft with the help of Yesusami, and has quit abusing alcohol. He remembers what he was like, as a 'possessed' alcoholic person. Annamma recollected how in the middle of the night she would go with her children in search of Joshua, because he might be lying somewhere in the street after drinking too much, but all that has changed after her prayers were answered and Joshua is now a very respectable person in the Paraiyar Christian community.

However, their struggle against evil spirits continued, as their daughter Rani became critically ill and was on her deathbed. Annamma and other others attributed Rani's sickness to renewed witchcraft attacks. Annamma never gave up hope in the healing Yesusami and prayed for Rani as she prayed for Joshua. One night as she was praying, Annamma had a vision of fire and light and Yesusami appeared and promised that Rani would be healed immediately and to everybody's joy Rani was healed. But, the struggle of their family against evil continued as Rani got married and had a baby boy, who quickly became gravely ill. Annamma again started to pray to Yesusami to help out her family, but on this occasion Annamma decided to make some promises to Yesusami. She made a *poruthanai* (promised) to hoist a flag with a cross on it on the hill top over looking the village and offer milk and sugar in a plantain leaf as an offering if her grandson was healed. And the boy was healed. Annamma told me that she believes it is possible to demand anything from Yesusami if she prays and makes an offering in return. Annamma has a strong faith and believes that Yesusami cares for her and the well-being of her family.

Thus, the aforementioned experiences suggest that daily encounters play a significant role in both shaping and supporting the Paraiyar Christian belief systems. Yesusami enables them to be connected with their community in a way that is often not socially possible. Relating human suffering and social abuse to Yesusami's power shows how the Paraiyar Christians encounter the less visible for tangible and visible benefits. Yesusami is constantly invoked and drawn into a mutual understanding, almost a covenant, one might say; even though this practice seemingly Christian, it is also undeniably loaded with local Hindu religious practices and traditions. This practical approach in relating to Yesusami is in effect a local religious practice – regardless of what the church authority deems as Christian.

Reciprocality of Yesusami

Dass, a vocal youth in the Paraiyar Christian community, has a reasonably uncomplicated understanding of God as nothing but a 'superior power' beyond human capacity to understand, who controls every aspect of human life. The Yesusami Dass believes in controls everything and acts or responds according to the lifestyle of human beings. The nature of an individual life depends upon and is determined by his attitude and good conduct; thus, if a person leads an evil lifestyle, his life will become one of struggle and suffering. In other words, Yesusami dispenses the good 'fruits' of life, as a reward for living a good life. There is hardly any room for *kirubai,* mercy or grace in this regard, because as he explains: 'God gives us lot of chances. If we don't learn from our past life style, I don't think he will forgive us!' However, he qualified his statement by observing that if there is lack of justice in the community in the form of equality, respect and sharing, one may not be able to understand or even know this Yesusami, because for Dass these qualities are prerequisites for knowing this Yesusami as the 'superior power'. The lack of these characteristics results in the absence of peace, which arguably seems to be an elusive entity among them. For him, this is a sensible model to approach God, as he commented: 'it is important to have moral standards by following what God has taught us; failure to do so will result in misfortune, which I think is the reason for the state of life among Christians'. He is of the opinion that unless the Paraiyars change their lifestyle from an 'eat-drink and be merry attitude', very little will improve in their lives. Dass connects the prevalence of 'misfortune' to God and to the outcome of human failure. He then goes on to observe that such misfortune can be changed by attending church and giving time to Yesusami, remembering him in all their ways. But, on the flip side, those Christians who experience relatively easier lives tend to take the moral high ground claiming that they are spiritually superior to those who suffer unfortunate events. Unsurprisingly, this attitude in turn fuels internal fights and quarrels among the Paraiyar Christians resulting in further social division. To avoid such unpleasant situations, Dass thinks that every individual should know their position in the community and live accordingly.

That Yesusami has created everybody equally and nobody is inferior to any one else is the firm opinion of Simon, another youth from the Christian community. He believes that everyone should understand this as fundamental to the nature of God, explaining that 'God is beyond all human conception and we may be able to interpret and describe it in our own way but we can't claim that we know the full details of who this God is'. According to Simon, this is the reason for the varied understanding of God among Paraiyar Christians in Thulasigramam. Significantly, he believes that no conception of God is complete, and hence people should stop claiming that they have the right knowledge of God: 'If everybody realises that their knowledge of God is inadequate, then there will not be any conflict'. He feels that relationships between human beings are far more important than religious affiliation, and moreover he is convinced that this is what God requires of humanity. Because of his belief, Simon claims not to discriminate against anybody on a religious basis.

However, Simon feels that God sometimes acts 'crazily' if he cannot understand why certain things happen in particular ways, and then he gets very angry with unreasonable and baffling acts of God. Simon's emphasis on relational rather than 'religious' affiliation, highlights the impact of the visible world on the less visible world. He also stressed the fact that human beings are responsible for their actions and should face the consequences of them. In the same line of thinking he believes that in the absence of respect and regard for other people God is absent as well:

> God dwells in all of us, in our conscience; God is not something or somebody that exists out there but within us. God becomes real through each of us, and when we fail to have a good relationship God can not be experienced. As long there is no equality and unity, worshiping God is a waste!

Simon's understanding of Christianity clearly articulates views of others in Thulasigramam emphasizing the aspect of justice in the here and now.

Reflecting on the reciprocity of Yesusami, Sanjeev, an active youth member of the church in Thulasigramam, observes from his own experience that 'whatever happens, one should give due respect to God and then only one shall be blessed'. He gives at least one rupee a day, an offering to the church in Thulasigramam and claims to occasionally receiving 20, 30 or 50 rupees back the same day from somebody as a gift or in kind. According to him when you give to God, God gives back with added blessing. He also declared that he got his present job as a ward boy in the local hospital in a similar manner after him having given his time and energy to Yesusami, so Yesusami promptly repaid him by providing a job: a perfectly utilitarian view, which the Gospel of Prosperity might applaud. He also extends this interpretation to the situation in Thulasigramam village as well. He asks, 'Why are there many people jobless and misguided? The answer is simple: because they have not given their time and energy to Yesusami'. He compares Thulasigramam to other villages and says that only in Thulasigramam are there many illiterates and day labourers, because these people do not fear God. Quoting scripture he paraphrases, 'If you don't treat the *koil* (temple) of Yesusami with respect, which is the body of God, you will receive a similar treatment from God!' Reflecting on the sensitive issue of caste discrimination, he feels that every individual should realize their potential and then strive towards getting out of the oppressive system. Interestingly, though he observes that, 'it is God who has created the inequality so that we human beings will look up to him and seek help,' a view commonly held among Paraiyars, who think that for once God is responsible for their *thalaividhi* (misfortune), but quick to add it is the same Yesusami who rescues them through the rough times in their life.

The above accounts of perceiving Yesusami contain interesting, but conflicting insights, characteristic of traditional Paraiyar understandings of god as an external superior power, blended with certain qualities of 'the Old Testament' God filtered through the central figure of Yesusami by Christian teaching. Dass has incorporated the Christian view of God as just and righteous with his traditional perception of god as an external power that controls human life. It is also important to recognize that the responsibility for achieving a good life is on people themselves and not on God, as God just dispenses 'fruits' according to human actions. Dass' opinion that most of the Paraiyars suffer because of their attitudes is a widespread Paraiyar Christian viewpoint, which sheds light on the tension between the day-to-day lifestyle of traditional Paraiyar culture and the eschatologically driven pietistic Christian understanding of human life as taught in the Church of South India.

Sanjeev's exchange based perceptions of Yesusami and the possibility of Yesusami intentionally creating inequality so that human beings will depend on him for survival does carry a *karmic* or fatalistic understanding of God within Christianity. Sanjeev also provides a window out of the caste system in this life, Christians could work their way out by good deeds. Put differently, human beings are not totally responsible for their misfortune, but God is also equally held responsible. The material and practical perception of Yesusami cannot be ignored in these observations. As discussed in the previous chapter the conceptualization of God takes place in and within the context of existence by incorporating and developing an understanding of the divine that addresses their situation. It can be argued within this stream of logic that the Paraiyar Christians think it is possible to control the actions of Yesusami, as a response to human action. The reality of Yesusami is directly related to the state of human relationships. Sanjeev pointed out that whenever he contributes money or time as an offering to God he does so with the expectation that he will be rewarded, what he calls a 'blessing' may be interpreted as an interesting reciprocal causal relationship with Yesusami. This awareness makes it possible to have a dynamic and open-ended perception of God. God is seen and understood as the source of all things: good, evil, misfortune, protection, prosperity and safety, all of which are beyond human comprehension. In such a context, appeasing God in order to receive blessings is very much a part of the system. God is understood as a personal, ever present yet less visible being, who acts instantaneously in their material physical world. It is easy to recognize the flow of various perceptions of God drawn from traditional religious arena in this account being reflected in their understanding of Yesusami. Yet it may well be that areas of their articulation, especially the benefits accounting from gifting or good actions, are assumed or expected by Christians beyond South India.

Yesusami, a communal God

Perceptions of Yesusami as a communal God in the Thulasigramam Paraiyar Christian community take different paths, contributing to diverse perceptions. The following descriptions provide a cross-sectional impression of views and the centrality of relational elements in the conceptualization of Yesusami. Deva, an elder in the Christian community, offers an important dimension to the understanding of Yesusami as God. He says,

> Yesusami is with me here in my hut, not in an isolated place in the sky. I can call him, talk to him and demand things from him anytime. When I pray to Yesusami he gets me the pension and the 'rum' bottles from the military canteen and I am thankful to him for that.

Observing the portrait of Yesusami on the wall in his hut, Deva explained that his perception of God through Yesusami gives him the freedom to interact with that God in his daily activities, even to the extent that he gets angry and swears at him when things are not going well, and venerates and showers him with praises when things are fine. In other words, Deva's experience highlights the fact that the worshipper almost owns the god/goddess they worship and utilize his/her services within their daily needs. It also points out that Yesusami actually lives with him, providing him not only with a pension but bottles of rum as well. Moreover, Yesusami's presence is real for Deva because he perceives God as living and interacting in the community, working for their benefit even at the most mundane and perhaps libational level. For Deva, being brought up as a Christian, Yesusami is the only God he knows and connects with spiritually. His view is not an isolated case as the majority of the Paraiyar Christian community subscribes to such a notion.

Poovamma, a widow, emphasizes the importance of proper relationships within the community in order to experience the presence of Yesusami. One word she often used to refer to the state of the Paraiyar Christian community is *maggipouthu*, 'decaying' beyond description. She claims that Paraiyar Christians are not happy to see others prospering in their community and want to drag them down to their own status. As she described,

> Characteristics like backbiting, jealousy, envy, instigating conflict, covetousness, and distrust abounds in this village. I feel that this community will

never prosper. They just have the name of Christians and do all the evil things. Even Hindus are frightened at the actions of Christians.

Poovamma alleges that while most of the Christians go to church, but when leaving pick fights and quarrel endlessly. She is convinced that because of such tendencies, Yesusami has punished her community to their present status of being Paraiyars (Untouchables) until they learn to live properly. She is very content with her life, even though she went through rough patches in the past. There were situations when the elders of the village advised her to leave her husband and marry somebody else, because he was an abusive alcoholic. She refused to do so and as she proudly recalled, she told the church elders she would live a good life by supporting her husband who was later diagnosed with tuberculosis.

That being said Poovamma was very upset with Yesusami when her husband died. She became so angry with Yesusami that she did not go to church, pray or participate in the life of the church for a couple of years. She felt let down by Yesusami and confessed that her faithfulness was not rewarded with her husband's healing. And she was upset that when she and her children were in dire need, nobody from the Christian community helped them, and asked 'how can one claim to know Yesusami, if you don't help a person who is in need right before one's eye?' And interestingly she questioned 'If you don't extend your hand to help somebody how you can expect Yesusami to help you?' For Poovamma, Yesusami becomes real only when people allow him to be real through kind and thoughtful relationships.

Underlining the communal nature of Yesusami, Peter, a respected youth leader, suggests that people are responsible for each other and that in the absence of respect, Yesusami is absent as well. For him Yesusami dwells in all of us, in our conscience and is therefore not something or somebody existing apart from humanity. 'Yesusami becomes real through each person, and when relationships fail Yesusami can not be experienced'. Peter, an idealistic young man, considers that *niyam* (justice) should be the essential quality of everyone who believes in Yesusami, since it is the main characteristic of Yesusami. As he asserts, 'Yesusami fought against unjust people in order to establish a community of equals. That's why he is God and if we believe in him we have to do the same'. Peter does not have problems attending festivals celebrated by his Hindu relatives as long as it brings happiness and facilitates cordial relationships. He also noted that his Hindu family also celebrates Christian festivals with him, underlying the fact that the relationships between relatives are far more important than inter-religious conflicts or distinctions. This is where he feels the church should play a positive role. For him, the Church is a community brought together by Yesusami and should therefore facilitate the experience of God in and for all, not just for Christians. Peter felt that the church is not fulfilling its task, because some of its members walk around with *thalaiganam* (head weight or pride) and 'ego', what he identifies as the key attitudes that fragment the community. According to Peter, when a person begins to behave in such a manner he obstructs Yesusami's presence in the community.

Drawing from the preceding insights it can be concluded that Paraiyar Christians perceive God as living in the community, which provides a sense of ownership for the worshipper. Yesusami is expected to obey the wishes and answer the prayers of the worshipper if they fulfil his desires. Furthermore, Yesusami becomes real only through proper human relationships, and if they are broken, the possibility of Yesusami's presence and blessings in the community is hampered.

Visions and corresponding life transformations

Visions of gods and goddesses are an integral part of the religious experience in Thulasigramam across all religious traditions. Visions in the lives of Esther, Jothi and Devi and the impact on their lives contribute significantly to their religious self-identities. Such incidents not only transform their lives but also provide the strength to continue on with their daily struggles.

Esther was childless for ten years after her marriage to Rathnam from the Paraiyar Christian community. She had converted to Christianity from Hinduism and faced hostility from her own relatives and family. Esther is physically challenged due to battling polio as a child and has difficulty walking. She began to gain some understanding of Christianity after her marriage to Rathnam, but could make little sense of the church's teachings. She faced humiliation and shame in front of others in the Paraiyar Christian community as she was unable to bear a child and was almost ostracized because of her 'barrenness'. During a church meeting, she heard someone preach about the love and compassion of Yesusami and the message that whoever asks God sincerely for help would receive it. As she explained to me, this message of Yesusami's love took firm root in her heart and she began to pray fervently to Yesusami, asking him to grant her a child so that her shame could be removed. Meanwhile, unable to bear the humiliation of being childless Rathnam took to drinking and became an alcoholic.

Amutha, Esther's neighbour, came to her rescue and began to narrate many stories from the Bible of barren women being blessed by God due to their fervent prayers and encouraged Esther to do the same. The couple lived on the foothill of *Oliva Malai* (mount olive), a hillock at the edge of the village used by the Christians for prayer. Esther decided to climb the hillock everyday and pray to Yesusami, near the crucifix planted by the Paraiyars Christians, until he answered her prayer. Esther pledged to climb the hill daily, hoist a flag with a cross symbol every week and offer any child she was granted back to Yesusami's ministry, if her prayers were answered. Days went by and Esther continued to pray faithfully until one night, she had an extraordinary vision of Yesusami, who promised that her prayers would be answered and that she would soon bear a son. Esther could not believe what she saw and kept the experience a secret lest anyone might think that she had lost her mind. A couple of days later Rathnam too had visions of Yesusami as a baby, in which he promised a child for them. Surprisingly Esther found herself pregnant within a week and realized that Yesusami's promise in the vision had actually come true. Esther now has a 7-year-old boy, Anthony, who she is hoping will become a priest for Yesusami when he grows up. She continues to climb the hillock and hoist her flag in honour of the promise fulfilled by Yesusami. So Rathnam believes that when people ask Yesusami, he answers those who are suffering and helpless. 'Prayer brings victory' was his ecstatic statement. Esther's experience of barrenness and social hostility is not an isolated episode as several other women in Thulasigramam have described having gone through similar experiences of Yesusami intervening in their lives and transforming their misery. The description of Yesusami by Esther can be closely linked to the local myth of a fertility goddess, *Vannathiamma* in the village, who is worshiped by the villagers and has been blessing barren women in a similar fashion. It could be argued that Esther places Yesusami in a similar mould due to her own Hindu background: but recast in as the Christian God.

Epitomizing the predominant experiences of rural Paraiyar women Jothi shared her painful story with me. Her abusive alcoholic husband, Samuel, beats her regularly and she is forced to take up hard labour in order to financially sustain the family. On many occasions Jothi pretends to take the goats into the forest in order to sit alone and cry out to Yesusami. She also has difficulties finding work on a regular basis due to the frequent failure of the monsoon rains and the fact that modern agricultural equipment is progressively replacing manual labourers. Yet with all her troubles she told me that she is very happy because she had been imploring Yesusami to ensure her husband stops drinking and abusing her violently. And after Christmas, according to Jothi her husband miraculously had a vision of Yesusami in the fields and consequently gave up alcohol. Earlier, he had lost faith in Yesusami as his prayers went unanswered. Samuel used to think that believing in Yesusami yielded nothing and was a wasted effort but after his encounter with Yesusami he drastically changed his mind and lifestyle.

Jothi told me that one of the problems with the men in Thulasigramam is that they spend most of what they earn each day either on drinking or eating, which badly affects the family. Now she is happy to some extent because her husband does not beat her anymore as in the past, and, she hopes that he will be completely cured from his addiction to alcohol. Jothi says, 'Yesusami appears like a child whenever I pray, and I feel like a child while praying to Yesusami as he takes care of me'. In Jothi's experiences, Yesusami is manifested both as a loveable, the fatherly figure who answers her prayers by intervening in the life of Samuel and turning him from alcohol, as well as a child. The often repeated element of personal encounters through visions enables Yesusami to be regarded not just as an external observer, but as a powerful force that can intervene in the human world and redirect the course of human life. In Jothi's opinion, Samuel would not have changed his lifestyle if not for his vision of Yesusami: he directly changed their lives.

A regular churchgoing family in the Paraiyar Christian community is represented by Devi and Arul. Even though they are both landless daily labourers in the Reddyars' fields, they make an effort to lead an orderly life. Unfortunately, their poverty complicates their efforts to lead a normal life. Their financial burdens result in misunderstanding and quarrelling between them, and quarrels become a daily feature of their lives even though they keep their church participation alive. Their worsening family situation and constantly ill children led Devi to attempt suicide many times as she felt that her prayers were falling on deaf ears and as she even saw her unsuccessful attempts as a failure to die. Illiterate, she memorized Psalm 23 and kept reciting it in the hope that one day Yesusami would answer her prayers. One day, disappointed and depressed while she was attempting to end her life, Yesusami and the Mary Matha (Virgin Mary) appeared to her in a vision during broad daylight and promised that all her troubles in life would go away if she stopped attempting to commit suicide. Understandably this was a life-transforming event for her. Even though her life has not changed drastically, she remains hopeful that her life circumstances will improve. Arul continues to pray and is still waiting for his own vision of Yesusami. Their son Wilson is partial blind and their daughter, married to Devi's brother, still suffers from untreated tuberculosis. Devi believes that by diligently following the instructions of Yesusami and Mary Matha given in the vision, their life will eventually change. The vision and the promise of Yesusami and the Mary Matha left a deep impact on the life of both Devi and Arul, which has given them new hope amidst adversity and hopelessness.

I argue that even though the visions of Yesusami and Mary Matha resemble their traditional Hindu religious experiences, it also stems from their own specific life struggles. Yesusami and Mary Matha are not just external observers, as often presented by the local church, but are actually regarded as participants and transformers, giving new meanings to the Paraiyar Christians understanding of their context.

Less visible world and its impact

According to most of the members of the Paraiyar Christian community spirits, both good and evil, hover over and live in the village. This is not just a claim but is backed by real experiences, including the spirits of the dead ancestors, as well as spirits wandering without a place to stay. Significantly, many of the events in the community were attributed to the works of spirits, thus giving the impression that the spirits play active roles in their everyday life. Let us examine a few aspects of this less visible world.

The world of spirits

The Paraiyar Christians relate with spirits in different ways; they are afraid and avoid them, they blame the spirits for their misfortunes and identify them with witchcraft causing pain and misery on others.[26] But there are also others who consider that the sprits of the dead ancestors guide them towards good and are beneficial to their lives. This phenomenon is common among many Dalit communities,[27] but here I will focus on some experiences from Thulasigramam, which offer significantly different insights.

Walking into the forest one day, Ramesh told me about his experiences of spirits in the village and how he believes that they come and go during the night. Even though they are very real to him, Ramesh is not greatly bothered about them as, believing that, 'they will hurt you only when you disturb them, otherwise they go on with their work'. While explaining his encounters with spirits in the village, he narrated the story of two little girls who fell in to a dried up well while playing in the fields and died. It is generally believed in the village that the spirits of those girls still hang around the particular well and the villagers claim to hear them crying from time to time. They have yet to harm anybody, and indeed there are many accounts of villagers being helped by their spirits when they were lost in the forest.

Encounters with evil spirits in the forest and fields by the villagers are normal and do not evoke much surprise. Most people claim to have had some sort of experience with such spirits, whether they are evil or benevolent, the difference discernable only by their actions. It confirms their belief in the spirit world and its proximity to human life. There is a belief in Thulasigramam that evil spirits originate from people who have died through suicide and murder, and harmfully linger around rather than resting. Until they stop being angry, they keep interfering in the lives of their living relatives and villagers. To remedy such a situation, the villagers, including Christians, sacrifice an animal (usually a chicken or a goat) to compensate for the life of the unhappy spirit. There are various signs and events that show the presence of evil spirits to the villagers. For example, I was instructed not to walk alone in certain parts of the village during high noon and or at midnight, as well as not to sleep alone in certain places during the night lest the evil spirits should harm me. This was believed to be more likely given that I was a stranger and an outsider. There appears no difference between the Christians and Hindus in their conception of the spirit world and its effect on human life.

There is also one day set apart in the local culture, *Mayana Kollai* (literally, 'graveyard robbery'), when people dress up in costumes of Hindu mythological characters and go to the burial grounds to offer food to the dead. During this festival, spirit possession is very common, as the spirits choose to come upon certain people and guide or warn them about their future. On this day anything can happen, and what does happen is done under the pretext of spirit possession. I also understand from the Paraiyars that on such occasions they have utilized spirit possession as an excuse to cause damage or demand things from the Reddyars; such ploys to utilize the spirits are not uncommon.[28] From the perspective of Paraiyars, this occasion helps them both to transgress the boundaries between the communities and to indulge in retaliatory activities. Apart from this, it is also said by some other villagers that their dead relatives come in dreams and visions in order to warn them about some impending danger. Swaminathan, an elderly person explained: 'It is a real world out there and one should not be stupid not to believe it: because of this many suffer'. This idea is in a sense one in which the visible and the less visible worlds are fully open to each other. Moreover, during such occasions, the boundaries between the visible and the less visible worlds are blurred and transcended.

Space and orientation are also similar sources of fortune or disaster in Thulasigramam. Rani lives in the house situated directly across the street from the church building. And while the entrance to her house faces the church, there is an old abandoned house occupying the space between her house and the church. After a few months she decided to close the entrance facing the church and make a new entrance on the other side of the house. She reasoned that she had been experiencing misfortune because her door was open to the ruined house which as is normal in Thulasigramam, became home to evil spirits, affecting nearby residences. The imposing church building standing right opposite the abandoned house is unable to prevent evil spirits from inhabiting the ruined house. Rani believed in Yesusami and in his power but equally respected the power of the local spiritual forces. Once, as I was coming out of her house, a cat crossed my path and she demanded that I stop, re-enter her house so that she can sprinkle water over my head and only then let me proceed, thus cancelling the power of the cat, the messenger of evil spirits. Whenever I travelled out of Thulasigramam on my motorcycle she would come and put a sign of cross sign on it, because I had to travel through a burial ground on my way – she believed that the cross would protect me from evil spirits in such places. Her belief system and worldview of spirits is built from Christian and local sources.

Among the Paraiyar Christians the tendency to attribute any unexplained occurrences to evil spirits could be traced back to their local tradition although the recent influence of the Christian Pentecostal fellowship in the neighbouring village cannot be overlooked. The Pentecostals also attribute unfortunate events to evil spirits and claim that the Paraiyar Christians need to join their prayer fellowship, regularly fast and pray in order to overcome them. If the Paraiyar Christians fail to follow the Pentecostal fellowship's instructions, they are told that their sufferings will increase as the evil spirits will know that they are unfaithful Christians and attack them more readily. Failure to subscribe financially to the Pentecostal fellowship is also presented as resulting in severe consequences in terms of spiritual attacks, even a simple headache being attributed to the work of evil forces. Another common reasoning among the fellowshipgoers is that sickness may come from an act of *sunyam* (witchcraft) being put on somebody as anyone can pay the *sunyakaran* (sorcerer) to invoke an evil spirit and cause misfortunes to fall upon an individual or family. The Pentecostal prayer fellowship claims that *sunyam* can be undone only by the power of Yesusami and then only through their pastor or somebody from the fellowship facilitating anointing of the Holy Spirit. Among Christians this perception carries strong weight due to the impact of the Pentecostal fellowship.

For example, Kanthi, a member of the prayer fellowship, firmly believes that there are many evil spirits in Thulasigramam and that they are the crucial reason for the poverty and misery of everyone in the village. She narrated her own story of being possessed, which resulted in her physical suffering with various diseases, until she was taken to this prayer fellowship where she was healed. Kanthi explains her healing as the anointing of Holy Spirit, who came upon a Pentecostal Christian who in turn anointed her. This has very close resemblance to the traditional village practices of spirit possession in the village community, only here it is identified as the Holy Spirit. Because of this similarity in practices many Paraiyars who are not Christians seek the help of the Pentecostal fellowships, and go for healing. It can even be observed that the prayer fellowship is almost in direct competition with the local *poojari* (local temple priest) and the *sunyakarn* (sorcerer) in attracting people in need of healing. In this context, the work of the Holy Spirit, as preached by Pentecostal Christians, is to set aright everything that has gone wrong due to evil spirits – in essence all calamity experienced by the village.

Appeasing the spirits of the dead

I was curious when one of Rani's relatives hinted that she needed to keep a particular food item in front of the picture of a dead person whom she loved. This act underlines the communities' relationship with the diseased or the spirits of the dead. While this may not be exactly like ancestral worship, it does have clear resemblances. Whenever she cooks a specific dish enjoyed by the dead person when he was alive, Rani places a plate of that food before the portrait of the deceased person. She also mentioned that the dead person would be very happy to see her gesture and the fact that she remembers him. Once, when she forgot to follow this routine, she hit her head unknowingly in the walkway, which literally jogged her memory, what she calls a 'gentle reminder' from the deceased person about her forgotten task.

It is also interesting to note that for Rani this person is almost alive and present in her home because she converses with his picture daily. This is not an insane or delusional conviction but rather common place in Thulasigramam. She also believes that by keeping him happy he will in turn be helpful in keeping away the evil spirits from her family. This is a good example of how the presence of the spirits of the dead relatives is perceived in this rural community. Rani also recounted how she does the same for one of the former priests, who became a bishop. When he was alive he would go to her house and whenever he visited the parish, she would prepare a particular meal which he enjoyed so much. One day when I went to her house I saw a plate of food presented in front of the picture of this bishop and that she follows the same practice. The word she uses is *padaikirathu*, which literally means 'offering' linking to the whole notion of worshiping the dead in order to appease them, as well manifesting benefits in the present day.

Sunyam and Mayam

The Paraiyar Christian community in Thulasigramam also demonstrated the prevalence of *Sunyam* (witchcraft) and *Mayam* (magic). Take the experience of Chandra, the wife of a retired Catechist, who firmly believes in the activities of evil spirits and their effects on the human life. She attributes most of the misfortunes that happen in the village to malicious forces which are evoked by some people against others, through local witches. She considers that her family suffers because somebody has put a spell on their well-being. Even though she is aware that she has lost some of her goats due to infectious disease, she attributes their death to the *sunyam* that has been placed on her family. Chandra claimed that someone must be jealous of her family's prosperity and therefore her husband and grandchildren frequently become sick, precisely because of the *sunyam*. She is of the opinion that evil spirits have tremendous control over human life and if they are not appeased they will cause misery for everyone. Interestingly, Chandra trusts that another way to challenge the evil spirits is to pray to Yesusami for him to control them. For that reason she carries a Bible with her most of the time as she believes that it contains the power of Yesusami who will protect her and her family from the evil spirits hovering over the village.

Ramamurthy is a recent widower with two young children and had been sick for a long time. Recently, his health deteriorated and he was diagnosed with advanced tuberculosis. Doctors strictly advised him to be admitted in a hospital and be treated especially since it is contagious and runs the risk of passing onto others in the village. But Ramamurthy chose to do otherwise and instead began attending the Pentecostal prayer fellowship, where it was prophesied that he was possessed by an evil spirit that was causing his sickness. They advised Ramamurthy to fast regularly and pray with them in their fellowship in order to be healed. Ramamurthy actually stopped taking his doctor prescribed medications further weakening his health. When he realized that he was not being healed in the prayer fellowship, he questioned them and was told that he was not praying with enough faith, thereby limiting God's power to heal him. Disappointed with the response of the Pentecostal prayer fellowship, Ramamurthy approached the local *Sunyakarn* (sorcerer) for help. Through a process of *kurisolvathu* (foretelling by communicating with the dead), the Sunyakaran gave him some suggestions. Along with following his instructions, Ramamurthy felt that it is important to keep praying to Yesusami, so that even if the Sunyakarn fails Yesusami might help him. He began to sleep on the church veranda, where I slept during fieldwork, hoping that he could impress upon Yesusami and remind him of his presence. Unfortunately, neither the Sorcerer nor Yesusami was able to heal him; however, in his desperation to be healed, it was irrelevant which spiritual force was responsible, as long as one was successful in healing him.

Alternative forms of healing were also actively practised in the village, even within the Christian community. One day, Muthu was bitten by a venomous scorpion and he suffered terrible pain and became unconscious. Instead of taking any medicine or rushing him to the nearby town for medical treatment, they went to Jayamma, a local village healer, to perform *mayam* (magic) for the bite. After a few moments of mayam, he was declared to be healed. The source of healing was kept a secret in fear that in divulging the truth the Mayam would lose its power. It was indeed fascinating to see Muthu back to full health after his treatment. It is rumoured within the community that more and more people are going to Jayamma to seek healing for their ailments. What is important here is that Jayamma is an important person in the Christian community and participates enthusiastically in church activities.

Surveying the above-mentioned experiences, the composition of the less visible world in the Paraiyar Christian community is fundamentally comprised of good and evil spirits, just like the understanding of their Hindu relatives. The struggle between these spirits to control the villagers is manifested and played out in the lives of every individual. Spirits are not inherently evil and can be manipulated to do good or evil acts.[29] Blessings and misfortunes are the outcomes of that struggle between the spirits. The Paraiyar Christians of Thulasigramam believe that the activities of the spirits can be controlled and manipulated through human intervention, particularly through offerings and appeasements. This perception assumes importance in the light of their poverty, which is attributed to the activities of the spirit world. The contribution of the Pentecostal fellowship gives a new dimension to this aspect by introducing the Holy Spirit and giving a new twist to human-spirit world interactions. The prevalence of ancestral worship among the community members also contributes to the belief that the spirits of the deceased play a role in individual and communal life. Examples of sunyam practice explained earlier pave the way for understanding how communities cope with the misfortunes in their life. These observations shed light on the fact that individuals and communities tend to choose their mode of interacting with the spiritual, less visible world.

Continuity in Paraiyar and Christian Paraiyar perceptions

The contextual conceptualization of the less visible world and its impact on the visible world is clearly evident in the preceding analysis of the Paraiyar Christian religious perception. This awareness stems from an approach that takes account of its social setting within which such notions are conceived for the individual and collective. The 'social eye' functions as an important tool in comprehending their religious views. Human determination and situatedness take precedence where the divine is conceived and leads to stressing the relationships between the divine and the human. From some of the examples discussed earlier it is clear that it is not possible to experience the divine if proper relationships among the community members are lacking. This paves the way for developing a causal and reciprocal relationship with the less visible world. Individuals and community members were able to establish a reciprocal communication with the divine while demanding certain specific responses from their gods and goddesses. As theoretically outlined earlier through the views of Merleau-Ponty, thoughts and actions belonging to the religious realm are very much conceived and couched within the social environment of individuals and communities.[30] That leads us to the important understanding of God as a communitarian being; since religious experience stems from the contextual conflictual situatedness of Paraiyars.[31] As most in the Paraiyar Christian community pointed out to me, they believe in a Yesusami who is with them in their homes and not confined to the church. Such an approach provides the possibility that they have control over the divine and reciprocally allow the divine to impact their lives. The Paraiyar Christian community addresses God as Yesusami, in their belief that he performs all the tasks that God is expected to play in the community. Yesusami encompasses all of the traits of the Christian God, but without a Trinitarian understanding. Most importantly, field experience showed how this idea is couched within the traditional Paraiyar understanding of the divine, which directly contradicts Azariah's claims (quoted at the beginning of this chapter) that Dalits, while converting to Christianity, leave behind all their traditional patterns of conceptualization.

There were clear instances of Yesusami being explained within a traditional Paraiyar understanding. If we closely observe Paraiyar conceptions of goddesses as presented by other researchers,[32] it would be easy to perceive that there is a parallel between the traditional Paraiyar notions of deities and Christian perceptions emerging from their daily life situations. Yesusami as a protecting and preserving God, punishing and healing, and intervening in human life are some of the aspects that exemplify the continuities of their sacred belief system. This prevalence undoubtedly rejects the idea that there is a definite discontinuity in the Paraiyar Christian perception of the divine. Instead, there is a synthesis of traditional Paraiyar and Christian worldviews, creating a hybrid, highly functional and contextually relevant perception of Yesusami.

As it emerged from many conversations, the feminine nature of the divine is preferred over the masculine, controlling and authoritative images of God. Similarly, many of the community members expressed that they get upset and angry with Yesusami, when he fails them and express their dissent individually and communally towards Yesusami, a characteristic true to keeping with the Paraiyar tradition.[33] There were also insights into the perception of the material and the spiritual worlds and the mutual impact they have upon each other. Understating of the spiritual world among the Paraiyar Christians, they have located the Holy Spirit within their inherited worldview. Another important aspect to stem from this approach is that Christians do not distinguish between this world and the spiritual world, but rather see no clear divisions between the two, nobody knows where the material world ends and the spiritual world begins. They rather believe that whatever happens, it happens in this world, a sort of non-dualistic approach to the universe. The decentralized and unmediated religious experience of Paraiyars needs to be understood in this context, which can be seen as a protest against the *Vedic brahmanism* that lays importance on rebirth and the retribution of *karma*. It is also interesting to observe these dynamics within the Christian community in which they expect Yesusami to work effectively in this world rather than promising eternal life in the next life.

In Thulasigramam, the dilemma of being a Paraiyar and a Christian simultaneously cannot be ignored. As highlighted earlier there are conflicts between the Paraiyar and Christian worldviews in terms of perceiving the visible and the less visible worlds. As Christians, the church teaches them that this world is inherently evil, which needs to be constantly overcome, and, as Paraiyars they have inherited the idea where one does not condemn the world one lives in, but rather embraces it. Paraiyars consider themselves to be part of the environment and the forces of nature, which essentially sustains their life. The Paraiyar worldview is interwoven within their surrounding context. Due to such a perception there is an obvious dilemma among Paraiyars to reconcile a pietistic Christian worldview that denies this visible world.

Fieldwork among the Paraiyar Christians of Thulasigramam shows that they have a functionalist and materialist understating of the religious arena, primarily rooted in their sensory experiences. As discussed earlier, most of the insights from the community reveal that their notions of the divine and spirits stem from their daily lived encounters and how they contribute towards the maintenance of their lives in the community. By giving significance to communal cohesion in order to experience the divine, they were able to achieve a certain amount of unity among community members. Failure to do so reflects in the misfortunes and suffering of individuals as well as in the village. As much as the social dimension is important, the individual contributes significantly to the collective by subscribing to a communal understanding of the divine.

In light of the discussion on the anthropological approaches to religion, this chapter set out to explore the way in which Paraiyar Christians conceive Yesusami, the less visible world and its effect on their everyday lives. These voices from Thulasigramam have narrated that the Paraiyar Christian experiences are not entirely 'Christian' in composition, but rather express an assimilative hybridity, which is relevant and meaningful in their marginalized context. Paraiyar Christians still continue to think in their traditional modes incorporating relevant Christian images and perceptions into their already existing worldview. It can be observed that there is a definite continuity in terms of their worldview. As argued in the earlier chapter, the Paraiyar Christian experience cannot be understood outside of their locatedness and the environment they inhabit. It also raises a crucial question of studying

Christianity as an exclusive religion in the Paraiyar context as it tends to downplay the complexity within the Paraiyar context. Studies of Christianity very often tend to privilege what people 'believe in' over what they 'practice', hence missing the significance of the dynamic interaction between belief and practice. The contestations and negotiations that take place between belief and practice within the lived social world of Paraiyar Christian community will be the focus of the following chapter.

5

Reproducing Social Hierarchies: Power and Community

> *Power must be analysed as something which only functions in the form of a chain. It is never localised here and there, never in anybody's hands, never appropriated as a commodity or piece of wealth. Power is employed and exercised through a net like organisation.*[1]

Foucault's observation offers a noteworthy insight into the collective experience of marginalization among the Paraiyar Christians in Thulasigramam, which points towards the reproduction of social hierarchies and fragmentation within the community. The church in the Paraiyar Christian community is the predominant site of such transactions in Thulasigramam. This chapter seeks to understand the issues of power and representation by examining the maintenance and continuance of the status quo. Of importance here are issues relating to non-political participation, lack of primary education and dominant Christian teachings regarding accepting one's own status and being subservient to the 'masters' of one's destiny. During our many long informal conversations, the people of the Thulasigramam Christian community shared their experiences of the local church in this regard.

Social power relations

Knowledge of a community involves understanding the dynamics of human relationships and the underlying principles upon which social roles are enacted. Interestingly, such familiarity takes place at multiple levels and is influenced by various factors controlling and guiding such functions. One of the ways to observe the negotiation and transaction of power is through social relationships. Moreover, defining 'power' still remains an elusive task to the social theorists. Steven Lukes states that 'power is an essentially contested concept',[2] owing to the perspective of the one who is defining it. But for the purpose of this chapter, a basic comprehension of power needs to be outlined. In its simplest form, power can be defined as the effective and assumed ability of a person or a group to affect, influence, direct and control the functions of the rest of the group. Power is essentially manifested and understood through the actions of human social relationships. Thus, as understood here, power is basically 'power over' or 'domination over' the other, and therefore dependent on the other. Steven Lukes defines power in relation to domination as 'the ability to constrain the choices of others, coercing them or securing their compliance, by impeding them from living as their own nature and judgement dictate'.[3] He further adds that 'domination occurs where the power of some affects the interests of others by restricting their capabilities for truly human functioning'.[4]

Power takes place in different forms and levels as expounded by Bertrand Russell[5] in his work of the same name; but for this chapter, it is essential to shed light on further dimensions of social power. In his book *Forms of Power*, Gianfranco Poggi gives a clear description of social power:

> Social power relations exist wherever some human subjects (individual or collective) are able to lay routine, enforceable boundaries upon the activities of other human subjects (individual or collective), in so far as that ability rests on the former subjects' control over resources allowing them, if they so choose, to deprive the latter subjects' salient human values. The chief among such values are bodily integrity; freedom from restraint, danger or pain; reliable access to nourishment, shelter or other primary material goods; the enjoyment of a degree of assurance of one's worth and significance.[6]

This characterization puts into perspective the functional nature of social power relations. It is important to note that through a religious framework, or faith system, power readily assumes much more significance as Nietzsche[7] and later Foucault[8] elucidated in their works, thus producing a slave mentality and willing to consent to power.[9] This process effectively lays the foundation on which any institutionalization of authority or structure can be built, with Christianity being no exception.[10] Martyn Percy presents a broad discussion on the issue of power in religious frameworks in his work *Power and the*

Church underlining the emergence of a structure around the Godhead or divine centrality, which in turn becomes the means for the establishment of a power relationship within a society.[11] With this brief working outline, we shall set forth to understand the way in which the perpetuation of subordination takes place within a Paraiyar Christian congregation in Thulasigramam through observing the functioning of the local church leaders and the priest, the fragmentation and reproduction of church hierarchy within the Christian community.

Deciphering hierarchy

On Sunday in Thulasigramam during the regular worship, the church is noticeably attended by a majority of women and children, with very few men around. From the beginning until the end of the service, it is Yovan, the local church leader, who makes all the decisions regarding what happens during the service. Since the ordained CSI priest only occasionally comes to the village, even he has to play a subordinate role and follow the local church leader's instructions. It was interesting to note that the local church leader's entire family holds key positions in the church: his wife is the church secretary, his son is the youth fellowship leader and his daughter is in charge of the women's fellowship. The rationale behind this family monopoly of the church positions is justified because theirs is the only 'educated' family in that community and therefore qualified to hold such posts. Because of his influence, the local church leader was able to secure good jobs for his children, since he was able to educate them up to the secondary level in the diocesan English medium school, to which other children from the village were not recommended. The local church leader's family also represent the Thulasigramam congregation in all of the diocesan activities. When a priest visits the congregation, the local church leader discourages him from eating with any other families in the parish citing their 'uncleanliness'. Within the Christian community, the local church leader virtually functions like a small landlord completely controlling the church property and even the congregants, since he can negotiate and recommend Christians for particular jobs, as well securing them government certificates or even lend them money. Yovan has been the local church leader for more than a decade and all of the information from the pastorate and the diocese about activities and programmes has to go through him. It is apparently clear that these choices are controlled by his family, who consequently enjoys most of the privileges provided by the church. The local church leader is the regular preacher and worship leader each Sunday, who consistently espouses a glorifying message of Yesusami, the suffering servant, and the sinfulness of the unworthy people – the congregation with the exception of his family. Furthermore, the sermons by the priest and local church leader about Yesusami are limited to his patience, tolerance, meekness, obedience, forgiveness and compassion, all of which are intended to encourage the congregation to accept their situation and continue to live literally as suffering servants. The community's perceptions of Yesusami, mentioned earlier, are nowhere to be found in his sermons. Many members of the Christian community have expressed their frustration at listening to the same sermon of 'condemnation' over and over again, his lack of interest and refusal to address their everyday struggle to find food and shelter.[12]

In Thulasigramam, the differences between the Christian and Hindu Paraiyars are sometimes difficult to discern, except for Sunday church attendance. It was very obvious from my conversations with the priest for that congregation, Arul who had no in-depth knowledge of the appalling conditions in which the Christians in Thulasigramam live, since he had eight other larger congregations to look after as well, and could be best described by the community as a visitor. In my observation, the diocesan authorities are only aware of the local church leader and his family, while the congregants are a mass of faces with no individual identities. The local church leader sees to it that the priest is well fed during his visit in order for him not to rely on or even approach other people in the village before rushing off to his other charges. It is essential to note that Thulasigramam had its first convert more than eight decades ago and that most of the community members are still in the same state of backwardness, with very few exceptions who were able to move out of the village to a nearby town escaping the vicious cycle of poverty and discrimination. This experience assumes significance in the light of the church being an 'institution' that has many schools, training institutes and other economic organizations, as pointed out earlier, which could be resources of emancipation for the impoverished Paraiyar Christians, who are still dependent on the local landlords or the state government for their survival. The local church leader has assumed a privileged powerful position, replicating and perpetuating hierarchical structures at all levels. To summarize in his own words,

> If I have not collected the donations to build this church, there won't be a church here. So I have the right to decide what is right and wrong in this church. Moreover if our family is not here there won't be any respect for these illiterates from the landowners.

From my fieldwork observations, it is clear that Yovan, the local church leader, has only a passing interest in the betterment of his parishioners, the 'illiterate' Paraiyar Christians of Thulasigramam. The preceding comment by the local church leader clearly spells out how he has usurped the power within the Christian community and holds everybody under his control.

The visible manifestation of hierarchy among the Paraiyar Christians in Thulasigramam has a significant impact on the life of the community. The hierarchy manifests itself in different ways, beginning from the local church leader assuming the high status and rank ordering of the individuals within the congregation being decided by him or face total exclusion from the church life. At the beginning of my fieldwork, the local church leader gave me a detailed gradation of the church members, ranking those who are 'good' Christians and those who are not, the latter essentially being people I should lookout for and stay away from. The list included broad categories such as alcoholics, thieves, the sinful, immoral and simply 'bad' people, which is similar to the categories presented by the Reddyars about the Paraiyars. He also instructed me not to have food with certain people citing unhygienic conditions, telling me, 'they are not clean, avoid having food with them'. In fact, he was very unhappy to find me interacting with some of those 'unclean' people in the community, particularly those who were not part of 'his group'. During the course of the fieldwork, it dawned on me that I was also looked at by the community as a person belonging to the local church leader's grouping and therefore people were keeping a distance from me. Only after I began to distance myself from him, did others begin to relate with me. To check my movement, sighting my unfamiliarity with the village context, the local church leader instructed Ramesh, a youth member of the church, to accompany me wherever I went, so that he could be aware of my conversations with the community members. When I avoided Ramesh, the local church leader became apprehensive and told me not to go by myself to visit houses. However, it quickly became clear that people opened up their intimate thoughts to me only when I went by myself. Analysing this experience, it is apparent that the local church leader was trying to establish with me or had already established a pattern of social interaction within the Christian community based on visible and invisible cleanliness. The community members religiously follow this structure, although some have grievances with this system, they do not have any forum to express their feelings.

To understand this situation it is perhaps helpful to look at the case of Raju, a relative of the local church leader. Hoping that he would continue his loyalty to Yovan he was made the church treasurer. However, Raju refused to follow his uncle's every demand and, after a few months of faithful service, began to disagree with some of his decisions. From Raju's account, he did not want to spend the poor Paraiyars' hard-earned money given as offerings to Yesusami for an elaborate and expensive function in the church to welcome the newly elected Bishop of the diocese. When the local church leader realized that Raju was being openly rebellious and openly antagonistic towards him, Raju was blamed falsely for misusing and swindling money from the church account. Many of the community members believed this accusation and began to condemn Raju at the local church leader's insistence. When I met with Raju, the local church leader was unhappy and began to warn me against his 'lies and corruption'. This apparent tension to control the community in all its complexity is palpable in the activities of the local church leader. In fact, he even recently challenged the Bishop when he planned to appoint a new local church leader for Thulasigramam, stating that he 'is the congregation' and no one can take that position from him.

One day I asked Isaac, an active young man from the Christian community, about his idea of 'justice'. He promptly replied to my question stating that justice actually means 'equality' – equality in terms of respect, recognition and regard. According to him, everybody should be treated equally, and the absence of equality means that there is no justice, and that the lack of both traits causes problems in the village. Such inequality obviously leads to serious problems and issues of hierarchy. This attitude triggers clashes and conflicts between many people, particularly within the Paraiyar Christian community. Sadly, Isaac thinks that as long as there is economic disparity within the church, such a reality is bound to continue indefinitely. So economic transactions, even though small, are central to the life of the community and manifest themselves in their church relationships. In the same line of thinking, he is also of the opinion that respect and regard are prescribed by society depending on the financial position of each person.

Interestingly, Isaac claims that this financial inequality is a new development among the Thulasigramam Christians. For him the church has become a victim in this regard, as those who give more offerings are considered to be more important and therefore only they have the right to speak up in the Christian community. 'If you want to be an important person in the church, give more money', quipped Isaac. This attitude in the church for him has caused severe divisions in the community, and since only a handful can contribute, others are sidelined and marginalized further. They do not have any right to raise their concerns and participate in the life of the church or help to make decisions. He feels that the church itself has become a source of division. Justice for him, as he said earlier, is all about equality, and what saddens him the most is that the church, which is mostly made up of Paraiyars, has a similar kind of segregation and discrimination to the caste system. He says that in his lifetime, 'I have not seen a committed Priest, none of them spent time in this village and they always came and went so fast! So the local church leader and the people do what they like!' The case of local church leader in Thulasigramam reflects the larger issue of the church as an institution where it is almost an unwritten law that if you do not have money then you are nobody within church hierarchy. One cannot assume important offices without appropriate personal financial backing. Many in the village believe that this has led to moral bankruptcy and serious erosion of credible leadership at the diocesan level. Isaac expresses the collective feeling among the Paraiyar Christians about the church, 'It has rather become an exclusive club of individuals and their followers. The promises made by the missionaries to empower the marginalised are still a distant dream for us!'

The hierarchy within the Thulasigramam Christians is formed by effectively accumulating power and gaining the ability to control the functioning of the community. The local church leader, through his 'religious' status as the leader of the congregation, takes upon himself the role of 'social authority' over the community. He presides over not only the church, but also, in effect, over the entire Christian community by appropriating all the channels of power. Once this system is in place, a hierarchy is formed on the basis of an individual's proximity to the church leader. If an individual questions this pecking order, then he may be pushed lower in order, probably on grounds of religious immoral behaviour. What is fundamental here is to recognize the fact that often religious status is translated into social status or vice versa. Combining this observation with an earlier illustration of geographical manifestation of hierarchy in the Paraiyar Christian community, one could develop a collective image of functional hierarchy in Thulasigramam.

Along with the neglect at the hands of the local church leader, another common grievance by this congregation is that the Priest hardly visits them in their homes. He only comes occasionally to administer communion and then leaves promptly to attend to his other parishes. It is very difficult for the Paraiyar Christians to even meet him in the town and consequently think that he spends all of his time taking care of the more financially stable town church and ignores them completely. The Priest admits to this facet and says that because the town church contributes significantly in terms of finance, he is forced to spend more time there and therefore the village church gets far less attention. Because of this, the Priest is unaware of the lived realities of these Dalit Christians as it appears that the larger church's need takes precedence at the expense of rural congregations. This is similar to Elizabeth Koepping's observation of the pastoral care in South Australia where, 'too often, individual or subordinate groups' need for justice . . . are ignored for the sake of collective (that is elite) face-saving which smoothes out the wrinkles, plasters over the sores, keeps to the rules'.[13]

To grasp further the gross negligence of the Priest towards this congregation, let me explain a sad situation that happened on a particular Sunday. The congregation was informed that there would be a communion service for which they all prepared, a rarity in Thulasigramam that only happens a few times each year. But to their dismay the Priest failed to show up, and since the local church leader is not authorized to conduct communion services, the special service was cancelled. Understandably, there was tremendous disappointment among the Paraiyar Christians as they had been waiting for approximately four months for their turn to receive communion from the parish Priest. Moreover, there was no word from the Priest regarding his absence, nor could he be contacted to reschedule. This incident prompted Peter, an active youth member of the congregation to observe, 'they (the Priests) never lived among us, so they have no idea what we go through every day. They don't care for us or what happens to us'. As it was observed during my fieldwork as well, the Priest came only occasionally to visit the congregation and left without spending any time with the people. Recalling the nature of the sermons preached by the local church leader and the Priest and their irrelevance to the lives of the congregation shows how out of touch they are. Many in the village attribute its backwardness to such attitudes from the Priests, who relegate their spiritual need as secondary to the larger wealthier congregations, despite the arrival of Christianity eight decades ago. Essentially in Thulasigramam there is no pastoral care for the Christian families and individuals. Their dissatisfaction is heightened by the fact that the local church leader controls all other aspects of church life. Peter, for example, expresses a collective frustration,

> I don't want to involve myself in the politics of the church, since it's run by one group of people who are economically better off than us. They think that they have the right to do everything. There is no responsibility given to others which has created lot of divisions among us. As long there is no equality and unity, worshiping Yesusami is waste!

Jeba, who earlier illustrated the motherly nature of Yesusami, offers another dimension to this perspective on pastoral neglect; she is wife of Paul, who is a musician in the church. Jeba has three children and lives in the village itself but Paul has another wife in a neighbouring village and lives in both places. When his polygamy became public knowledge, Jeba was heartbroken and attempted to commit suicide on numerous occasions and painfully failed in her attempts. Many in the village blamed Jeba for the situation; accusing her of being such a terrible wife that Paul went off in search of someone else. This attitude from the community hurt Jeba further and caused her to suffer from severe depression. During this episode, Paul for his actions was not corrected or reprimanded and he continued to carry on living between his two families. Most importantly, the church elders also took a similar stance, neither reprimanding Paul nor intervening in the situation but chastizing Jeba instead. The Priest also took the advice of the church elders and stayed away from this incident and while Jeba did not receive their support or counselling, but she drew strength and support from Yesusami. She tearfully recollected to me,

> When I was going through my painful period, everybody in the community judged me as the person responsible for the situation, even the priest, and due to bad counsel, he branded me as a bad influence among the community and advised others to keep away from me.

According to Jeba, the men of the village, including the priest, oppressed her and treated her no better than garbage, failing to help her rebuild her family life. The church elders' and the Priest's failure to intervene in her life resulted in Paul continuing his double life and while allowing him to be a significant member of the church due to his closeness with the local church Catechist. With her children's future in mind Jeba succumbed to pressure and accepted Paul's other wife, as long as he continues to support them. Jeba still thinks that if the Priest and church leaders had intervened and instructed Paul he would have given up his second family. It must be noted that this disparity between how the church reacted to Jeba and Paul is also based on gender inequality. In other cases where there is a disagreement between a husband and wife, the church elders and local church leader usually side with the former party. The insensitivity and lack of pastoral care from the part of the Priest demonstrates the marginalization of not only rural Paraiyar Christians but also of the women within the same community.

Politically removed church

Field observations among the churches in South India reveal that the region remains captive to its missionary heritage and does not involve itself in the socio-political lives of its congregants but stresses the importance of 'the spiritual' life.[14] But the political nature of religious institutions in Tamil Nadu is highlighted by David Mosse in the following terms, 'in the Tamil countryside, religious institutions and their festivals have long been central to the exercise of dominance and control in local and regional political systems'.[15] If that is the case then by political disengagement, the local church could potentially disempower Dalit Christian communities. Moreover, the CSI does not frequently support their sociopolitical representation or the Indian legislature, denying the privileges provided by the government to the Dalit and Backward Class communities. When the Paraiyars became Christians, they are left in an ambiguous situation due to lack of political participation resulting in lose of privileges for social mobility.[16] When Dalit Christians are subjected to humiliation and exploitation, very often the church teaches them to endure their politically disabled and vulnerable sate, as to emulate Christ, the suffering servant, all the while looking forward to their reward in heaven. Lancy Lobo observes,

> the Church is selectively political and most often collectively incompetent. The clergy are disinterested in social matters such as unemployment, poverty, drought, corruption and political misrule. In such structural matters, they stay away and do relief and service.[17]

With the above-described context in mind, a few of the following narrated experiences will explain the indifference of the church as an organization towards the social well-being of its members, especially in Thulasigramam.

Prabu, a middle-aged member of the Paraiyar Christian community, feels that the church has done very little in terms of supporting the people in Thulasigramam. He recollects various occasions in the past when the Christian community was under attack, due to caste conflict and religious tensions, during which the local church never supported their cause, openly stating that in the case of caste tension, there is very little that the church can do. Prabu narrated an incident that took place a few years ago in the village, an event that is vividly remembered by almost everyone in the village regardless of caste or religious affiliation. One day, Dass, a young man in the Paraiyar community, while he was walking to the fields, was attacked by a few young men from the Reddyar community, who swore at him and insulted him. This unprovoked attack resulted in retaliatory efforts as Dass came back and told everyone in the village about the incident, inciting some of the men in the Christian community to seek revenge for what they saw as an unjust act of aggression. Initially they dug up the road disrupting traffic, making it impossible for the Reddyars to commute in their vehicles, while some others refused to go to the fields for work. This further angered the Reddyars, who came into the Cherie and blackmailed the Paraiyars to return to work, threatening them with job cuts. This tension began to gather momentum, and one day Dass and some of his friends stopped a young man from Reddyar community and severely attacked him. This action instigated an open conflict between the Reddyars and the Paraiyar Christian communities. Interestingly, Paraiyars from the Hindu community considering the severity of the situation and fearing retaliation refrained from supporting their Christian Paraiyar counterparts. After violent clashes broke out, the local police were forced to intervene and defuse the situation, and take a few members from both communities into custody for investigation. Unsurprisingly, the Reddyar men were released early due to their political connections in high places, while the Paraiyar Christians were stuck at the police station without any outside help. The police registered a case against the Paraiyar Christians as instigators of the violence that caused communal tensions in the village. While still in custody, the Paraiyar Christians sought help from the church authorities, particularly to defuse the situation and to secure their release. But the church authorities refused to be drawn into the 'village caste conflict' and withheld their support. Some of the local political parties also denied their support, as the Christians did not support them during the previous elections. The Paraiyars from the Christian community understandably felt betrayed and let down but eventually found support from a non-governmental organization, which came forward to argue for their case and get them out of police custody. This incident left an indelible mark on the memory of Paraiyar Christians, most significantly the failure of the church authorities to act during a crucial situation. This episode is consistent with church teachings, which neither encourages nor discourages political participation among its members, a teaching that turns a blind eye towards caste discrimination and social injustice. This recollection of Prabu sheds light on the very important attitude of the church as an institution to intervene in the local life of Thulasigramam.

In the past, the Paraiyar community had to depend on the Reddyars for their basic necessities like water and electricity, a food ration shop and other essential facilities. Apart from the intricate hierarchy within the caste system, the Paraiyars were further marginalized due to the fact that they had no control over the political system, making the Paraiyars perennially dependent on the Reddyars. The Paraiyars are voiceless in the proceedings of the local politics, without which no welfare programmes could be brought to their locality. The youth from the Christian community would like to participate fully and take on leadership roles but are promptly discouraged by their Priest and the local church leader stating that it is not their duty and that they should not join the 'bad' politicians. According to Dass, this attitude of the church and its leaders adversely affects the Christians, as well as indirectly supports the continuation of Reddyar dominance.

Besides being the main character in the above-mentioned incident, Dass is also an active member of the youth fellowship and frequently comes into conflict with the local church leader because of his grievances against the leadership in the Christian community and its advice against entering into the political arena. Most of the youth in the village share his frustration as they are unable to raise concerns with the village authorities, since they do not belong to any established political group. They feel that this constrains if not prevents possibilities of bringing development into the village, particularly from non-governmental organizations. Due to the lack of political support from Paraiyar Christians, the political parties do not treat them respectfully and their concerns are therefore not forwarded to higher civil authorities who process welfare programmes. Recently, Thulasigramam was classified as a reserved constituency for the local *Panchayat* (village administrative committee) elections, which means only a person belonging to a Scheduled Caste can contest in election.[18] However, according to the Paraiyars (both Christians and Hindus), they are locally prohibited by the Reddyars from nominating and electing candidates from their communities. In the past, prior to this legislation, and against the instructions of the Reddyars, the Paraiyar Christians had tried to nominate their own candidate but did not get enough votes, since the Paraiyars from the Hindu community gave no support and the Reddyars physically and verbally threatened the Christian candidates and any of their supporters.

In such a polarizing environment, the Paraiyar Christians felt that with the recent designation as a reserved constituency, it was as good a time as any to contest the election and represent themselves in the Panchayat elections. After some thought, most of the Christians felt that even if they managed to present a candidate, the Hindu Paraiyars would not support him, under pressure from the Reddyars, so they requested that the Hindu Paraiyar community put forward a candidate. After much initial resistance, both Paraiyar religious groups began to take the proposition seriously. The Reddyar community was angered by this move and again threatened dire consequences. Following long deliberations, the Paraiyars, both Hindu and Christian, agreed upon a candidate from the Hindu community and eventually won the local Panchayat elections. Dass recollected that the local church elders were upset during this whole process, as they believed that it is not the task of Christians to 'play politics'. In fact, some of the Christians were reprimanded by the Catechist for their active involvement during the election process, creating a further internal rift in the Christian community.

Many from the Christian community have similar opinions about Prabu and Dass, attributing the continued backwardness of the village towards the negative attitude of the church leadership. According to most Paraiyar Christians, the lack of political participation results in the lack of public amenities and the failed implementation of various projects for the betterment of the Paraiyar village. In other words, the indifferent attitude of the local church leadership effectively disconnects and isolates the local Christian community, which forms about 30 per cent of the Thulasigramam village population. It also jeopardizes any possibility of development for the Christian community, facilitating the perpetuation of domination and dependency.

Dissonance and fragmentation

The popular opinion among the Paraiyar Christians of Thulasigramam is that church as a fellowship and community has almost ceased to exist, acting merely as an institution and a bureaucratic organization. Moreover, resources, time and energy are being spent for the preservation of this mechanism, and the few elite avail its benefits. There is little room for accommodating new church initiatives or reviewing its past failures. In this process, the church is losing significant ground and importance among the Paraiyar Christians. One such issue is the emphasis on the external mission of the church still preaching about converting the Hindus while grossly negating the importance of Dalit community's needs in rural congregations. Arguably, the mission of the church in Thulasigramam and adjoining areas has become programme-oriented rather than people-centred. To grasp fully this notion among the Paraiyar Christians in Thulasigramam, some voices are put forward.

Spiritualizing suffering

Simon, the only undergraduate student in the village, expressed his frustration with the church partly because of the fact that the sermons keep condemning him as a 'sinner' every time he comes into the church. He feels that his life is boring and mundane and when he keeps hearing about his supposedly sinful nature it makes him feel miserable. Because of his dissatisfaction with such sermons he prefers to walk out of the Sunday service and sit in the street rather than staying in the church; an open show of disdain for the church and its leaders. Many youth share Simon's opinion. During my fieldwork it became apparent that the most common theme of sermons in the village is sin and how sin is keeping everyone under bondage and justifies their present condition. Their socio-economic realities of discrimination and poverty are given a spiritual twist through sermons in which their sinful nature is emphasized and presented as insurmountable. According to one preacher whom I heard during my stay, he said, 'the only way out of your miserable life is to confess your sin and wait upon the Lord to save you'. For the Paraiyar Christians, this preacher and others in his position have resigned themselves to the excluded state of Dalit Christians, encouraging the subjects of their sermons to do likewise. In fact, the preacher suggests that during this process of salvation the Paraiyar Christians should respect their masters and do their work diligently without murmuring – to be suffering servants.

Another sermon theme preached at the church in Thulasigramam is that of eternal life in the kingdom of God, where even the streets will be paved in gold, there will be an absence of poverty and impoverishment, and life will be perfect all of the time. The Christian leaders implore the people not to worry about this world, but rather to prepare for the joys of eternal life with prayer and faith. Besides the future promises of heaven, teachings on prosperity also flourish particularly due to the influence of charismatic movements in the church. Interestingly, in both the CSI and Pentecostal churches, socially negative external influences on the lives of individual Christians are completely ignored. Sermons in the CSI church elevate the promises of the world to come, while the Pentecostal church preaches the need for faith for the affirmative changes. The Paraiyar Christians are told that whatever they ask for in the name of Jesus Christ, it will be surely given to them.[19] Yet in cases where if one does not receive what one asked for in prayer, then the failure is judged to be a lack of faith or sinfulness of the person in question, not Yesusami's refusal to respond. Again, the issue at hand is situated within the individual and not outside influences. These stereotypical sermons preached Sunday after Sunday create a negative impact especially on the youth as well as some of the elders who are frustrated with the stagnation of their lives in the village. These sermons collectively reinforce traditional notions and subscribe to the prevailing structures, ensuring that there will not be any radical change in the mindset of people who might prompt a break from the norm. The victim's victimization is, therefore, justified and, even to some extent, glorified!

Karuna, a youth member of the Christian community, is of the opinion that there is absolutely no unity in the church because different people are dragging it in too many different ways. He explained that there are some in the church who are head strong and behave like masters and overlords of the rest of the congregation. And the opposite is also true that there are some who refuse to take up responsibility when given the opportunity saying that they are not 'good' enough. According to him, everyone in the Paraiyar Christian community is accountable for the present status of disunity in Thulasigramam. He feels that the church elders are not doing anything to bring unity to the community and are also prohibiting the youth from achieving their own goals. He hopes that when the church elders realize and take steps to address such problems, there will be a change, a time of trustworthiness and respect for everyone.

Meanwhile, Vijay, son of Nathan, the church treasurer, explained his version of the internal conflicts between different families in the church. One reason that he pointed out was that some of the members think their church festivals should be much grander than the Hindu festivals conducted by the Reddyars.[20] Others opposed this idea as extravagant, since it would be an unnecessary expense for the church and would deplete the little resources they have acquired. This resulted in the congregation being divided into different groups, those supporting and those discouraging large-scale festivals causing internal conflict and confusion, which manifests itself in different ways. There are also questions being raised regarding who can run the church and whether or not just one family should decide everything regarding its maintenance and daily running.

Another example of open frustration happened one Sunday when most of the young men decided not to come into the church and instead sat on the street outside while the service was underway. Even when they did join the congregation they showed their resentment by walking out of the service once sermon began. It was a very clear show of rebellion against the church hierarchy, or to be precise, against the local Catechist and his family who tend to control the proceedings of church life. Although as mentioned earlier, the whole village is related to each other, either through blood or marriage, they show their anger by refusing to participate in the activities of the church. They have split into different groups based on kinship and individual issues, blaming each other for the poor church attendance. As Vijay mentioned above, a major issue is festivals and whether or not they should be coupled with feasting, and more specifically with the dish, *Biriyani*, a special meat and rice dish in South India. It is customary that any celebratory event should be centred around the sharing of food and enjoying the company of one another. One of the groups demands that church congregational offering should be used within the community rather than just keeping it in the bank. They feel that the church is obliged to give back to the community by feeding it especially during Christian festivals. An interesting insight came from one member who suggested that, 'offerings from the community should be utilised for the community and not stored up in an unknown place'.

Amutha, a widow and a mother of two children, is an active member of the church, participating, contributing financially and taking leadership roles. But she has a negative impression of some of the church elders because she is a woman, and a poor one at that. According to Amutha's account, the church elders were waiting for a suitable time to 'teach her a lesson'. And as she anticipated when her son proposed to marry a woman from another village and actually held the wedding in the bride's village at a civil registrar's office, the marriage was not accepted by the church elders in Thulasigramam. They complained that it was an improper marriage and that no rules were followed, hence it could not be recognized. Amutha believed that this was just a ploy to victimize her by the local church hierarchy, which suddenly took a moral high ground against her and her son. According to Amutha, the elders also gave false information to the Priest who, as mentioned earlier, had not visited the village congregation in long time and therefore accepted their version of the story and refused to accept the marriage as a legitimate act. Amutha claims that all these actions were aimed at her by the elders because she had raised a few uncomfortable questions about the running of the church and the handling of money in the church account. She also recollected how her daughter, Vimala, was victimized by those who stopped most of their support for her daughter's education by insisting that she did not deserve their financial support. As an outcome, Vimala could not continue her education and took up working in the fields for a living.

Amutha's woes did not end there as she continued her work in the church and the village by organizing women and helping them to invest small amounts and take loans from the bank. This financial support has helped women in agricultural work and is being utilized for educating their children. She also encourages the women of the Christian community to assert themselves and take an active part in church life. Again, this work of Amutha did not go down well with the church hierarchy, and when she was arranging her daughter Vimala's wedding, the local church elders did not help her in any way and even instructed the Priest not to participate in any of her family's celebrations. As the Priest needed the support of the local church leader, he chose to follow their instructions. They also instructed other women not to entertain Amutha and painted her as a bad influence on the community. According to Amutha, all these actions were an outcome of her taking an active role in church life, challenging the male domination of the church and empowering woman.

As has been noted in the previous chapter, one recent development in the Thulasigramam village community is the establishment of a Pentecostal fellowship in the neighbouring village. It has been presented as the alternative for the disgruntled Christians in that area. There are also claims that the prayers offered in the fellowship are answered more consistently than in the Thulasigramam church. This claim began to attract more and more people from the villages. One Sunday, there was not a single person apart from the local church leader and myself in the church. We were told that everybody has gone to a special fasting prayer day in the Pentecostal fellowship. Only then did the local church Catechist come to realize the impact of the Pentecostal fellowship in his community. After enquiring, people shared that the brothers from the fellowship visited them and prayed for them in their houses. Moreover, they promised that whatever they asked for in prayer to God, they would definitely get, if they did so in faith. Some of the Christian members from the village took an interest in the Pentecostal message and began to attend their fellowship regularly. Many of the Paraiyar Christians cited that the pastoral care provided by the fellowship was unmatched in the CSI church in Thulasigramam, because neither the local church leader nor the Priest took any interest in visiting their houses or enquiring about their well-being. The Pentecostal fellowship became a potent, viable alternative in the face of the carelessness shown by the Christian elders in the village. This development has created a serious rift between those who began attending the fellowship and the local church hierarchy, further alienating the former from the life of the church. Those who attended the Pentecostal fellowship meetings also started looking down upon the Christian community in Thulasigramam, because they are not as 'holy' as they are. It also brings an interesting dynamic into the communal relationship among the Paraiyar Christians across villages.

'The church is like a prison, we are not allowed to do anything that brings us life, we feel like captives and trapped' is a candid statement made by one of the young members in the Christian community. According to Simon, one of the youths, members of his age group lack religious instruction and guidance, since there is hardly anybody to provide leadership for the Christian community, apart from those who have assumed privileged positions. Most of the youth feel that the church and its functionaries encourage their members to accept their status and never try to challenge. Any attempt for change even within the church is almost unthinkable, as they are ridiculed for their young age and told to keep quiet. This further fuels resentment and avoidance among the young members in the Christian community. The youth want tangible results from their participation in the church, but the elders and the local church leader keep tangible results for themselves. For instance, earlier the youths used the church premises for communal activities, such as games and social gatherings, but recently a compound wall has been erected, stopping anybody from entering the compound except on a Sunday, when the local church leader opens the gate. Now the youth have nowhere to congregate apart from sitting in the street and chatting and are then promptly criticized by the Catechist, as 'jobless fellows'. This continuing tension between the church hierarchy and the youth is reflected in church life. For their part, the church elders see the youth as misled by some of the people in the community who want to destabilize the Christian community.

While glancing through the wide-ranging opinions of women, men and the youth about their experience of the church and its leadership, it is safe to conclude that frustration and fragmentation seems inevitable in the Christian community of Thulasigramam. The various factors narrated above express the anguish and distress of many Christians in the community. The women and youth feel completely let down by the church due to its teachings and male-dominated attitudes. Others feel that there is lack of pastoral care, which they have now found in the Pentecostal fellowship. All these aspects have become stumbling blocks in the life of the Christian community of Thulasigramam.

Neglect of public welfare

> In more than eighty years of Christian life in Thulasigramam there is only one graduate, no teachers, no Government or diocesan employees, not even church workers! Almost all of them are daily labourers. That reflects the backwardness in terms of education and employment and the negligence on the part of the church to provide opportunities and empower the poor rural Christians is very obvious.

This statement, observed by Nathan, sadly continues to hold true in many rural congregations in spite of churches being one of the key players in the field of education, employment and healthcare. Because of the missionary emphasis on 'holistic mission', the church still runs a significant number of schools and hospitals but they have become exclusive elite centres, beyond the reach of poor rural Christians. An attitude of 'tokenism' still exists in the church, which benefits only those who are close to the powerful leaders. The major detour to the churches' involvement in the educational and employment field is important. From data collected during fieldwork, in the Vellore diocese alone there are more than 15 higher secondary schools belonging to the diocese, six professional training institutes, three teaching and training hospitals and various other initiatives which were initially started by the missionaries to educate the rural people. Although these are still functioning, they are now predominantly used by people who can afford private education in the towns and urban centres. The pity is that these educational opportunities do not frequently reach the people in need, like the community under study. Although there are clear measures and policies in place to help the underprivileged, they are often not implemented by the local church authorities, as shown in this village congregation. In fact, this happens to be the most important grievance of the Paraiyar Christians in Thulasigramam community – they are aware of the possibility for advancement but cannot avail themselves of such opportunities.

The above-mentioned situation actually leads to some of the Paraiyar Christians exploring the possibility of different kinds of opportunities. Many in the Paraiyar Christian community observed that avenues such as education, professional training and employment actually are open to the underprivileged people are utilized by only a few who are in the 'right and powerful' group in the Christian community. For instance, Nathan and Selvadass, being the right-hand men and relatives of the local church leader, have access to many of these benefits along with the Catechist. Both families use their status in the church to provide education for their children in the diocesan schools and find jobs and professional training outside of the village. Recently, Selvadass even moved out of the village to a nearby town, but retains the community lay leader position in the church. Intriguingly, neither the local Catechist nor the community leader lives in the actual village and takes no initiatives to guide the education of any other children apart from their immediate family.

Among the Paraiyar Christians of Thulasigramam, there are more than 23 young school children below the age of 17 who go to various schools near the village. They walk approximately four miles or travel by bus to a neighbouring town to attend a private or government school, despite the existence of a government primary school in the village itself. Unfortunately, this is a school dominated by children from the Reddyar community and the teachers overtly or covertly practise untouchability. Malini, a mother of two in the Paraiyar Christian village, recollected her experience how her son and daughter were made to sit separately in the class room and severely beaten for failing to do home work. Similar experiences were shared by many in the Paraiyar Cherie, which forced them to send their children to a different school in the neighbouring town. For the purpose of paying school fees for their children, many in the Paraiyar Christian community take loans from the Reddyars, exacerbating their economic dependency. Hence, most of the Paraiyar Christian parents have decided to send their children to a different school and as such have to pay a large percentage of their incomes for school fees, often beyond their economic means. This situation argues badly for the role of the church in such a rural and backward area. It is startling to watch parents pay what are exorbitant amounts to send their children to school in neighbouring villages when a governmental school is just down the road.

Selvi and Yacobu succinctly expressed their helplessness in bringing up three children below the age of ten. Yacobu works in a poultry farm run by one of the Reddyars for meagre wages. Similarly, his wife Selvi is a farmhand in the fields, and whatever they earn is barely enough for the family food consumption and on top of which they have to pay for the education of their children. They have approached thelocal church leader and the priest numerous times for help to get their children admitted in one of the diocesan boarding schools, but their plea fell on deaf ears. Before I left the village they were about to take one of their children out of school due to financial problems.

Mala, the wife of Prabu, tearfully narrated the story about her sister Jeya, who lived in the same village and was married to Raju. They had one daughter and Jeya become pregnant again. In Thulasigramam, the villagers depend on the mobile primary health clinic that comes once in a month to administer health check-ups and treatments as the government-run clinic no longer functions, as it is the case in many villages across India. During her pregnancy, Jeya developed complications and became very ill and had to go to a government clinic in the nearby town, because the mobile clinic was not in the village, but she was refused help. Mala took Jeya to a mission hospital in another town and sought medical assistance. The mission hospital offered to treat her on the condition that they get some sort of a recommendation from the Priest or a concerned church authority, in this case the local Catechist. Mala went to the local church leader for help, but he refused to do so, citing that they never come to the church. Repeatedly, Mala somehow got to the Priest' office, in the nearby town, only to be told that he was away. Having failed to secure a recommendation letter, Mala took Jeya back to the hospital and pleaded them to give her medical assistance, but sadly rejected again. Meanwhile, Jeya developed further complications in her pregnancy, from which she eventually died leaving behind a 2-year-old daughter and Raju. Mala regrets that if only she had secured a recommendation from the church or found some guidance she could have saved her sister's life. Mala's story strikingly captures the insensitivity that prevails in the community and the 'mission' institutions. Jeya was let down by the mission hospital, the Priest and the local church leader, though all of them could have come to her aid. In the same way, even though the mission hospitals run by the 'Church' have a mandate to help the poor including Christians, it is hardly the case as observed above. This situation actually points to a broader issue of negligence in health care for the underprivileged within and outside of the church. Most of the mission hospitals have become inaccessible for the poor Christians as they cannot afford the treatment and need recommendations. With the government going the way of privatization and the church also following closely on its heels, there seems to be little hope for the underprivileged in the society. Mala's story clearly underlines that development often has no place for the marginalized.

My fieldwork among the Christian community exposes the false idea that the church plays a key role in empowering downtrodden communities. Nathan observed in the beginning of this section that there was only one Christian graduate from the entire village in its 80-year history of Christianity. This sheds light on the fact that there is a lack of interest in emphasizing the importance of education among the church elders, the priest and the local church leader. Further, there is no mechanism in the local church to guide young students towards higher education. The lack of education is of course a vicious circle ensuring that the Paraiyar Christians remain subservient agricultural labourers, strengthening their dependence on the Reddyars. Most of the children have to drop out of school, either because their parents' could not pay the school fees or had to begin working in order to earn money to support their family. The government-run primary school is in a very poor condition, with only one teacher handling nearly 60 students. The situation of school children within the Paraiyar Christian community reflects the sheer failure of the church as an institution to live up to the promises it has made in the past and the promises it continues to make. The inability to access health and employment resources also makes life difficult for the Paraiyar Christian community. Sadly, the various resources owned by the church are denied to its own poorer members who cannot benefit from them to better their lives.

Replication of hierarchy

The story of the Thulasigramam Christian congregation exemplifies the functioning modalities of control and access to resources available to the community, also indicating the effect upon the nature of communal relationships. The preceding narrations also describe the reproduction of hierarchies within the Christian community arguably to its detriment. In an interesting study conducted among Catholic Christians in Tamil Nadu, David Mosse discusses the process of replicating hierarchies and how opportunities of equality have been subverted by few, as well as locating it within the larger discussion of the Dalit situation in South India.[21] Significantly, this approach is different from that of Michael Moffatt, who argued for passive internalization of caste hierarchy, though he ignored other forces at play.[22] However, Robert Deliege argued in his work that there is no visible hierarchy (or structural replication) within the Paraiyar Community while critiquing the 'consensus and replication' idea of Michael Moffatt.[23] As much as I agree with him in critiquing the 'passive consensus' proposed by Moffatt, my own observation in the Thulasigramam Paraiyar Christian community suggests that even though Paraiyars consider equality as an important character of the community, they do replicate hierarchy on the basis of their position within the Christian community. For example, the local church leader in Thulasigramam has assumed significance by appropriating all of the available responsibilities and resources in the church. With his family and relatives firmly holding important positions within the church, the power to control does not leave the family circle.[24] Even the Priest is made to become part of this vicious circle due to his minimal presence in the lives of his parishioners. The perpetuation of this structural hierarchy continues to work in the following ways; it is due to the special knowledge of the system that the local church leader has and the villagers do not, because the situation of the community is justified and interpreted in spiritual terms by the local church leader every Sunday, describing it as the outcome of their sinful lives. As illustrated earlier, most of the teachings and sermons tend to glorify the 'suffering servant' and promises a better life to come after death. In using such Christian rhetoric, Paraiyar Christians are spiritually force-fed to accept their situation and submit to the spiritual authority of the local church leader and church hierarchy. Knowledge or lack of it thereof becomes the main factor of sustaining this system of power relations, making the largely illiterate villagers rely upon the local church leader for everything, from reading a letter to burying them. Once this dependency syndrome comes into effect, the local church leader assumes an almost irreplaceable status in the community. He either assumes it coercively by his own means or the community itself complicity hands it over to him. He takes extreme care that no one meets the priest or other a church official without his knowledge and in essence has become a 'power broker' between the Reddyar landlords and the Paraiyar Christians if any dispute between them arises. He continues to be the head of church hierarchy in Thulasigramam, as long as he maintains the status quo keeping the Priest's interests (since his support is essential for the Priest in controlling the pastorate) and keeping his parish subservient to him. In this complex power game, the unassuming Paraiyar Christians often believe in the word of God as espoused by the Catechist, which contributes to the continuation of rank ordering thereby establishing a functional hierarchy. Even though there are many opportunities for the Paraiyar Christians to change their lifestyle, they are seldom utilized because they seem out of their reach. However, Hugo Gorringe suggests that such compliance may not be consensus, 'for people may both participate in a culture and resist it at the same time',[25] as it was explained earlier through the subversive expressions of the Paraiyar Christians. In general, this experience from Thulasigramam not only underlines the observation by Mosse that the Catholic Church in Tamil Nadu is able to challenge caste domination through its own institutionalization, but also further suggests that the institutionalization of the Protestant church provides new forms of hierarchy and exclusion within the Christian community.[26]

It could be discerned from the previous discussions that any hierarchy flourishes in a situation of subordination, dependency and fragmentation. Once such a hierarchical system takes root, it provides room for the abuse of power by those who are able to usurp it through their position in the community. In the case of the Christians in Thulasigramam, the local church leader is able to occupy such a position and establish himself as the sole authority or a gatekeeper of the church and Christian community. In order to maintain this graded system, any efforts by individuals within the Paraiyar Christian community to destabilize status quo are met with disdain and legitimized with a religious colouring by the powerful.

The discordant voices within the community who find the courage to lament the lack of political participation, education, healthcare and employment facilities are quietly dealt with as 'anti-Christian'. This situation within the Paraiyar Christians mirrors how the caste-dominated society functions. Hence, it is safe to conclude that the Christians in Thulasigramam have come to replicate the same hierarchy it initially attempted to change. Such a reproduction of hierarchy seems to be the experience of Dalit Christians across India,[27] as power is the ability to have access to resources and use those resources for the betterment of the person. The preceding interpretation puts into perspective the consistent continuation of the 'Dalitness' of Dalits across India.[28]

The above-mentioned situation in Thulasigramam clearly depicts that a particular family, that of the local church leader, has unequal access to the resources provided by the church. As long as the family of the local church leader remains faithful to the Priest, both parties benefit. Additionally, this arrangement enables the Priest to be part of another hierarchy. It becomes apparent that the Catechist would be powerless if he were unable to take advantage of the system keeping the congregation ignorant about the resources available to them or effectively diverting their attention from seeking those resources. Their spirituality is used to justify the perpetuation of their situation.

What cannot be forgotten is the fact that the local church leader is still a Paraiyar Christian, but since the Christian community has effectively accepted him as their 'Spiritual Landlord' to some extent, they accept their subordination to him with the knowledge that they do not have much choice. It is apparently clear that the role of the Priest is restricted to conducting the sacramental rituals, rather than providing pastoral care, thereby paving the way for the local church leader to assume such a prominent role. It is important to bear in mind that it is the position of the 'local church leader' which needs to be critically looked at and not the individual, as he or she could be replaced. With the insights from the Paraiyar Christian community in Thulasigramam, one could effectively conclude that the churches in South India have provided an effective structure in facilitating dominant hierarchies, furthering socio-economic dependence and reproducing cultural subordination. Having said that, there is also a conscious replication of hierarchy, yet one cannot ignore the resistance and subversions that take place within the Paraiyar community, which will be the focus of the following chapter.

6

Social Efficacy: Religious Symbols, Performance and Subverting Local Customs

> *It is well known that in South India, temple rituals are fully entangled in political process. From pre-colonial kingship through colonial rule and continuing today in both rural and urban communities, temple rituals have remained a vital means of asserting control over territories, garnering social constituencies and articulating and contesting relations of rank within communities.*[1]

This critical observation made by Diane P. Mines on the central place of religious life and temple rituals in Tamil Nadu prompts further careful examination of the religious practices among the rural Paraiyar Christians of Thulasigramam in South India. A closer observation of the lives of the Paraiyar Christians reveals that they do not just perceive and passively consume the Christian religious symbols, spaces, worldviews and rituals with which they are presented, but rather, take an active role in interpreting, reshaping and utilizing them for their own ends. In this process, they reflect and even redress the community's needs and ambitions within its complex caste-dominated and marginalized social context in which religious affiliation crucially defines their sociocultural boundaries and identities. This chapter seeks to highlight the contestation and negotiation employed by the Paraiyar Christians within the matrix of caste and religious conflicts. First, it develops a fundamental understanding of symbolic representation within the anthropological approach to the study of religion. Second, it briefly observes various aspects of how the Paraiyar Christians negotiate their social position through religious symbolism, creative strategies and subversive social actions.

Understanding religious symbolism

Symbols, signs and rituals are located within a cultural social convention performed by individuals and communities. Symbols are not merely representations, but carriers of meaning provided by the observers and the performers, which not only instruct but also enable the user to make new meanings.[2] Symbols are vehicles of interpretation as they are malleable and can be made to fit particular needs and uses of an individual or community.[3] Clifford Geertz suggests that symbols are 'imprecise' cognitive constructs, facilitating 'subjective' communal expression.[4] Symbols also provide space for the community to infuse meanings in order to serve their specific objectives.[5] Culturally, symbols play a significant role in reinforcing cultural boundaries while reconstituting them since, as Geertz observes, 'symbols are shaped by psychological and social factors, while they in turn also shape psychological and social reality of the signifier'.[6] Material symbols become relevant and alive because of the meanings actively infused and inferred by human cognition.[7] Meanings are ascribed through symbols and gain prominence particularly when contrasted with other symbols.[8]

Symbolism is a form of social knowledge and, according to Geertz, in the religious arena, symbols assume 'sacredness' by mediating ontological and cosmological knowledge and guiding people to 'live realistically'.[9] As suggested earlier, religion is located within culture and society and in the communal and individual aspects of human life, profoundly influenced by emotional elements.[10] Geertz proposes the possibility of religious symbols and rituals assuming sociopolitical and metaphysical significance in the light of specific existing contexts.[11] Moreover, symbols and rituals within religious spheres represent communal consciousness and provide meaning for the individual's existence within the group. However, symbols within a religious context make things that are not visible visible, transform the 'transcendent' into the 'immanent' and make things that are inaccessible accessible to human contact. As Eller suggest,

> spiritual concepts, beings and forces, which are not "present" in the ordinary sense, are made present, made physical, made "flesh" by sacred symbols and objects. These entities "break through" normal reality in specific forms; such forms are an eruption of the supernatural in the natural and social.[12]

Taking it further and emphasizing the social impact, Victor Turner opines that 'symbols instigate social action', since symbols and rituals provide an instructional structure facilitating social order or 'Communitas'.[13] Religious symbols and knowledge become important to people only when they are able to use them, to make sense of their experiences, which eventually shape their social attitudes in the world in which they live.[14] Having gained this basic grasp of understanding the relevance of symbolism within a socio-religious milieu, it is also important to recognize the ambiguous nature of interpreting symbolism because of the constantly changing social world of human communities.[15] With this background, let us observe some aspects of the Paraiyar Christian community of Thulasigramam, which might shed light on the aspect of human communities utilizing religious symbols and socially subversive actions for negotiating their social space.

Utilization of religious symbols and sacred artefacts

Thulasigramam has been the place of various social and religious conflicts in the past. Continuing tensions of caste conflicts between the Reddyars and the Paraiyars compounded by the wider religious conflicts between Hindus and Christians form the complex environment within which the following observations were made. Historically, in Thulasigramam, these conflicts not only were rooted in the community but were also sometimes instigated by people from outside the village with vested interest. Five observations give the basis for further discussion regarding the utilization of religious symbolism and ritual performance for contesting their social status.

The cross on the hilltop

The cross on the hilltop near the Paraiyar Cherie (colony) has an interesting and noteworthy history. Near the central part of Thulasigramam there is a hillock on top of which is a small temple dedicated to the Hindu lord *Murugan*. Interestingly, there is another slightly higher hillock on the southern edge of the village, close to the Paraiyar Cherie, and some of the Paraiyar Christians came up with the idea to use the higher hill near closer to their home for prayer and meditation. One day they went up the hill, cleared some of the bushes and placed a cross there, and since then, they have consciously claimed it as a *Punitha Idum* (sacred place) for the Christian community. Observing this development, the Hindu Reddyars objected and warned a group of the Paraiyar Christians to remove the Christian symbol or face dire consequences. When they felt that the Paraiyar Christians were not responding to their threats, they instructed the Hindu Paraiyars to place a *Trisulam* (trident) symbolizing the Hindu god Shiva on the same hill near the cross, thereby directly challenging the Paraiyar Christians. Considering this to be an insult, the Paraiyar Christians gathered together and decided to rename the fought over hill as *Oliva Malai* (after the biblical Mount Olive) and built an altar with a large cross, and moreover fenced off access to the hill path, effectively claiming the hill as the private property of the Christian community. The Paraiyar Christians have made a formal legal application to their elected politician through their local church to declare the site as a Christian sacred space and include it under the ordinance of church maintenance. But the Reddyars still consider the land on which the cross is situated as an illegal occupation and continue to make efforts to clear it.

Some Paraiyar Christians claim that their prayers have been answered after making a pilgrimage to the hilltop and hoisting a flag with a cross on it. As mentioned earlier, Esther, a devout Paraiyar Christian woman, revealed that when she was barren and despised by the community, she used to go to this particular hilltop cross and pray for long hours. One night Jesus appeared to her in a dream as a child, and within a week she found herself to be pregnant. This news spread around the community and the hilltop cross began to gain importance within the Christian community and the village. Based on such experiences, a myth around the hilltop cross began to take shape and, consequently, the Hindu Paraiyars also became interested in it, hoping that they also would receive the benefits of praying to Yesusami near the hilltop cross. It is also important to recognize the implication of such a belief within the community that one could experience or encounter Yesusami on the mountain top, thus making it a sacred space. This mountain top and the cross have become a place of spiritual concentration for the community, by importing spiritual power to the site by the community itself.

Apart from the perceived miraculous powers of the cross on the Oliva Malai, it is actually far higher than the hill where the Lord *Murugan* temple is located. Examining this in the light of a comment made by a Paraiyar Christian youth, 'our cross is higher than their *Murugan*', provides a very powerful insight. The cross is effectively used as a tool to claim literally 'higher ground' above the gods of their oppressors, the Reddyars and the Hindu Paraiyars in a context where the Christian Paraiyars are poorly treated. The hilltop cross becomes a means to contest their socially and religiously inferior status while claiming a denied higher status through their religious affiliation, they use the perception that the verticality of one's religious association in many occasions determines the social ranking within the community. The location of the cross on the hilltop, a favoured place of Hindu deity worship across India, thus communicates the message of contestation by the Paraiyar Christians, effectively literally claiming higher status for them not just spiritually, but most significantly in the social realm.

The holy Bible: A source of the sacred

The Bible is often considered to be a *parisutha*, a holy book, and is treated with great reverence within the predominately illiterate Paraiyar Christian community. It is also believed to contain enormous powers within it, which can be used for personal as well as communal benefits. During fieldwork, Chandra, an elderly lady in the Paraiyar Christian community and wife of a former catechist, disclosed her belief in the miraculous power of Yesusami, made possible through the Bible, which she believes contains 'His' Power. One evening, visibly upset, she went to the church and prayed with her Bible in hand; afterwards, she returned home and entered her backyard. I was surprised to see her place the Bible on the heads of some of her sheep and pray for healing. Upon enquiring she explained that she was praying for her sick sheep, which were affected with a contagious infection. After a few of them had died, she decided to use the power that she saw latent in the Bible to protect the sheep. She firmly believed that the Bible had the power to heal if she placed it upon the sheep while praying to Yesusami. Chandra also added that if the sheep die, her only source of living would be gone. She recollected that from her previous experiences when she and her husband would visit sick people, they would pray with the Bible by placing it upon the ill person who would frequently be healed. For Chandra, the Bible contains magical healing power within itself that is released when she prayed to Yesusami with faith and good intention. She also confided that she often keeps the Bible under her pillow while going to sleep to avoid bad dreams by keeping evil spirits from reaching or harming her. She admitted to this practice for more than five decades and claims to always find it to be beneficial.

Chandra is not alone in this type of practice as several other women and men from the Paraiyar Christian community share this belief in the power of the Bible. Many in the community use the Bible for various reasons apart from reading and learning scripture, primarily because most are illiterate. In some houses, it is kept in an elevated place along with portraits of Yesusami and sometimes even with other deities, decorations and candles, almost performing *poojai* (worship) to it. The Bible as a religious sacred object almost becomes a magic tool used to prevent misfortune in personal, social and economic life. Chandra infuses new meaning into the use and role of the Bible in her life primarily through her faith and past experience. But this process does not stop there as it permeates into other aspects of her life as well. It can be observed that religious sacred objects, like the cross and the bible, can take on new roles other than what they were intended for as ascribed by the users. In the case of the Christian Paraiyar community in Thulasigramam, this process effectively gives a new meaning to the religious sacred objects. The bible in this context not only contains 'spiritual text' but 'spiritual power' as well, making it a source of sacred itself.

Portraits of Yesusami and Mary Matha

Yesusami and Mary Matha (Virgin Mary) are the predominant portraits present in most households of the Paraiyar Christians in Thulasigramam. Interestingly, there is not a single portrait of either figure within the church building because the local church leader believes that Christians should not worship idols (i.e. portraits), which is also the official stance of the local church. Contrary to this view, many of the Christians in the community worship and venerate pictures of Yesusami and Mary Matha privately within their homes. Peter, a young member of the Paraiyar Christian community, explained that he spends five minutes every morning in front of Yesusami's portrait before leaving for work. He believes that this 'prayerful act' provides him safety, strength and peace every day. In another instance, Nathan, the local guardian of the church and respected member of the community, decided to farm rabbits with the help of a loan arranged by his employer. Prior to receiving the baby rabbits, he prepared a shed for the rabbit cages, inside of which he hung a portrait of Yesusami. When asked why, Nathan replied that by placing the picture of Yesusami with the rabbits, he ensures their protection and well-being, as well as making sure that his business venture would be prosperous. He further added that the portrait of Yesusami is equivalent to the real presence of Yesusami among the rabbits and promises good safety and better profit.

This practice is widely prevalent among the Paraiyar Christians in Thulasigramam. Yacobu, who works in the poultry farm of a Reddyar, keeps a portrait of Yesusami in his tent while working. He believes that this picture helps him work well and consequently to earn a good reputation from his manager. Rani, an elderly widow in the Christian community who maintains the church premises for free, also offers a good insight into the way images of the divine are perceived in the community. She has portraits of Yesusami, the Mary Matha and a deceased former bishop hung on a wall of her house. These portraits occupy a special place in her wall and are adorned with decorations, much like the Hindu shrines. One day she had food items placed in front of the portraits and when I asked, she explained that she continues to make the same dishes the bishop liked when used to visit the village when he was alive. Her gesture of hospitality was extended to the portraits of Yesusami and the Mary Matha next to the deceased bishop, hoping that they would consume it, and in return bless her. In the past she claimed to see the foods disappear.[16]

The visual interaction with the portraits of the divine and hopeful extraction of power with them among Thulasigramam Paraiyar Christians provides useful insights into the relationship between divine images and devotees. Moreover, these images have practical implications on the lives of Paraiyar Christians. As David Morgan explains through extensive research on the usage of divine images in the Indian subcontinent, the devotees and viewers of divine portraits and images enter into a relationship, a 'covenant' with the image and use it to interpret socio-spiritual empowerment.[17] Besides viewing what is going on in the community from the perspective of religious symbols one could suggest that there is an element of religious 'charm or fetish' in this form of religious behaviour.[18] Moreover, these observations highlight the material expression of belief and the sensory experience of religious faith.[19] As explained earlier, the Paraiyar Christian community amply demonstrate that images and portraits of the divine assume a real presence through their psycho-social interpretations producing functional value in their lives.

The Palm Sunday procession

Among the most awaited Christian religious observances in Thulasigramam, the Palm Sunday procession, that celebrates the triumphant entry of Jesus into Jerusalem, is one of the most significant highlights of the year. There is great excitement about, and preparation for, the carrying of palm leaves, singing of Tamil lyrics and the procession around the streets of the Paraiyar Cheri. Within the Christian community, this religious spectacle is an important demonstration of Christian Paraiyar religious affiliation, as well as a vehicle to proclaim (loudly) their changed status, from that of religiously impure Hindu Paraiyars to 'Christians'. On the previous day, young people go around the Paraiyar Christian houses and instruct them all to participate in the Palm Sunday procession. The procession starts from the church, continues through the main road and into the street populated by Hindu Paraiyars, where they gathered right in front of the Hindu temple boisterously singing Christian lyrics.

It was interesting to observe and analyse the multiple dynamics involved in this event. At one level, they displayed their unity as Paraiyar Christians and the new religiously 'acceptable' status they had achieved by becoming Christians. On another level, carrying a symbol of Yesusami they demonstrated their proximity to the core deity of their faith, which was denied to them as Hindus because Hindus see Paraiyars as ritually polluting and unable to access the Hindu deity. As Hindus, the Paraiyars were prohibited from touching Hindu iconography or high-caste Hindus and therefore took particular pride in going in procession around Thulasigramam with their Christian symbols. Even though many of them actually did not know the religious history of Palm Sunday, they nevertheless attached value to the event, since it was the only time they were able to go around the village as a 'Christian' group. The Palm Sunday procession by the Paraiyar Christians clearly exemplifies how a ritual practice takes on new connotations pertaining to the context in which it is performed. The Palm Sunday procession creates a platform for the Christian community to come together in spite of their inner conflicts and differences, while providing a united stance to contest their previous religiously impure status by showcasing their proximity to the Christian deity.[20] This religious performance is loaded with socio-religious meaning for the struggle against dominance and status change within the stronghold of the caste structure. As Victor Turner observed, religious ritual performances with localized contexts create a particular meaning and can instigate and facilitate new 'communitas'.[21] Within Thulasigramam, the Paraiyar Christian community were able to achieve a new status as well as to break through the religious untouchability of their past.

Other Christian festivals

In Thulasigramam, there is increasing interest among the Christians to celebrate and conduct major Christian festivals like Christmas, New Year and Easter in a grand manner overshadowing the Hindu festivals predominantly organized by the Reddyars. The Paraiyar Christians take extreme measures to raise funds and organize for those celebrations. During Christmas, New Year and Easter occasions they arranged for expensive decorative lights for the church building and loud stereo systems so that the whole village could see and hear their celebrations. Many of the Paraiyar Christians were very clear that their festivals should be better and grander than the Hindu temple celebration organized by the Reddyars. Taking a cue from the Hindu temple festivals, the Christians have decided to organize a large meal for the whole Thulasigramam village during Christmas and Easter. It needs to be mentioned that the felt purpose among the Christians was to outshine the Reddyars, that being perhaps more crucial than actually celebrating the birth and resurrection of Jesus Christ. There is genuine interest to celebrate festivals among the Paraiyar Christians, but one cannot miss the competitiveness shown by the Paraiyar Christians to organize grand religious fiestas, thus exemplifying their strategy to claim a position that was denied to them in Hindu religious practices. The competitiveness among Christians in organizing grand festivals is not an isolated occurrence but can be seen around the world and is true for other religious traditions. Paraiyars, according to the village restrictions in Thulasigramam, could only be spectators and never the creative organizers of religious celebrations. So, as Christians, they can now physically organize and celebrate Christian holidays like Christmas and Easter, and have thus an added gusto and gaiety, which was denied to them before. It also sends a message to the Reddyars that as Christians, even as Paraiyar Christians they cannot just be pushed aside in the village. This process demonstrates their capacity to act as a coherent and resisting group.

Another example is the annual harvest festival at *Annaicuttu*, a village near Thulasigramam, where many of the rural Christian communities from the northern part of the district gather to celebrate and give thanks to Yesusami for the harvest that season. At first instance it could be mistaken for a Hindu temple festival, because the church building resembles a traditional Hindu temple and people come with offerings such as chickens, cattle, agricultural products and so on. Many believers even offer their hair as offerings in response to the blessings they have received from Yesusami as a result of their prayers offered during the previous year. This practice is characteristic of popular local religious practices that are widely followed among Hindus as well. Christians, predominantly Paraiyars, plan and organize this celebration on a grand scale, which thereby resembles and even overshadows other Hindu temple festivals in that area.

Such celebrations are becoming increasingly popular in the area, and there are now more than ten different festivals organized in different parts of the region annually. The phenomenal growth and popularity of these harvest festivals in the rural areas have caused serious tensions between the Paraiyar Christians and local high-caste landlords. Interestingly, the Paraiyar Christians have utilized the harvest festivals to mobilize both local and neighbouring Paraiyar Christian communities allowing them to celebrate in a grand style the blessing received from Yesusami through that year's harvest. It can also be observed that there are definite political undertones to such festive gatherings, which very often angers the local land-owning communities.

Subverting local customs

Subversion of the accepted social behaviour and norms contributes to the constructions of religious identity. Subversive elements have the potential to create value for the oppressed communities. Within the Paraiyar community, stealing from the farms and fields owned by the Reddyars is not surprisingly considered to be a punishable action. Stealing has to be qualified here; it is not an action intended to inflict misery upon the landlords but to express their right to a share of the crops. On many occasions, members from the Paraiyar Christian community narrated their brave adventures in the Reddyars lands stealing tender coconuts, mangoes, bananas and rice, just to mention a few items. Simon and Dass, two Paraiyar Christian youths, were famous for their exploits, especially during the night. Comically, their adventures have become a regular feature of village gossip. Whenever they gather together, they would plan to visit one of the farms and take a substantial amount of fruits. After stealing the produce, they often stay and consume what they took at the actual scene of the crime so to speak, bragging about their bravery to their friends. They do not perceive stealing as a serious ethical problem, but rather their right to take a few of those 'fenced' products for which their parents have worked so hard. Such night time activities of the Paraiyar Christian youth have prompted the landlords to electrify the fences surrounding their lands in order to protect their crops, but the youths still find some way to continue stealing. This interaction is actually a manifestation of the tension that exists between the land-owning Reddyar community and the impoverished Paraiyar community. Even though the elders of both communities would agree that such actions should not be permitted and punished when they do happen, the young men from the Paraiyar Christian community continue to steal with the tacit support from their community. It is a subversive method of negotiating their right into the plenty which was 'fenced off' from them.

Another example of similar mischievous behaviour is as described in the previous chapter, the digging up of the road in random places by the Paraiyar Christian youths. This became a source of expression of their anger and disagreement with the Reddyars. The government had laid a tarmac road in the village in the area primarily used by the Reddyars and the occasional public transport vehicle. The road runs through the Paraiyar settlement, but most of the users are the Reddyars, who own vehicles and drive too fast in the Paraiyar Cherie, almost killing a couple of children and injuring several women. Because of these threats the Paraiyar community demanded that a speed breaker should be put on the road so that the speeding vehicles can are forcibly slowed down, but their requests fell on deaf ears. One night, some of the Paraiyar Christian youths gathered and dug deep potholes in some parts of the road near their houses, thereby forcing the vehicles to go slowly. Since their homes were directly adjacent to the road, they felt that it was the rightful expression of their anger in the face of the failure to respond to their concerns. The Paraiyar Christians argue that carrying out punishable action such as stealing and digging up the road to protest against gross negligence and violation of their rights was permissible within their community ethos.

Other subversive activities include desecrating Hindu religious sites by urinating or defecating on or near the idols in temple and *puthuu* (holy anthills), which are worshiped by the Reddyars.[22] A few years ago within the Paraiyar Christian community Prabu and his friends went to the temple in the village and urinated and defecated on some of the Hindu idols during the night in response to the prohibition to participate in some of the village festivals conducted by the Reddyars. Nobody talks about it publicly, as the Reddyars are still not aware of the 'culprits'.

This subversion is also expressed in their attitude and body posture. I observed that there was certain body language used by the Paraiyar Christians, which (sometimes) could be misleading, especially in cases when it might seem as though they are acting respectful to the Reddyars, but in actuality they are doing quite the opposite. To illustrate this point, when Paraiyar men and women sit on the veranda, and a Reddyar passes by, they are traditionally compelled to stand and pay their *mariyathai* (respect) by taking off the *thoundu* (a piece of cloth) over their shoulder. However, nowadays after making the respectful gesture they immediately use the *thoundu* to clean the *veranda* making it look as if they stood up just to clean the place where they were sitting, thereby giving a different meaning to a traditional practice. What goes on during such actions is that some in the Paraiyar community demonstrate and express their protest against their subordination by subverting the accepted social norms in order to undermine the authority of the Reddyars. These defiant actions not only demonstrate the anger latent within the Paraiyar Christian community but also challenge and contest the boundaries that are laid out in principle and in practice among the different caste communities in the village. What is intriguing is that these subversive actions were presented to me as happening only among the

Christian community, since Hindu Paraiyars, who are religiously affiliated with Reddyars, would not attempt such actions. Hence, Christian Paraiyars enjoy the freedom to express their anger in such visible acts.

It seems that these subversive behaviours have become part of their daily existence and have almost become a new custom. It may be due to the fact that they have to fight constantly for their survival in an exploitative social setting that subversion becomes the means to negotiate their place and space within such an exploitative setting. However, it could also be due to their functional understanding of religion, which finds its expression in Christianity. The following section will attempt to elaborate on this idea.

Materializing belief

To understand the use of religion in the Paraiyar Christian community, the experience of Ramamurthy is helpful. As mentioned earlier Ramamurthy is a widower and a chronic tuberculosis patient. He came regularly to the church in the hope that his sickness would be cured. However, it was his approach to prayer that I found interesting to observe. He said 'if I ask God for healing, it has to happen today; otherwise I'll look at other options!' Although there was no significant change in his health condition, he still hoped that he would be healed one day. After worshipping for a couple of months in the CSI church, he went to the Pentecostal prayer fellowship in the neighbouring village to be prayed for. He did not stop there as he even went to consult a local healer for remedy and eventually admitting himself into a government hospital.

A very functional understanding of religion is to be found in Ramamurthy's and other Paraiyar Christians' perception of religion. It may be termed as an 'expression of desperation' by the local church catechist and a couple of other Christians, but the fact was that Ramamurthy's expectation of Yesusami was that he would be cured of his illness, a hope that provided his persistence. If he did not find remedy in the local church, he was determined enough to look for it in other possible places. This perception of religion is prevalent among the Paraiyar Christians of Thulasigramam and to a large extent determines their relationship with the church and religion in general. To illustrate further this point is the example of Jebanesan, who said, 'I go to God only if there is some need'. Jebanesan is a known alcoholic in the village, who works with some of the illicit liquor brewers. Although he was ridiculed in the Paraiyar Christian community for his lifestyle and actions, his opinion further bolsters the Paraiyar Christians' approach to God. The Paraiyars by default are a community with a lot of needs due to their overarching state of poverty; therefore, it is perhaps not surprising to observe that their predominant mode of relating with God is through the fulfilment of their tangible and material needs in life.

'If I come to church, who will feed my kids and family?' was a profound question asked by Saroja, a middle-aged mother of two children in the Paraiyar Christian community, when asked about her absence in the church on a particular Sunday. This illustrates the notion that many of their decisions were made in view of the present moment and not the 'future'; such an answer in no way undermines her faith, but only demonstrates her practical approach to life. Her first priority was to provide for her family's daily needs and only when they were met did she attend to the practice of her faith. Within the context of the growing difficulty in getting a day's work, Beulah makes the choice to work and earn a living rather than sitting in the church, singing and praying. She added to her explanation 'Yesusami would understand my situation; he (Yesusami) will not get angry if I don't go to church once in a while'. It is important to grasp her religious perception and the priorities in her life. Although she felt sorry for not going to church, she was more concerned to provide a meal for the family through her work, choosing their material and immediate needs over her spiritual needs. This experience was shared by Paraiyars across the Christian community. There was even one Sunday when the service had to be cancelled since nobody turned up as most had gone to the paddy fields for rice harvesting. The popular perception among Hindus in Thulasigramam was that the Paraiyars are unfaithful in their religious practice and do not fear God, but on the contrary, the Paraiyar Christians pursue pressing practical life issues with the hope that Yesusami will understand their absence in the church service on a Sunday morning.

Deva's candid statement mentioned earlier, 'When I pray to Yesusami, he gets me the pension and the 'rum' bottles from the military canteen and I am thankful to him for that', encapsulates the way he perceived God and understood the tangible nature of belief. Primarily Yesusami was realized through daily life experiences. I would argue that the Paraiyar Christians have a very personal, participatory and real dimension to the conception of their faith. This statement needs to be located within a pietistic missionary understanding of Christianity, in which alcohol consumption was considered to be sinful and religiously prohibited. Deva's perception of Yesusami not only transcends the narrow confines of denominational Christianity, but also provides a fascinating and functional dimension of Yesusami attributed through the experiences Paraiyar Christians. Most importantly, God is conceived to be among the Paraiyar Christians and not constrained in an isolated place, thus giving them the freedom to interact with that divine presence. When God fulfils their needs, he gains importance and currency in the Paraiyar Christian community gaining their allegiance and faith. From the preceding observation it is possible to suggest that the material aspect of religion is core to the Paraiyars' conceptualization of a worldview, hence providing space for exercising their agency in negotiating the evolving context.

Negotiating social change

The claiming of new status through the location and height of the hilltop cross, the magical power of the Bible to transform personal and social problems, the hope and protection provided by the portraits of Yesusami and Mary Matha, the creation of a new 'communitas' through the solidarity expressed in the Palm Sunday procession, the celebrations during the Christians festivals and deliberate subversive acts all happen within the socio-religious domain, but are infused with different meanings by the actors themselves. The above-mentioned observations contribute to the continuing struggles of Paraiyar Christians to contest their inferior status as 'outcastes' living in the Cherie and in the process gain a new status within a subordinated social reality. Religion becomes one of the major means of negotiating their identity and status within the caste-dominated village community. As observed earlier, these religious symbols and practices along with the freedom to exercise their subversive actions are given new meaning for a specific purpose of personal and social transformation. These are also utilized to negotiate and redraw the existing cognitive and social boundaries, as well claiming higher status in the midst of caste discrimination and socio-religious untouchability. The process of receiving and practising religious symbols and rituals are used to attain certain goals, while providing a sense of religion functioning as an agency for change.[23] As explained earlier, within the context of alienation from necessary resources and imposed subordination by the caste system, Paraiyar Christians in Thulasigramam do feel that they have the potential and power to change their lives with the religious resources provided to them within Christianity.

Many of the practices and performances analysed in this chapter are fashioned to unsettle and contest hierarchies, thus providing new space for religious and communal expression. They are innovative strategies for subverting social structures and negotiating identities. The creation of sacred space not only provides a rallying point for the community to mobilize but also facilitates an impetus for social change. The case of the hilltop cross is not only spiritually important for the community but also becomes an avenue for others to interpret it in subversive terms. Thus, even the public religious performances, such as Palm Sunday procession, are meant to draw the community together and infuse the occasion with subtle message of reclaiming lost status. It is in this context that we need to understand the pragmatic approach to belief and the usefulness of sacred objects in the everyday lives of the individual and community. Collectively, the subversive actions within the spiritual domain are played out in public to alter perceptions and notions in the social realm.

Victor Turner observes that due to the need to escape from the structural compulsions, people might adopt certain cultural expressions, which may be not only religious, but also heavily ritualized.[24] Having said that, such ritual performances might be in direct conflict to governing structures and even question their authority. Turner hints at this process in which the 'inferiors symbolically usurp' certain practices to subvert the structure to realize the communitas.[25] In the light of Turner's understanding of ritual performance, it can be said that these acts of the Paraiyar Christians are concrete protests against the existing dominant social structure and not just conservative sublimation to the status quo. As Geertz argues, certain actions cannot be just treated as epiphenomenon and as spectacles,[26] because performances are antagonizing, decentring and subverting processes.[27]

Symbols and ritual performances have the power to break human limits and create the possibility of new communities. The impacts of the less visible world and its visible representations have a significant impact on the lives of people as was demonstrated in the previous chapter. Thus, it can be argued that the hilltop cross, the Bible, the Palm Sunday procession and the Christian festival celebrations are visible representations of the less visible world. Along with other discursive and subversive processes, these become strategic tools of identification, negotiation and transformation across socio-economic and religious fields, providing new space for the Paraiyar Christians of Thulasigramam, both individually and socially.

7

Lived Religion

The lived religion of the Paraiyar Christians as encountered in this book is messy, conflictual, multi-layered, dynamic and context-bound. The overall purpose of this volume is an attempt to understand the grounded and complex nature of 'religion' within the Paraiyar Christian community of Thulasigramam. Having gone through the details of Paraiyar life, this chapter consists of three sections. It first develops a comprehensive understanding of the Paraiyar worldview based on observations made in earlier chapters, shedding light on the notion of religion within the Paraiyar community and communal identity. Second, the chapter finds similarities and divergences with other works focusing on lived religion, thus offering a wider perspective on the complexity of religion. And the final section concludes with the theoretical suggestion of a synergetic view of religion in the case of Paraiyar Christians and beyond.

Locating religion among Paraiyars

> Religions are not finished products: they constantly hand themselves over to their adherents. They are susceptible to continuously being crafted into meaning-giving and meaning-making symbolic dwelling places.[1]

While observing religion among Paraiyars, this remark by Sathianathan Clarke could be applied to the experiences from Thulasigramam. Paraiyars have clearly demonstrated their ability to live with more than one prevailing religious worldview. Even though the dominant religious persuasions may demand undivided adherence, Paraiyars have shown the human capacity and agency to influence such views and change their course of action. What comes out of this study is the malleability of religion that renders meaning to the Paraiyar social existence. Such a process is possible because religion does not preoccupy itself only with the sacred but also takes significant interest in the social. The discourse on the role of religion in societies should take into account the fact that the sacred is part of the social, and as the Paraiyars have amply shown are mutually dependent. Religious beliefs and worldviews are grounded and embodied in the community experience, and without tangible social expression, religion is irrelevant and futile. Moreover, religion in its broadest sense provides an additional texture to Paraiyar life. Working with the hypothesis that religion is a process that functions as a window into the complex social life of people and their aspirations to be human in a society, I shall summarize my views in what follows.

Self and the community

The self-conceptualization of the Paraiyar Christian community in Thulasigramam is a dynamic, discursive and contextual strategic process. It is important to grasp the polyvalence of the cognitive conceptualization of the self through differentiation with the 'other' in Thulasigramam, an 'other' that may not always be fixed. As elsewhere, self-conceptualizations of people in the community are intricately woven within their religious and cultural consciousness, which is firmly rooted in the particularities of spatial location. Individuals and communities operate and shape their worlds primarily by belonging to a system, by internalizing it, actively shaping or subverting it, which is often directed by (even if working against) dominant notions.

Self-conceptualization takes root within and outside of a community with multiple reference points, primarily expressed through relationships. Throughout this book, I have argued that the identity of Paraiyar Christians in Thulasigramam is constituted and determined by their specific location within the caste system and their physical location – their social and spatial locatedness. As Paraiyar Christians, my fieldwork subjects negotiate being Paraiyar, Christian and Paraiyar Christians embedded in a specific locality with its own spirituality. It is also important to recognize the fact that none of these processes function within a vacuum, or in isolation, but constantly interplay and interpolate each other, contributing to the construction of social identity. My research shows that Paraiyar Christians switch back and forth between their Paraiyar (i.e. their local Dalit) and their Christian identities, and sometimes a confluence of elements from both finds meaning in their communal and individual life. As Paraiyars they continue to conceive their status in terms of their local norms, but challenge it with their Christian identity as and when required. This continuation of alternate identities is due to various factors such as economic dependence, lack of education and employment and their own agency. I argue that the Paraiyar Christians in Thulasigramam continue to think as Paraiyars into which their Christian identity must fit. Both identities are essentially determined by the religious categories of the Vedic Hindu system and the religion of the Christian missionaries, with the former identity often overshadowing the latter identity. While I do not want to undermine the role of conversion and the individual religious experience of Paraiyar Christians, it is important to recognize the fact that certain aspects can only be understood in opposition to the other village caste communities such as the Reddyars, Arunthathiers and Hindu Paraiyars; indeed, the category of Paraiyar Christian is a relational one.

Collective identity provides the framework for individuals to draw upon their own self-perception. It is in this context that the communal identity asserted by religious affiliation and cultural norms, as in the case of the 'outcaste' Paraiyars, gains significant importance. As observed earlier, in the Paraiyar community, there is a necessity in subscribing to such a self-perception due to their status as well as effectively choosing to identify oneself with a particular identity. Amidst this process of identity formation one needs to recognize that the community that is also being formed along the same lines, drawing and redrawing boundaries in order to accommodate their embraced social status. We have seen that Paraiyars operate from coexisting multiple religious reference points, challenging the notion of singular religious adherence. Elsewhere in India, religion is often seen as the main factor in identity formation, both at the individual and collective level. But even though Paraiyar Christians are in a disadvantageous position due to their caste identity, they are able to effectively use the system for their advantage by being Christians as well as Paraiyars. The impact of this can be seen internally and externally, as well as spiritually and socially. Thus with their religiously predetermined outcaste status, Paraiyars negotiate their livelihood using another religious belonging without capitulating to either of them. Religious affiliation and corresponding identity formation in the case of Paraiyars reconfigures conventional perceptions of religious belonging.

Worldview

The Paraiyar Christian religious worldview is one that is locally conceptualized. I assert that the individual and the community consider their social setting as the epistemological ground for their self-conceptualization and worldview. As explained earlier, notions of the less visible world often stem from tangible, conflict-ridden daily existence and vice versa. This dynamic relationship between the visible and less visible worlds reflects and provides space for the formation of relationships among individuals, gods and goddesses. Such a framework of relating also means that in the absence of proper relationships between individuals within the community, their experience of the gods and goddesses are often blocked. Thus, between the less visible world of gods and goddesses and the visible world of individuals and communities, there is a causal and reciprocal relationship. Most importantly, Paraiyar Christians hold the less visible world and the visible world together as a complete unit in which human beings and spirits interact daily, for they do not have a dualistic understanding of the universe. This means that the religious experiences of Paraiyars are characteristically often decentralized and unmediated. A significant implication of such an understanding is that that gods and goddesses become communal beings, with a specific sense of ownership by the community, which in the Paraiyar context can be accessed by all, male and female. Here, the dilemma of being both a Paraiyar and a Christian emerges. They simultaneously live with different worldviews within which they find meaning for their life. First, there is the Vedic religion which is driven and structured by Varna ideology, second, the Paraiyars' holistic, conflictual and subversive perception of the universe, and third, the exclusive and all-pervasive Christian church. Paraiyar Christians live with all of the above-mentioned frames of reference, resulting in a fluid, yet functioning *middle* position.

The previous chapters on the Paraiyar worldview have shown that the Paraiyar Christian worldview is more complex than is often perceived. But as the Paraiyar Christians in Thulasigramam shared through the facets of their life experiences, it is possible to integrate Christian understandings of Yesusami within their inherited notions of Hindu gods and goddesses, less visible realities living with them, indeed within them and not in some removed or even elevated place. For the Paraiyar Christian community,

Yesusami is their God, who performs all of the tasks expected of a God in the Paraiyar community. Yesusami encompasses all of the traits of a Christian God couched within the local Paraiyar understanding of the gods, but without a Christian trinitarian understanding. As explained earlier, Yesusami is not Jesus Christ, part man, part divine, but rather he is Jesus, who is experienced as God the Father and also as the Holy Spirit combined. It is as though Yesusami is a god, not because he is God incarnate in man, but because he acts similarly to how other Paraiyar gods and goddesses function. In the Paraiyar conception, Yesusami is not understood as part of three different beings as it is often rather inadequately understood in the Christian tradition, but as one god who potentially functions in different ways, a belief congruent with the local Hinduism. As recounted by many women and men in the Paraiyar Christian community of Thulasigramam, Yesusami is seen as a protecting and preserving god, as well as a punishing and healing God who intervenes in and transforms human life. It needs to be stressed that there is no discontinuity in the Paraiyar Christians' perception of the gods and goddesses, but rather that there is a confluence of local Paraiyar and Christian worldviews, giving forth a polyphonic, highly functional and contextually relevant perception of Yesusami. The feminine nature of Yesusami as expressed by the Paraiyar Christian community undermines the distant, controlling and authoritative image of God the Father, characteristic of Christianity as they have heard it presented in the local church.[2] Their understandings of Yesusami give space for expressing anger, dissent or protest, either individually or communally. Paraiyar Christians expect Yesusami to work effectively in this world, rather than promising an eternal life in return for a virtuous life. Paraiyar Christians certainly have a functionalist and materialist perception of religion, primarily rooted in their experience.[3] In the Paraiyar Christian community, communal cohesion facilitates the experience of Yesusami, failure to act for the collective good results in misfortune and suffering of the individual as well as the community.

The daily reality in which Paraiyar Christians live argues for the self-aware reconceptualization of their religious worldview. This is possible because of the Paraiyar decentralized and unmediated approach to religion. The notion of gods and goddesses is conceived within the community, thereby providing space for individuals and the community to access the divine in various forms.

This approach is fascinating given the fact that Paraiyars are shunned from Hindu sacred space because of their religiously impure status. The Christian image of Jesus Christ is given a complete makeover through Paraiyar cultural norms and experiences. Yesusami is relevant, useful and accessible for Christian Paraiyars, thus enabling them to participate in village life as Paraiyars, as well as allowing them to subvert the system as and when needed. Paraiyar Christians are thus able to move beyond and move within religious boundaries due to their dynamic appropriation of worldviews.

Social agency

Human communities are symbolic constructions within which an individual may find meaning for existence.[4] When such a community is directed by domineering class and ownership ideology, which is here expressed in discriminatory casteism, an individual (or a community), within his designated place, will either accept the system and his place within it or contest, negotiate and subvert it in order to change such a system.[5]

Previously, I argued that the Paraiyar Christian congregation in Thulasigramam reproduces (but not necessarily passively) hierarchical structures similar to the caste system. This was done by controlling access to the resources within the community, which largely determines the nature of that community's relationship. The local church leader and his family, along with a few of his relatives, have appropriated all of the possible responsibilities and benefits within the church consequently controlling and directing the lives of their parishioners. The Christian priest, who seldom visits the village and if so only briefly, fits into and thereby supports this power structure. In this context, caste hierarchy is reproduced by the local church leader, who functions as the gatekeeper, what I have called the 'Spiritual Landlord' phenomenon. He utilizes Christian spiritual notions, such as 'being submissive to the master' in order to impose and perpetuate a rigid structural hierarchy within the Christian community.

Exclusion from social power relations only enhances subordination, thereby further marginalizing the Paraiyar Christians. The lack of pastoral care for Christians in Thulasigramam results in internal fragmentation and disillusionment, enabling rigid hierarchies to flourish within the Christian community. Once such hierarchy (already an innate feature of the caste-based system) takes root in the Christian community, it provides room for the abuse of power by those who are able to usurp it through their position in the community. There is no room for the community to voice its grievances, since this would undermine the established authority, rendering the hierarchy ineffective. In a nutshell, the Paraiyar Christian community in Thulasigramam continues to perpetuate the hierarchy found in caste society, but re-rendered through the new framework of Christianity. This aspect of reproducing hierarchical systems is experienced among many other Dalit Christian communities as encountered in Tamil Nadu.[6] The denial of agency to access resources and to transform their lives is still a dream among many Dalit Christian communities. This situation seems almost inescapable, since the church as an institution reflects and assimilates the oppressive and exploitative caste hierarchy within its framework.

Nevertheless, the Paraiyar Christian community has shown explicit discontent and efforts to subvert such hierarchies through a range of discursive processes. Various means of negotiation and subversion, such as establishing a cross on a hilltop, conducting grand Christian festivals and processions and desecrating religious spaces, facilitates a new understanding of community among the Paraiyar Christians, excluding the Reddyars and Hindu Paraiyars. Such activities not only challenge the established village system based on caste ideology but also provide space to evolve an alternative to the subordination of outcastes in the village.[7] In Thulasigramam, as elsewhere in India, the caste system is a religiously ordained and prescribed system within Hinduism, against which Paraiyar Christians can utilize various Christian religious practices, as mentioned earlier, to contest their status as ritually impure untouchables. Paraiyar Christians are able to negotiate effectively their identity and alter their status within the caste-dominated village by giving new meaning and context to the religious symbols and practices they have inherited through converting to Christianity.

In India, caste ideology is sustained by cognitive and social boundaries rigidly implemented by most communities. The Paraiyar Christians in Thulasigramam are located in such a context, yet have created a quasi-alternative context through which they are able to utilize the symbols, rituals and practices within Christianity to unsettle, redraw and challenge the existing cognitive and social boundaries. These are innovative strategies for subverting social structures and negotiating identities. This is possible because the Paraiyar Christians have a strong sense of agency and need for immediate social change. Their often antagonizing, decentring and subverting interpretations of symbols and ritual performances have the power to redraw their boundaries and create a new understanding of community.

As outline earlier, the Caste system functions in such a way as to restrict and dominate the social life of people. Often, this structural process is guided by religious authorities, making it difficult for individuals and communities not to adhere by it. The Paraiyar community exemplifies this aspect as being played out in both Christian and Hindu communities. Developing subversive religious symbols and performances creates a new sacred space within the community in the absence of one. They can access and control this sacred space, while at the same time challenge the norms and structures that excluded them in first place. What becomes apparently clear in these transactions is the malleability of religious space, which is created and infused with specific meaning in order to serve a particular purpose. The direct material impact cannot be undermined. Various accounts from the Paraiyar community, both at the individual and community level points to the fact that their engaged worldview provides them with the impetus to shape the world around them. So even the replication of hierarchy needs to be seen in this light. It is not passive submission, but active participation that provides them with self-conceptualized identity. Again, narrow religious definitions fail to account for such subversive practices. Paraiyars have clearly shown that they can operate with more than one worldview and that they can belong to more than one religious meaning-making system without internal dissonance. Observing the Paraiyar community in all its complexity, one is reminded of the need to go beyond narrow perceptions of religion and workings of religious spaces in order to develop a synergetic view of religion that takes into account all of these competing and conflicting processes.

Gleaning beyond the Paraiyars

Having elucidated the complex yet creative life of Paraiyars, we now turn our attention to broader understandings of 'lived religion'. For this purpose,

I shall briefly draw upon three works from different contexts in order to accentuate the story of the Thulasigramam Paraiyar Christians. In the process we shall observe the tension between the socio-anthropological method of studying religion, which tries to dissolve overarching categories, and the sociological approach, which operates from an *a priori* definition of religion. The following discussion highlights the need to reconcile both of these theoretical processes.

The Borneo Kadazan Christians

Elizabeth Koepping in her ethnographic work *Food, Friends and Funerals* focuses on the lives of Borneo Kadazan Christian communities, living beside Muslims in the same community. As with the Paraiyar worldview, Koepping suggests that irrespective of their religious belonging the Borneo villagers operate with the *adat*, an all-embracing frame of reference and meaning-making system for their lives within the local community.[8] The *adat* provides the villagers with an understanding of the living, the dead and the spirits. Additionally, it also bestows mundane life, like growing rice, human interrelationship and commensality, with a significant role in their daily lives. Even though these villagers are Christians, they operate within this worldview because the place they live demands such an observance. According to one of the villagers, following the *adat* was not a matter of choice, as living on the lands compelled him to observe these local village practices which go beyond any singular religious belonging. This worldview also suggests that there is a spiritual facet to all things mundane; hence, the spiritual force or *tatod* should be respected. They, in turn, facilitate the social order of the community. In other words, they were able to conceive their own identity primarily by belonging to their particular place. This insight resonates with the self-perception of Paraiyars, who consequently also facilitate their own individual and communal identities. The behaviour of individuals and the community has a direct impact on the well-being of the village. Koepping describes the fact that many Anglicans in the village continue to believe in the power of the *adat* and Christianity, providing them with 'a view which was coherent, had meaning and made logical sense'.[9] Reflecting on the interaction between

Christianity and the local religion in Kadazan villages, Koepping observes that they 'maintain identity, absorb comprehensible aspects of a new way as well as refine the old way over time'.[10]

Observing the Holy Spirit healing services in the Anglican churches, Koepping suggests that the sheer variety and perceptions in existence were a testimony to the localized view of these rituals.[11] There is clear evidence of how Islamic symbols, such as the bright light and white cloth of the Muslim Seer and the 'morally neutral state', referred to as 'Kadazan coolness', can be found in the experience of receiving the Holy Spirit among Anglican Christians in this region. Thus, the Anglican Christians in Kadazan interpret their own Holy Spirit healing services through the prism of village practice which itself has Islamic elements.

Moreover, the Kadazan villagers also use their Christian identity to express their ethnic and cultural identities. However, the Christians' conversion to Anglicanism did not occur without conflict. When Christianity severed the 'sacred' and the 'secular', the Kadazans had difficulty in accepting this process, as they had a clear knowledge of the less visible world ordering their social and communal relationships. The early conversion process breached the integrity of the community, but as Koppeing later on observes, they were able to reconcile these different frames by blurring the boundaries and implicitly referring to other frames of worldview.[12] While critiquing the limitations of a syncretic view that concretizes various strands, Koepping observes,

> fluidity in applying ideas and practices does not derive from confused identity, but clear ties to locality and shared relations to the inherited visible and less visible world which makes one 'holy' whole with the reciprocal obligations and demeanour. Confusion is relevant more for those outsiders who believe in boxed religions. When village clusters still maintained internal authority and external alliances, the skill, power and certain healing and cleaning rites of Islam were integrated into costal Borneo locality, identity and praxis affecting adat, Islam and Muslim influenced Christians . . . whether following Christian or Muslim *agama* common to all villagers are *adat* based values of reciprocation and social balance and rejection of anger, shamming and bragging.[13]

The Sabah residents from the Christian and Muslim religious groups effectively use their own channels to practise *ilmu,* a local Muslim belief in the capacity to access and harness hidden power through Muslim Seers and koranic texts. On the pretext of being residents of Sabah, the local Christians use their own scriptures in the fashion of *ilmu* for healing. Koepping observes that this practice of the 'healing and harnessing of *ilmu* may seem to be syncretic, yet some of the residents have expressed their ability to keep the various streams separate in their minds, using them in combination depending upon the situation.[14] The pragmatic use of belief among Paraiyar Christians underlines these experiences. From the Paraiyar perspective, the concept of a non-dualistic worldview and multi-layerity are central to their identity, whether they live in Borneo or Thulasigramam. Social efficacy plays a crucial role in directing their actions and their beliefs. As demonstrated in both contexts, the social locatedness and communal belonging have significant bearing on the construction of religious worldviews. This process highlights the centrality of human agency without which 'religion' as a system would be non-existent. Moreover, from these observations, religion cannot be reduced to some sections of human society but needs to be applied to society in its totality. These observations from the context of Borneo and Thulasigramam villagers living within multiple frameworks of reference and worldviews clearly exhibits the central notion that 'lived' religion is beyond narrow understandings of religion. It suggests the complex yet pragmatic approach of a synergetic view of religion as lived in the presence of multiple worldviews and religious belonging.

Religion in English everyday life

Timothy Jenkins begins his ethnographic account of life in the English parish of Comberton in Cambridgeshire with a broad understanding of religion that has a significant role in shaping the entire local society.[15] As he explains,

> religion, without seeking to absorb other institutions, is peculiarly concerned with the aspiration to be human in a particular form and therefore with living satisfactory and responsible lives, both singular and in common, reflectively and actively.[16]

Observing the everyday life of the parish, Jenkins offers an insight into 'religion' that reflects the social organization of the village itself. Jenkins presents the various competing structures within the community and notions concerning the village and the villagers, as well as the ideas about 'the church', 'the clergy' and 'the congregation'. In this context, the church functions as a symbol of village identity and through its services makes the community formation possible. He also records the relationship between and within these categories and how they shape the culture of the village life itself.[17] This symbiotic relationship between the church and the village was also clearly articulated through the lives of Paraiyar Christians. The church as a symbol gave Paraiyars an identity that they were able to build upon and in so doing gain a new social status that was otherwise denied to them. These observations underline the fact that religious institutions not only provide spiritual care but also pave the way for social reordering.

Following his account Jenkins interestingly offers a description of the annual Whit Walk procession in Kingswood.[18] This annual event draws people from all Christian denominations, walks of life and members from the Guides, Scouts and Boys Brigade as well as the Salvation Army. The procession features a tableau depicting the life of Jesus Christ and the miracles associated with him. Jenkins argues that the Whit Walk cannot be simply taken as a Sunday school procession but rather as 'an assertion of local identity: the declaration of a kind of person, of a particular history and of a territory'.[19] Participation in this event goes beyond church membership and reflects the local lived expression of religion. Yet, Jenkins reminds his reader that the Whit Walk participants exhibit a variety of beliefs and motivations, 'different perspectives that do not necessarily add up into a coherent picture'.[20] The procession demonstrates how 'men and women, notables and congregations, marchers and spectators, respectable and feckless' generate multiplicity of voices.[21]

Jenkins also traces the evolution of the Whit Walk as a collective expression of respectability through participation. As mentioned earlier in the study of the Palm Sunday procession in Thulasigramam, the Whit Walk echoes the social processes in which the community proudly displays its associations. In both these events, the local identity is affirmed with a twist, only to reclaim a new identity, thereby regaining a new status and legitimizing a new community. In both processions, the intentions of the individuals, organizers and institutions are diverse, yet as a collective celebration they are able to achieve far beyond the original purpose of these events.[22] Jenkins captures the means by which a religious festival becomes the site for expressing a variety of social aspirations. In his own words, Jenkins observes,

> in the Whit Walk, religious institutions (or values, as we might prefer to call them) are present, for conversion and membership are clearly expressed. Membership of such voluntary organisations has a quasi-legal status, for it concerns individuals and collective rights. Moral values and orderings are displayed in a complete and convincing way; as are economic values, conceptions and status. Social morphology is exhibited, for everything that happens presupposes the longer-term existence of both families and wider groupings and the aesthetic element is present in the dramatic display, the banners paraded and the performance of the bands. In short, in the Whit Walk, we are dealing with the totality of a local society.[23]

Religious expression in Comberton and Thulasigramam cannot be considered wholly as something concerned with the other worldly but rather needs to be seen as an effective means to shape social reality. Through ritual acts such as the Whit Walk and Palm Sunday processions, the interwoven nature of religious belief and the lived reality of the local community come to the fore. The community generates its self-perception from its religious belonging and, in turn, the Church provides the social and ritual space which is utilized by the community to achieve its own ends.

The Famished Road

The Booker Prize winning novel *The Famished Road*[24] by Ben Okri captures the religious fervour of Africa through the characters of living and dead spirits, particularly through the eyes of Azaro, the *Abiku* or spirit-child. The theologian Mabiala Justin-Robert Kenzo highlights the religious themes within the novel particularly resonant in the African context.[25] Kenzo argues that *The Famished Road* 'represents religion as a construct' in which 'human actors take various elements they find from a variety of sources, some endogenous and others exogenous to Africa, in order to construct their own religious identity'.[26] As a work of 'magical realism', Okri's novel creates a parallel universe that draws together 'the modern worldview, with its empirical outlook, and the African worldview'.[27] This constructed worldview presents the supernatural as part of the ordinary life of people. The detailed description of the parallel universe fully encapsulates the African lived reality. It is not just magical but also a practical reflection of reality. Joining with other critics Kenzo suggests that the worldview present in *The Famished Road* 'is deeply grounded in and thoroughly imbued with the existential reality of Africa'.[28] Kenzo summarizes this worldview as 'a single coherent world in which the spiritual dimension of life is intrinsically linked to the physical which it shapes'.[29] Similarly, the visible and less visible world of Paraiayars resemble this coexistence of the spiritual and material world so central to African religious experience. The universe captured in *The Famished Road*, 'though conceptually coherent, is not existentially harmonious, but cacophonic'.[30] According to Kenzo, there are also undertones of post-coloniality in which an African worldview grounded and imagined within the matrix of African traditional experiences is striving to break free of the colonial theoretical predicaments.[31] Reflecting on the religious overtones of *The Famished Road* Kenzo writes,

> Okri's fictive universe is profoundly religious. In it one constantly hears about 'obscure prophesies', 'sacrifices', 'burnt offerings of oils and yams and palm-nuts', 'prayers', 'libations', 'chants', 'secret shrines', 'priests', 'priestesses', 'innumerable gods', 'feathered gods', 'the God of the Road', and so on. As a matter of fact, religious ceremonies with their rites and rituals remain daily occurrences within this universe. Remarkably, though, no one religious tradition emerges as the one established religion. Rather religion is dissipated over all other social practices, which it permeates; and religious identity is a construct in a state of flux.[32]

This dynamic and gathered understanding of religion is crucial not only for African traditions, in which 'the religion dissipated over all other social practices', but is also found among Kadazan Christians, Paraiyars and English village life. Furthermore, through its numerous references to Islamic scripture and biblical narratives, *The Famished Road* points to a synergetic view of religious beliefs. A worldview which is not conflated or collapsed to create something new, but rather in which 'each belief is treated with respect and is given equal weight as an interpretative grid for life's riddles'.[33] Among many points that arises from this analysis of *The Famished Road*, Kenzo highlights how Okri

> shows that the religion that plays a role in Africa is not a ready-made package that is passed on from one generation to the next (or from one

> context to the other). Rather, religion in Africa is most likely to be a hybrid construct. Africans, as any other people for that matter, are not passively shaped by their cultures. Instead, they skilfully and creatively construct their identity borrowing insights from whatever resources they have available to them.[34]

The Famished Road narrates African religious traditions as viable options within other religious traditions, not in competition but in collaboration. Most importantly, the novel's theme of 'human creativity, industry, and determination' as the source of liberation and transformation from a predetermined existence is replicated not just in Africa but also in remote corners of Borneo, South India and Cambridgeshire.

Lived religion: A synergetic view

> There are times in life when the question of knowing if one can think differently than one thinks, and perceive differently than one sees, is absolutely necessary if one is to go on looking and reflecting at all.[35]

The need to 'think differently' is pertinent in our discussion of the contextual portrayal of lived religion. Earlier, we surveyed wide-ranging plausible perspectives of what constitutes and shapes religious belonging. However, examining complex discursive processes among Paraiyars and the accounts of Koepping, Jenkins and Okri, we gather that religion not only provides multi-layered belief systems but also comes to shape self-perception, designate social status and provide numerous ways in which communal existence is negotiated. Paraiyars in particular are able to develop their individual and collective identity by utilizing various means available to them through their religious belonging, be it Christian or Paraiyar. Moreover, the conceptualization of an engaged worldview prevalent among the discussed communities shows that they are happy to live within multiple worldviews. Lived religion in the above-mentioned contexts is understood as moving beyond the functional and substantial levels and is thus woven into the fabric of individual and social life. Hence, any narrow understanding of religion, without contextual references fails to capture the reality of religious belonging.

Given the discussion of worldview and religion as presented in this book, it would perhaps be reasonable to term the religious phenomena as 'religious syncretism' or even 'religious hybridization'. Surveys on the subject of religious syncretism like those of Eric Maroney,[36] Birgit Meyer,[37] Jim Kiernan[38] and David Mosse[39] elaborate on the ways in which different religious forms are synthesized through absorption and accommodation. These authors themselves explain that there are limitations to the syncretic approach to religion in that it fails to take into account historical encounters, agency and the role of religious authority.[40] Further, the works of Daniel Goh[41] and Pattana Kitiarsa[42] on the subject of religious hybridization in Chinese Religion and Thai Buddhism demonstrate the inadequacy of syncretism and argue for the need to approach the dynamic movements within religion through the prism of 'hybridity'. Within post-colonial studies, the concept of cultural hybridity, as articulated by Mikhail Bakhtin and Homi Bhabha, has gained significant currency and has been effectively used to study various developments within religion.[43] Even though 'hybridity' as a theoretical concept critiques essentialism, as Ella Shoat observes, 'as a descriptive catchall term, hybridity per se fails to discriminate between diverse modalities of hybridity, for example, forced assimilation, internalised self-rejection, political co-option, social conformism, cultural mimicry, and creative transcendence'.[44] Furthermore, it problematically assumes that when two or more cultural systems are combined or selectively mixed, it produces a third space which carries the best or the worst of both worlds. But in many cases this is simply not true as people do not necessarily and consciously mix worldview and religious beliefs to produce something new, but rather they comfortably live with multiple belongings. These belongings may be ruptured and fissured, but there within lived religion is found to be dynamic and fluid. As Clarke suggests, religions 'are susceptible to continuously being crafted into meaning-giving and meaning-making symbolic dwelling places' and therefore cannot be considered to be homogeneous and finished products.[45] As argued throughout this book, lived religion is not simply multiculturalism, inter-religious dialogue or a shallow tolerance of multiple religious worldviews, but is constructed from various religious and social sources through contestation and creative interplay. Moving beyond the syncretic and hybrid theories of religion, I suggest that a synergetic view may be more fruitful.

Synergy simply means a collective engagement of individuals which produces a significant effect at the end.[46] It can also be defined as a 'co-operative effects', literally the effects produced by things that 'operate together' particularly when it produces a significant impact. Explaining this term in the context of life sciences Peter Corning argues that

> a synergy perspective suggests a paradigm that explicitly focuses on both wholes and parts, and on the interactions that occur among the parts, between parts and wholes and between wholes at various 'levels' of interaction and causation.[47]

Furthermore, synergy also implies the ability of individuals or communities to act collaboratively in order to produce meaningful and relevant results. Viewing religion from this perspective provides interesting insights.

Paraiyar Christians and other religious adherents discussed in this book have shown that the texture of their life is dynamic and creative. Such a lived religious reality thrives on the co-operative efforts of individuals and the collective. Religion thus elucidates and transcends narrow preoccupations, thereby encompassing human life in its entirety. Such an understanding may alarm some in asserting that everything in human life is 'religious'; however, a synergetic perspective simply implies a symbiotic relationship between the part and the whole of lived religious expression. The focus then is on the centrality of human agency and not on supernatural, otherworldly occurrences or objects. As amply demonstrated by Paraiyars and elsewhere, 'religion' as a system would be non-existent, or at least socially irrelevant, without human agency and creativity. However, I am not suggesting that religion is simply a figment of human imagination or invention, but that the less visible world is experienced and shaped by human beings within the visible world. As illustrated by the Paraiyar experience, the notions of the less visible primarily stems from their tangible conflict-ridden daily existence, thus making the supernatural part of the ordinary. Because of the grounded nature of their worldview, it consequently provides space for the formation of dynamic relationships among individuals, communities and deities. Hence religion does not preoccupy itself only with the sacred but also takes a significant interest in the social as well. The preceding observations reiterate the fact that religion comes not pre-packaged, as if somehow void of human creativity and industry. As such, lived religion cannot be restricted to religious institutions and dogmas, but transcends them through experiential practice. In this framework, religion shapes communal and individual identity, thereby reforming the cultural caste norm of being 'Outcaste' Paraiyars, even if only religiously expressed.

Lived religion, as we have gleaned from this work, presents itself as malleable, decentralized and unmediated, providing space for negotiation and subversion within a community. Religious symbols, rituals and practices are utilized to unsettle, redraw and challenge the existing cognitive and social boundaries. We have seen how religious belonging is employed to loosen dominant ideological predicaments, be they colonial, caste or institutional structures. In the various contexts described in this book, lives are lived within the matrix of religion and therein expressed. Therefore, multiple religious reference points are not necessarily an anomaly but rather a confluence of worldviews, giving forth a polyphonic, highly functional and contextually relevant religious experience. A synergetic view of religion affirms that religious belonging is multi-layered, not through the conflation or collapsing of religious beliefs, but rather as the consequence of dynamically negotiated daily life.

The liminality of simultaneously being a Paraiyar and a Christian was evident throughout the experiences gained in Thulasigramam, resonating with my own personal encounter. It was also a journey into the community of Paraiyar Christians living at the village's edge, excluded and alienated, but still able to find meaning due to their religious belonging. This research, which began as a quest to understand my own roots and to grasp the texture of life lived in the margins, both at societal and religious levels, has brought to the surface the fact that it is only in such places that lived religion abounds.

Notes

Preface

1 S. Clarke, *Dalits and Christianity: Subaltern Religion and Liberation Theology in India*, Delhi: Oxford University Press, 1998, p. 62.

2 T. Jenkins, *Religion in English Everyday Life: An Ethnographic Approach*, Oxford: Berghahn Books, 1999, pp. 14, 36. I use the term 'religion' not in its narrow institutional sense but as Jenkins points out, 'religion' as a process that functions as a window into the complex social life of people and their aspirations to be human in a society, both individually and communally, which is relevant in the context of studying Paraiyar Christians in Thulasigramam.

3 Thulasigramam, a pseudonym for the south Indian village which was the focus of this research.

Chapter 1

1 The concept of 'Hindu' or 'Hinduism' is highly contested because it is not in the same mould as other 'World Religions'. It rather refers to a wide variety of theology, mythology, cultic practices and philosophies spread across India. For want of a better term, I will be using Hinduism referring to religious practices in India. Moreover, some would argue that caste system as an expression of the *karmic* theory is not historically viable. But as the complexity of defining Hinduism illustrates, there could be differing opinions on this issues. For more on this debates see J. L. Brockington, *The Sacred Thread: Hinduism in its Continuity and Diversity*, Edinburgh: Edinburgh University Press, 1981 and J. Lipner, *Hindus: Their Religious Beliefs and Practices*, London: Routledge, 1994.

2 U. Sharma, *Caste*, Buckingham: Open University Press, 1999, p. 5.

3 M. Milner, *Status and Sacredness: A general Theory of Status Relations and An Analysis of Indian Culture*, New York: Oxford University Press, 1994, p. 46.

4 U. Sharma, *Caste*, Buckingham: Open University Press, 1999, p. 35.

5 M. Milner, *Status and Sacredness: A general Theory of Status Relations and An Analysis of Indian Culture*, New York: Oxford University Press, 1994, p. 50.

6 U. Sharma, *Caste*, Buckingham: Open University Press, 1999, p. 36.

7 M. Milner, *Status and Sacredness: A general Theory of Status Relations and An Analysis of Indian Culture*, New York: Oxford University Press, 1994, p. 48.

8 Ibid., p. 46.

9 O. Mendelsohn and M. Vicziany, *The Untouchables: Subordination, Poverty and the State in Modern India*, Cambridge: Cambridge University Press, 1998, p. 7.

10 R. Deliege, *The Untouchables of India*, Oxford: Berg Publishers, 1999b, pp. 27–50. Deliege provides an extensive analysis of caste system, particularly examining the works of L. Dumont (*Homo Hierarchicus: The Caste System and its Implications*, Chicago, IL: University of Chicago Press, 1980), Berreman (*Hindus of the Himalyas: Ethnography and Change*, Berkeley, CA: University of California Press, 1963), M. Moffatt (*An Untouchable Community in South India: Structure and Consensus*, Princeton, N J: Princeton University Press, 1979) and A. Beteille (*Caste, Class and Power*, New Delhi: Oxford, 2002). See also J. C. Webster, *The Dalit Christians: A History*, Delhi: ISPCK, 1992, pp. 2–5. Michael in his book traces the sociocultural and political history of Dalits while explaining the origin of caste through Varna system and untouchability, *Introduction*, in S. M. Michael (ed.), *Dalits in Modern India*, New Delhi: Vistaar Publications, 1999. And also Shriram, *The Fourfold Hierarchy*, in S. M. Michael (ed.), *Dalits in Modern India*, p. 50.

11 D. R. Nagaraj, *Flaming Feet*, Bangalore: South Forum Press, 1993, p. 6.

12 M. N. Srinivas, *Social Change in Modern India*, Madras: Allied Publishers, 1966, p. 31.

13 'Harijan' is a term coined by M. K. Gandhi, meaning 'children of God' referring to the children of temple prostitutes, which was considered patronizing and degrading by the Dalit leaders.

14 J. Massey, *Down Trodden*, Geneva: WCC, 1997a, p. 3.

15 J. Massey (ed.), *Dalit Solidarity*, Delhi: ISPCK, 1995, pp. 9–14.

16 M. E. Prabhakar, *The Search for a Dalit Theology*, in A. P. Nirmal (ed.), *Reader in Dalit Theology*, Madras: Gurukul, 1991, p. 45.

17 www.censusindia.net, for a detailed statistics on Dalit Population in India see Sukhadeo Thorat, *Dalits in India*, New Delhi: SAGE, 2009.

18 S. K. Thorat and R. S. Deshpande, *Caste System and Economic Inequality: Economic Theory and Evidence*, in G. Shah (ed.), *Dalit Identity and Politics*, New Delhi: SAGE Publications, 2001, pp. 57–70.

19 *Broken People*, New York: Human Rights Watch, 1999. This book describes in detail the violence meted out to the Dalits irrespective of their religion over a period of past 50 years. It highlights the sexual abuse and physical violence and the innumerable murders that happened in the Dalit communities.

20 S. Paswan (ed.), *Encyclopaedia of Dalits in India; General Study*, vol. I, Delhi: Kalpaz Publications, 2002, p. 296.

21 K. R. Narayanan, 'The President Speaks' in *National Council of Churches Review*, 2000, 120(3): 243–55.

22 S. M. Michael, *Introduction*, in S. M. Michael (ed.), *Dalits in Modern India*, pp. 12–32.

23 S. M. Michael, *Dalit Encounter with Christianity: Change and Continuity*, in R. Robinson and J. M. Kujur (eds), *Margins of Faith: Dalits and Tribal Christianity in India*, New Delhi: SAGE Publications, 2010, p. 52.

24 M. Azariah, *A Priest's Search for Dalit Theology*, Delhi: ISCPK, 2000, p. 28.

25 S. Paswan (ed.), *Encyclopaedia of Dalits in India; General Study*, vol. I, Delhi: Kalpaz Publications, 2002, p. 303.

26 The presence and effect of the caste system within the South Indian churches and the current experience of Dalit Christians will be dealt in the following chapter.

27 M. E. Prabhakar, *Christology in Dalit Perspective*, p. 403, and D. Monikaraj, *Mission, Evangelism, and Conversion*, p. 458, in V. Devasahayam (ed.), *Frontiers of Dalit Theology*, Delhi: ISPCK/Gurukul, 1997.

28 V. Devasahayam explains in detail in *Pollution, Poverty and Powerlessness–A Dalit Perspective*, pp. 20–1 and also K. Wilson in *Towards a Humane Culture*, in A. P. Nirmal (ed.), *A Reader in Dalit Theology*, Madras: Gurukul, 1991, pp. 152–3.

29 M. Azariah, *A Priest's Search for Dalit Theology*, Delhi: ISCPK, 2000, pp. 28–9.

30 D. Monikaraj, *Mission, Evangelism and Conversion*, in V. Devasahayam (ed.), *Frontiers of Dalit Theology*, p. 458.

31 J. Massey and S. Shimray (eds), *Dalit-Tribal Theological Interface: Current Trends in Subaltern Theologies*, New Delhi: TSC/WSC, 2007. This anthology provides a good foundation on Dalit Theology.

32 A. P. Nirmal, *Towards a Christian Dalit Theology*, in R. S. Sugirtharajah (ed.), *Frontiers in Asian Christian Theology*, New York: Orbis Books, 1994, p. 31.

33 According to 2001 India Census, Paraiyars number about 9 million in Tamil Nadu alone. www.censusindia.gov.in/Tables_Published/SCST/dh_sc_tamilnadu.pdf. Moreover, the generic term *adi-dravida* referring to untouchables in the census could also mean Paraiyars and other untouchable castes; in that case, the number of Paraiyars will be significantly higher.

34 R. Deliege, *The Untouchables of India*, Oxford: Berg Publishers, 1999b, p. 74; also see Sri John, *Psychoanalysis of Myths in Dalit (Paraiyar) Culture*, in J. Massey and S. Lourdunathan (eds). *Breaking Theoretical Grounds for Dalit Studies*, New Delhi: Centre for Dalit/Subaltern Studies, 2006, pp. 119–33.

35 R. Deliege, *The Untouchables of India*, Oxford: Berg Publishers, 1999b, pp. 74–5.

36 R. Deliege, *The Untouchables of India*, Oxford: Berg Publishers, 1999b, p. 75. He provides an extended discussion on Paraiyar origin myth in the chapter titled 'Untouchable Myths of Origin'.

37 S. Clarke, *Dalits and Christianity*, Delhi: Oxford University Press, 1998, p. 66.

38 S. Clarke, *Dalits and Christianity*, Delhi: Oxford University Press, 1998, p. 67, also see C. Joe Arun, 'From stigma to self-assertion: Paraiyars and the symbolism of the parai drum', *Contributions to Indian Sociology*, 2007; 41; 81, and R. Deliege, *The Untouchables of India*, Oxford: Berg Publishers, 1999b, p. 25.

39 M. Bergunder, 'Contested Past: Anti-Brahmanical and Hindu Nationalist Reconstructions of Indian Prehistory', *Historiographia Linguistica*, 2004, xxxi(1): 68.

40 A. Ayrookuzhiel, *Essays on Dalits, Religion and Liberation*, Bangalore: ATC, 2006, p. 17.

41 K. Ilaiah, *Why I am not a Hindu: A Sudra Critique of Hindutva Philosophy, Culture, and Political Economy*, Calcutta: Samya, 1996, pp. 71–101. Here in this work, Kancha Ilaiah provides the similarity between various Dalit communities in its religious and cultural worldviews that transcends the diversity of the Indian subcontinent. He also discusses in detail the conception of deities in the Hindu and Dalit philosophical worldview. For a more traditional understating of Hindu Worldview, see J. Lipner, *Hindus: Their Religious Beliefs and Practices*, London: Routledge, 1994.

42 J. N. Mohanty, *Classical Indian Philosophy*, Oxford: Rowman & Littlefield Publishers Inc., 2000 and R. King, *Indian Philosophy*, Washington: Georgetown University Press, 1999. Both these works provide a good overview on the influence of Vedic corpus on other Indian philosophical writings.

43 *The Laws of Manu*, translated by G. Buhler, Oxford: Clarendon Press, 1886. Manu describes the creation of four varnas as following in the first chapter, '1.87 . . . in order to protect this universe He, the most resplendent one, assigned separate (duties and) occupations to those who sprang from his mouth, arms, thighs, and feet.

1.88. To Brahmanas he assigned teaching and studying (the Veda), sacrificing for their own benefit and for others, giving and accepting (of alms).

1.89. The Kshatriya he commanded to protect the people, to bestow gifts, to offer sacrifices, to study (the Veda), and to abstain from attaching himself to sensual pleasures;

1.90. The Vaisya to tend cattle, to bestow gifts, to offer sacrifices, to study (the Veda), to trade, to lend money, and to cultivate land.

1.91. One occupation only the lord prescribed to the Sudra, to serve meekly even these (other) three castes.

1.92. Man is stated to be purer above the navel (than below); hence the Self-existent (Svayambhu) has declared the purest (part) of him (to be) his mouth.

1.93. As the Brahmana sprang from (Brahman's) mouth, as he was the first-born, and as he possesses the Veda, he is by right the lord of this whole creation'.

44 A. Ramaiah, *The Dalit Issue: A Hindu Perspective* in J. Massey (ed.), *Indigenous People: Dalits*, Delhi: ISPCK, 1994, pp. 6, 80–1, also see the following selection from *The Laws of Manu*, translated by G. Buhler,

'8.270. A once born man a Sudra, who insults a twice born man with gross invective, shall have his tongue cut out, for he is of low origin.

8.271. If he mentions the names and castes of the twice-born contumely, an iron nail, ten fingers long, shall be thrust red hot into his mouth.

8.272. If he arrogantly teaches brahmanas their duty, the king shall cause hot oil to be poured into his mouth and into his hears.

8.281. A low caste man who tries to place himself on the same seat with a man of a high caste shall be branded on his hip and be banished, or (the king) shall cause his buttock to be gashed.

9.334. But to serve brahmanas who are learned in the Vedas, householders, and famous for virtue is the highest duty of a Sudra, which leads to beatitude.

11.85. By his origin alone a brahmanas is a deity even for the gods, and his teaching is authoritative for men, because the Veda is the foundation for that'.

45 *The Laws of Manu*, translated by G. Buhler, 2.172.

46 A. Ramaiah, *The Dalit Issue: A Hindu Perspective*, in J. Massey (ed.), *Indigenous People: Dalits*, Delhi: ISPCK, 1994, p. 8.

47 R. Nath, *Why I Am Not a Hindu,* Patna: Bihar Rationalist Society, 1993. In this brief booklet he says, 'The system of *varnashramdharma* is upheld by popular Hindu epics like *Ramayana*, *Mahabharata* and *Bhagvat-Gita*. In *Ramayana*, for example, Ram kills Shambuka simply because he was performing *tapasya* (ascetic exercises) which he was not supposed to do as he was a *Shudra* by

birth. Similarly, in *Mahabharata*, Dronacharya refuses to teach archery to Eklavya, because he was not a *Kshatriya* by birth. When Eklavya, treating Drona as his notional guru, learns archery on his own, Drona makes him cut his right thumb as *gurudakshina* (gift for the teacher) so that he may not become a better archer than his favorite *Kshatriya* student Arjuna. *Bhagvat-Gita*, too, favors *varna-vyavastha*. When Arjuna refuses to fight, one of his main worries was that the war would lead to the birth of *varna-sankaras* or offspring from intermixing of different *varnas* and the consequent "downfall" of the family'.

48 M. K. Gandhi, *Hindu Dharma,* New Delhi: Orient Paperbacks, 1978, p. 9.

49 Ibid., p. 57.

50 A. Sharma, 'Sankara's Life and Works as a source for a Hermeneutics of Human rights', in B. J. Malkovsky (ed.), *New Perspectives on Advaita Vedanta*, Leiden: Brill, 2000, p. 109. In this essay, the author tries to bring in a new perspective in reading Sankara, but the incidents that he quotes were so isolated that it can't be taken as the essence of his philosophy.

51 C. Ram-Prasad, *Knowledge and Liberation in Classical Indian Thought,* New York: Palgrave, 2001, p. 163.

52 C. Ram-Prasad, *Advaita Epistemology and Metaphysics*, London: Routledge Curzon, 2002, p. 6.

53 C. Ram-Prasad, *Knowledge and Liberation in Classical Indian Thought,* New York: Palgrave, 2001, pp. 173, 215.

54 V. A. George, *Self-Realization 'Brahmaanubhava': The Advaitic Perspective of Sankara,* Washington: The Council for Research in Values and Philosophy, 2001, p. 28.

55 Ibid., p. 38.

56 Ibid., p. 41.

57 Ibid., p. 51.

58 J. T. Appavoo, *Dalit Religion*, in J. Massey (ed.), *Indigenous People: Dalits,* New Delhi: ISPCK, 1994, pp. 112–13 and A. Ayrookuzhiel, *Essays on Dalits, Religion and Liberation,* p. 7ff.

59 S. Clarke, *Dalits and Christianity: Subaltern Religion and Liberation Theology in India*, Delhi: Oxford University Press, 1998, p. 72.

60 J. C. B. Webster, *Religion and Dalit Liberation*, New Delhi: Manohar, 2002, p. 25.

61 K. S. Muthu, *Dalit Deities*, Madurai: the Dalit Resource Centre, 2005, p. 21.

62 J. T. Appavoo, *Dalit Religion*, in J. Massey (ed.), *Indigenous People: Dalits*, p. 116.

63 Ibid., p. 118.

64 Ibid., p. 120.

65 Ibid., p. 117.

66 F. Wilfred, *The Sling of Utopia*, Delhi: ISPCK, 2005, p. 141. He uses the term 'subaltern' as an inclusive term to refer to the marginalized groups under Hindu dominant worldview.

67 Ibid., p. 142.

68 Ibid., p. 144.

69 D. R. Nagaraj, *Flaming Feet*, Bangalore: South Forum Press, 1993, p. 55.

70 S. Clarke, *Dalits and Christianity*, Delhi: Oxford University Press,1998 , p. 101.

71 R. Deliege, 'Replication and Consensus: Untouchability, Caste and Ideology in India', *Man*, 1992, 27(1): 155–73.

72 Joe C. Arun, 'From stigma to self-assertion: Paraiyars and the symbolism of the parai drum', p. 84. R. Deliege records a similar observation in his work, 'Untouchability and Catholicism, the Case of the Paraiyars in South India', *Comparative Studies of South Asia, Africa and the Middle East*, 1998, XVIII(1): 32.

73 *Reddyars* were the former warrior caste, who took up agriculture and migrated to Tamil Nadu from Andhra Pradesh, a South Indian state. They are the major landowners in Thulasigramam and act as the dominant caste. In the absence of Brahmins (the 'high caste' Hindus) in the village, Reddyars assume the place of the 'local high caste' in the village hierarchy.

74 See Joe. C. Arun, 'From stigma to self-assertion: Paraiyars and the symbolism of the parai drum' and Robert Deliege, 'Replication and Consensus: Untouchability, Caste and Ideology in India'.

75 *Arunthathiers* are the community that works with leather products and supposedly migrated from Andhra Pradesh.

76 Initial hiccups in my research were prevalent, particularly related with conducting interviews, as I had been trained to tape record and take notes during my conversations. But to my dismay, whenever I took out my digital recorder, people immediately stopped talking. So I had to adapt to the situation by abandoning the digital recorder path and depend on my memory to remember the unstructured and often random conversations. Most of the insights quoted in this volume were part of longer conversations with the said individuals that happened over the period of my stay in the village and other parts are retrospectively recollected summaries, reconstructed as a narrative. The challenge for me, as for any researcher, was to remember the issues they raised in their previous conversations and invite them to reflect further.

Sometimes, such an approach had a positive response and at other times I was disappointed by their unwillingness to expand upon earlier comments. Most importantly, many of the conversations took place while they were working near their houses or during walks to the fields or forests. Because of such situations, it was hard to carry a notebook along to note down my conversations and thus I had to record them when I could. Hence, it is possible, that my accounts are not a perfectly accurate word-for-word rendering of the conversations, but recorded in my own words, giving room for my thoughts. Thus the research draws from random notes taken every day during my stay in the village and also from cumulative recollection of conversations as remembered by me later during the week. The longest conversation on any given topic did lasted no longer than thirty minutes, and although some were shorter, they were the continuation of a broken narrative. Therefore, the challenge was to review my notes and extracts, and to clarify the details, which may otherwise have been unclear at a later date. Hence, the quotes and conversations in this book are not provided with a specific date and time. It has to be mentioned that my own social and theological thinking did impact my recording of the events and conversations in the field, about which I shall reflect later.

77 C. A. Davies, *Reflexive Ethnography*, London: Routledge, 1999, pp. 67–76 and H. F. Walcott, *Writing up Qualitative Research*, Thousand Oaks: SAGE Publications, 2001, p. 73.

78 P. Atkinson, *The Ethnographic Imagination: Textual Construction of Reality*, London: Routledge, 1990, pp. 129–55.

79 H. F. Walcott, *Writing up Qualitative Research*, Thousand Oaks: SAGE Publications, 2001, pp. 8–10, 19.

80 R. Hertz, *Introduction: Reflexivity and Voice*, in R. Hertz (ed.), *Reflexivity and Voice*, London: SAGE Publications, 1997, p. xii.

81 C. A. Davies, *Reflexive Ethnography*, London: Routledge, 1999, p. 6.

82 E. Koepping, *Food, Friends and Funerals*, Munster: LIT, 2008, p. 11, while discussing the complexity of the issue of 'belonging' in a research context, she explains the ambiguity of insider–outsider debate in anthropological research. See also T. Jenkins, *Religion in English Everyday Life: An Ethnographic Approach*, pp. 132, 216.

83 I. Baszanger and N. Dodier, *Ethnography: Relating the Part to the Whole*, in D. Silverman (ed.), *Qualitative Research: Theory, Method and Practice*, London: SAGE Publications, 1997, pp. 9–10, C. Geertz also argues for a similar understating in his book, *Local Knowledge*, New York: Basic Books, 2000b, p. 59.

84 J. Miller and B. Glassner, *The 'Inside' and the 'Outside': Finding Realities in Interviews*, in D. Silverman (ed.), *Qualitative Research: Theory, Method and Practice*, London: Sage, 1997, p. 111.

85 R. Deliege, *The World of the 'Untouchables': Paraiyars of Tamil Nadu*, translated by D. Phillips, Delhi: Oxford University Press, 1997, and 'Replication and Consensus: Untouchability, Caste and Ideology in India', in *Man*, 1992, 27(1): 155–73.

86 D. Mosse, 'Idioms of Subordination and styles of protest among Christian and Hindu Harijan Castes in Tamil Nadu' in *Contributions to Indian Sociology*, 1994, 28(1): 67–106, and 'The Politics of Religious Synthesis', in C. Stewart (ed.), *Syncretism/Anti-syncretism: The Politics of Religious Synthesis*, London: Routledge, 1994.

87 L. Vincentnathan, 'Untouchable Concepts of Person and Society', in *Contributions to Indian Sociology*, New Delhi: SAGE Publications, 1993.

88 H. Gorringe, *Untouchable Citizens*, New Delhi: SAGE Publications, 2005.

89 J. C. Arun, 'From stigma to self-assertion: Paraiyars and the symbolism of the parai drum' *Contributions to Indian Sociology*, 41: 81–104, 2007.

Chapter 2

1 R. E. Frykenberg, *Christianity in India: From Beginnings to the Present*, Oxford: Oxford University Press, 2008, p. 92.

2 St Thomas Christians were totally integrated into the local caste system at the top and into the political and economic system, providing soldiers for the local *Raja* and engaging in the pepper trade.

3 R. Robinson, *Sixteenth Century Conversions to Christianity in Goa*, in R. Robinson and S. Clarke (eds), *Religious Conversions in India*, New Delhi: Oxford University Press, 2003, pp. 291–322 and S. Clarke, *Conversions to Christianity in Tamil Nadu*, in R. Robinson and S. Clarke (eds), *Religious Conversions in India*, New Delhi: Oxford University Press, 2003a, pp. 323–50 in R. Robinson and S. Clarke (eds), *Religious Conversions in India*, New Delhi: Oxford University Press, 2003. Both these articles provide a comprehensive overview of the complex conversions between the fifteenth and eighteenth centuries in southern India.

4 To understand the gravity of the oppressive nature of the caste system, references are made to situation in the Protestant, Orthodox and Catholic

churches. Due to the scarcity of documentation on this subject, Pentecostal churches are not included in this chapter.

5 R. E. Frykenberg, *Christianity in India: From Beginnings to the Present*, Oxford: Oxford University Press, 2008, p. 100.

6 S. Neill, *A History of Christianity in India*, Cambridge: Cambridge University Press, 1985, p. 403. For a detailed history from the Thomas Christians and the arrival of Portuguese missionaries in India see G. M. Moraes, *A History of Christianity in India*, Bombay: Manaktalas, 1964.

7 K. Ballhatchet, *Caste, Class and Catholicism in India, 1789–1914*, Surrey: Curzon, 1998, p. 7.

8 J. Massey, 'Christian Dalits in India: An Analysis', *Religion and Society*, 37(3): 43, 1990.

9 D. B. Forrester, *Caste and Christianity*, Curzon: London, 1980, p. 14.

10 S. Manickam, *Mission Approaches to Caste*, in V. Devasahayam (ed.), *Dalits & Women*, p. 67. B. R. Ambedkar, a pioneer in Dalit thought expresses a similar anguish over the failure of the missionaries to check 'the social evil of Caste'. Ambedkar as quoted by Anthoniraj Thumma, *Dalit Liberation Theology*, Delhi: ISPCK, 2000, p. 87.

11 R. E. Frykenberg, *Christianity in India: From Beginnings to the Present*, Oxford: Oxford University Press, 2008, p. 144.

12 J. W. Kaye, *Christianity in India: An Historical Narrative*, London: Smith Elder, 1859, p. 252.

13 J. Massey, 'Christian Dalits in India: An Analysis', *Religion and Society*, 1990, p. 44.

14 D. B. Forrester, *Caste and Christianity*, Curzon: London, 1980, p. 42.

15 A. Balachandran, 'Catholics in Protest: Lower-Caste Christianity in Early Colonial Madras' *Studies in History*, 16(2): 250, 2000.

16 J. C. B. Webster, *The Dalit Christians: A History*, Delhi: ISPCK, 1992, pp. 37–8.

17 A. Daniel, 'Approaches of Mission and Church towards the Indian Caste System', *Religion and Society*, 42(2): 6, 1995.

18 Sr. C. Graham, *The Church of South India: A Further Stage in Development*, a booklet published on behalf of the appeal committee for women's work in the Church of South India, 1956, p. 8.

19 A. M. Abraham Ayrookuzhiel, *Essays on Dalits, Religion and Liberation*, Bangalore: CISRS/ATC, 2006, p. 174.

20 D. B. Forrester, *Caste and Christianity*, Curzon: London, 1980, p. 84, in a chapter titled 'Liberal Missionary Attitude to Caste', Forrester further discusses

in detail the prevailing ideas about caste and various arguments for it and against it among the missionaries who influenced the life of the church during that time.

21 P. Dayanandan, *Dalit Christians of Chengalpatu Area and the Church of Scotland* in G. Oommen and J. C. Webster (eds), *Local Dalit Christian History*, Delhi: ISPCK, 2002, pp. 18–64 and see also J. Massey, 'Christian Dalits in India: An Analysis', *Religion and Society*, pp. 40–53, 1990.

22 They included Paraiyar, Pallar, Nadar, Vellala, Mala, Madiga and Izhava communities, just to mention a few. Though they were all Dalit communities, they had their own inner caste dynamics and hierarchy.

23 CMS Pamphlet, *Travancore: Then and Now*, from the Centre for the Study of World Christianity archives, New College, University of Edinburgh.

24 For example, Madras diocese includes most of the Scottish mission fields, though it falls into other states like Andhra Pradesh and Karnataka.

25 N. Koshey, *Caste in the Kerala Churches*, Bangalore: CISRS, 1968, (booklet) also see K. Kawashima, *Missionaries and A Hindu State: Travancore 1858–1936*, New Delhi: Oxford University Press, 1998.

26 N. Koshey, *Caste in the Kerala Churches,* Bangalore: CISRS, 1968.

27 J. W. Gladstone, *Christian Missionaries and Caste in Kerala*, in M. E. Prabhakar (ed.), *Towards a Dalit Theology*, Delhi: ISPCK,1988, pp. 104–12.

28 G. Oommen, *Pulaya Christians of Kerala: A Community in Dilemma*, in G. Oommen and J. C. Webster (eds), *Local Dalit Christian History*, Delhi: ISPCK, 2002, pp. 83–97.

29 The Sudhra Caste is the fourth and lowest caste category in the fourfold caste hierarchy in the Indian caste system, the others being Brahmin, Ksathrya and Vaisya.

30 G. Shiri, *Plight of Dalit Christians in Karnataka*, in V. Devasahayam (ed.), *Dalits & Women*, Chennai: Gurukul, 1992, p. 93 and 'In search of roots: Christian Dalits in Karnataka and their struggle for the liberation', *Religion and Society*, 40(4), 1993.

31 D. B. Forrester, *Caste and Christianity*, Curzon: London, 1980, pp. 84–5.

32 M. Azariah, *The Unchristian Side of the Indian Church*, Bangalore: Dalit Sahithya Academy, 1985, p. 10.

33 M. Azariah, *The Churches Healing Ministry to the Dalits*, in J. Massy (ed.), *Indigenous People: Dalits*, p. 320.

34 J. D. Maliekal, 'Identity-Consciousness of the Christian Madigas story of a People in Emergence', *Jeevadhara*, 61(181): 25–36, 2001.

35 M. E. Prabhakar, 'Caste-Class and status in Andhra Churches and Implications for Mission Today: Some reflections', *Religion and Society*, 28(3): 9–35, 1981. See also D. B. Forrester, *Caste and Christianity*, Curzon: London, 1980, p. 79.

36 Clarinda Still discusses in detail a similar phenomenon while working among the Madigas in Andhra Pradesh. 'Caste, Identity and Gender among Madigas in Coastal Andhra Pradesh', *Journal of South Asian Development*, 4(1): 7–23, 2009. Also see, Ashok Kumar, *Legally Hindu: Dalit Lutheran Christians of Coastal Andhra Pradesh*, in R. Robinson and J. M. Kujur, *Margins of Faith: Dalit and Tribal Christianity in India*, New Delhi: SAGE Publications, 2010, pp. 149–68.

37 J. C. B. Webster, *The Dalit Christians: A History*, Delhi: ISPCK, 1992, p. 180.

38 Ibid., p. 173.

39 S. M. Michael, *Dalit Encounter with Christianity*, pp. 57–61.

40 S. G. Kurian, 'Struggle for Survival-Experience of Christian Dalits (in Vijayapuram Diocese) in Kerala', *Religion and Society*, 42(2): 14, 1995 and 'Kerala: the Christian Dalits Experience-a Case Study of the Palais Diocese', *Religion and Society*, 45(4), 1998. Augustin Andrews also discusses this problem in his unpublished thesis, *The Problem of Caste in the Church: A Challenge to the Praxis of Theology of Liberation with Special Reference to the Church in Tamil Nadu,* Unpublished Thesis, Edinburgh University, 1993, pp. 11–12.

41 R. Robinson, *Negotiating Boundaries and Identities: Christian 'Communities' in India*, in S. S. Jodhka (ed.), *Community and Identities*, New Delhi: SAGE Publications, 2001, p. 233.

42 C. Devanesan, *The Educational Ministry of the Church: Priorities for the Mission of the Church*, Madras: CSI, 1982, pp. 26–7.

43 L. Lobo, *Dalit Religious Movements and Dalit Identity*, in W. Fernandes (ed.), *The Emerging Dalit Identity*, New Delhi: ISI, 1996, p. 174 see also his article *Visions, Illusions and Dilemmas of Dalit Christians in India*, in G. Shah (ed.), *Dalit Identity and Politics*, New Delhi: SAGE Publications, 2001, pp. 242–57.

44 A. M. Abraham Ayrookuzhiel, *Essays on Dalits, Religion and Liberation*, Bangalore: CISRS/ATC, 2006, p. 176.

45 J. C. B. Webster, *The Dalit Christians: A History*, Delhi: ISPCK, 1992, p. 177.

46 Godwin Shiri, *Plight of Dalit Christians in Karnataka*, in V. Devasahayam (ed.), *Dalits & Women*, Chennai: Gurukul, 1992, p. 95

47 R. S. Sugirtharaja, *Postcolonial Reconfigurations*, London: SCM Press, 2003, p. 119.

48 D. C. Scott (ed.), *Keshub Chunder Sen*, Madras: CLS, 1979, p. xii.

49 These are translated as 'Truth', 'Intelligence', and 'Joy'. D. C. Scott (ed.), *Keshub Chunder Sen*, p. 228.

50 D. C. Scott (ed.), *Keshub Chunder Sen*, Madras: CLS, 1979, p. 228.

51 D. C. Scott (ed.), *Keshub Chunder Sen*, Madras: CLS, 1979, pp. 224, 228 see also R. H. S. Boyd, *An Introduction to Indian Christian Theology*, New Delhi: ISPCK, pp. 28, 37.

52 R. H. S. Boyd, *An Introduction to Indian Christian Theology*, New Delhi: ISPCK, p. 64.

53 J. Lipner (ed.), *The Writings of Brahmabandhab Upadhyaya*, vol. I, Bangalore: The United Theological College, 1991, p. 24.

54 R. H. S. Boyd, *An Introduction to Indian Christian Theology*, New Delhi: ISPCK, p. 73, see also J. Lipner (ed.), *The Writings of Brahmabandhab Upadhyaya*, vol. I, Bangalore: The United Theological College, 1991, pp. 94–145.

55 Ibid., p. 153.

56 S. J. Samartha's book *The Hindu Response to the Unbound Christ* published in 1974 clearly shows the continuation of Vedic philosophy in Indian Christian Theology. S. J. Samartha, *The Hindu Response to the Unbound Christ*, Madras: CLS, 1974.

57 K. P. Aleaz, 'Pluralistic Inclusivism: A Viable Indian Theology of Religions', *Asia Journal of Theology*, 12(2): 265–88, 1998, for the problems of such approaches to theology see my article, A. Jeremiah, 'K. P. Aleaz and 'Inculturation': A Subaltern critique of Indian Christian Vedanta', *Asia Theological Journal*, 21(2): 398–411, 2007.

58 R. H. S. Boyd, *An Introduction to Indian Christian Theology*, New Delhi: ISPCK, pp. 228–54.

59 V. Devasahayam, *Authentic Christianity*, in V. Devasahayam (ed.), *Frontiers of Dalit Theology*, Delhi: ISPCK/Gurukul, 1997a, p. 257.

60 G. Oommen, 'Dalits' Socio-Religious Aspirations and Christianity', *Religion and Society*, 49(2–3): 148, 2002. Oommen explains in this article the struggle and dilemma of Dalit converts due to the Christianization of their existence.

61 V. Devasahayam, *The Norms of Theology*, in V. Devasahayam (ed.), *Frontiers of Dalit Theology*, p. 4.

62 J. Massey and L. Fernando (eds), *Dalit World-Biblical World: An Encounter*, New Delhi: Centre for Dalit/Subaltern Studies, 2007. This collected work sheds light on the complex relationship between Dalit and Biblical world.

63 M. E. Prabhakar, *Christology from Dalit Perspective*, in V. Devasahayam (ed.), *Frontiers of Dalit Theology*, Madras: Gurukul Lutheren Theological College and Research Institute, 1997, p. 426.

Chapter 3

1 S. M. Parish, *Hierarchy and its Discontents*, Philadelphia: University of Pennsylvania Press, 1996, p. 7.

2 T. Jenkins, *Religion in English Everyday Life: An Ethnographic Approach*, Oxford: Berghahn Books, 1999, p. 36.

3 L. M. Alcoff, *Visible Identities, Race, Gender, and the Self*, New York: Oxford University Press, 2006, p. 9.

4 R. Deliege, *The World of the 'Untouchables': Paraiyars of Tamil Nadu*, S. Clarke, *Dalits and Christianity*, and L. Vincentnathan, '*Untouchable Concepts of Person and Society*', as mentioned earlier, my research differs from such researches as I move beyond some of their arguments.

5 The Christian Paraiyar community was the main focus of this ethnographic research, but there were few occasions were Hindu Paraiyars also contributed to the conversations.

6 R. Jenkins, *Social Identity*, London: Routledge, 1996, p. 119.

7 J. Weeks, *The Value of Difference*, in J. Rutherford, (ed.), *Identity: Community, Culture and Difference*, London: Lawrence & Wishart, 1990, p. 88.

8 P. Bourdieu, *Outline of a Theory of Practice*, translated by Richard Nice, Cambridge: Cambridge University Press, 1977. In Chapter 2 titled 'Structures and the Habitus', Bourdieu discusses in detail the concept of 'habitus' within the human social setting. p. 78ff.

9 P. du Gay, *Organizing Identity*, London: SAGE Publications, 2007, p. 46.

10 R. Jenkins, *Social Identity*, London: Routledge, 1996, p. 80.

11 J. Weeks, *The Value of Difference*, in J. Rutherford (ed.), *Identity: Community, Culture and Difference*, London: Lawrence & Wishart, 1990, p. 89.

12 K. Woodward, (ed.), *Identity and Difference*, London: SAGE Publications, 1997, pp. 2, 30.

13 Ibid., p. 21.

14 R. Jenkins, *Social Identity*, London: Routledge, 1996, p. 29.

15 R. Jenkins, *Social Identity*, London: Routledge, 1996, p. 50, see also J. Rutherford, *A Place Called Home: Identity and the Cultural Politics of Difference*, in J. Rutherford (ed.) *Identity: Community, Culture and Difference*, London: Lawrence & Wishart, 1990, pp. 9–27.

16 S. Hall, *Cultural Identity and Diaspora*, in J. Rutherford (ed.), *Identity: Community, Culture and Difference*, p. 222.

17 P. Gilroy, *Diaspora and the Detours of Identity*, in K. Woodward (ed.), *Identity and Difference*, London: SAGE Publications, 1997, p. 314.

18 R. Jenkins, *Social Identity*, London: Routledge, 1996, p. 20.

19 Ibid., pp. 89–102.

20 H. K. Bhabha, *The Third Space*, in J. Rutherford (ed.), *Identity: Community, Culture and Difference*, p. 216, see also H. K. Bhabha, *Location of Culture*, London: Routledge, 1994, pp. 184–5.

21 P. du Gay, *Organizing Identity*, London: SAGE Publications, 2007, p. 53.

22 H. Bhabha, *The Third Space*, in J. Rutherford (ed.), *Identity: Community, Culture and Difference*, London: Lawrence & Wishart, 1990, p. 210, see also H. K. Bhabha, *Location of Culture*, London: Routledge, 1994, pp. 222–3.

23 S. S. Jodhka, *Introduction*, in S. S. Jodhka (ed.), *Community and Identities*, New Delhi: SAGE Publications, 2001, pp. 19–29.

24 A. P. Cohen, *The Symbolic Construction of Community*, Routledge: London, 1993, p. 74, see also for broader discussion on 'community' by M. Mayo, *Cultures, Communities, Identities*, New York: Palgrave, 2000.

25 A. P. Cohen, *The Symbolic Construction of Community*, Routledge: London, 1993, p. 97.

26 R. Jenkins, *Social Identity*, London: Routledge, 1996, p. 107.

27 A. P. Cohen, *The Symbolic Construction of Community*, Routledge: London, 1993, p. 12.

28 It may be recollected that I was eventually 'placed' in the community through my position in the web of kinship as a relative of one of the community members in Thulasigramam.

29 R. Deliege, *The World of the 'Untouchables': Paraiyars of Tamil Nadu*, Delhi: Oxford University Press, 1997, p. 177ff.

30 A. A. Yengoyan, 'Clifford Geertz, Cultural Portraits, and Southeast Asia', *The Journal of Asian Studies*, 68(4): 1222, 2009.

31 T. Pillai-Vetschera, *Ambedkar's Daughters: A Study of Mahar Women in Ahmednagar District of Maharashtra*, in S. M. Michael (ed.), *Dalits in Modern India*, New Delhi: Vistaar Publications, 1999, p. 231.

32 As explained while introducing the caste system, relationship based on purity-pollution is one of the important signifiers of various caste groups.

33 It is worth noting that even Dalit 'theologians' portray the Dalit Christians as weak and vulnerable people, a stereotype that Paraiyar Christians are trying to shed in Thulasigramam.

34 The idea of individuals constructing their own identity in opposition to others was outlined earlier and also suggested by K. Woodward, *Identity and Difference*, p. 21.

35 L. Vincentnathan, '*Untouchable Concepts of Person and Society*', pp. 57–9.

36 R. Deliege, '*Replication and Consensus: Untouchability, Caste and Ideology in India*', p. 167.

37 H. Gorringe, *Untouchable Citizens*, p. 170ff. Gorringe discusses in detail the centrality of physical space in the Dalit Identity construction.

38 It is interesting to note the rank ordering around sacred sites as highlighted by Yel, which I think reflects in the social ordering in Thulasigramam as well. Ali Murat Yel, *Appropriation of Sacredness at Fatima in Portugal*, in E. Arweck and W. Keenan (eds), *Materializing Religion: Expression, Performance and Ritual*, Aldershot: Ashgate, 2006, pp. 221–35.

39 L. Vincentnathan, '*Untouchable Concepts of Person and Society*', pp. 53–82, in this article Vincentnathan explores various concepts of self hood within the Hindu caste system and the untouchable communities.

40 Although, since then the explosion of mobile phone usage has revolutionized this aspect in many rural parts of India, including Thulasigramam.

41 D. Mosse, '*Idioms of Subordination and Styles of Protest Among Christian and Hindu Harijan Castes in Tamil Nadu*', p. 73, see also H. Gorringe, *Untouchable Citizens*, p. 125.

42 S. M. Michael, *Introduction*, in S. M. Michael (ed.), *Dalits in Modern India*, New Delhi: Vistaar Publications, 1999, p. 12. In this book, he traces the sociocultural and political history of Dalits while explaining the origin of caste through Varna system and untouchability. And also Shriram, *The Fourfold Hierarchy*, in S. M. Michael (ed.), *Dalits in Modern India*, New Delhi: Vistaar Publications, 1999, p. 50.

43 For example, such practice is not unique to Thulasigramam; to understand the prevalence of such notions in other cultures my experience in Scotland could be helpful. While working in an Episcopalian congregation in Edinburgh, I encountered one woman, from Scotland, who refused to take communion while she was menstruating. She claimed that this made her impure and unworthy of communion.

44 P. Bourdieu, *The Biographical Illusion*, in P. du Gay (ed.), *Identity: A Reader*, London: SAGE Publications, 2000, p. 300.

45 R. Jenkins, *Social Identity*, London: Routledge, 1996, p. 123.

46 T. Pillai-Vetschera, *Ambedkar's Daughters: A Study of Mahar Women in Ahmednagar district of Maharashtra*, in S. M. Michael (ed.), *Dalits in Modern India*, New Delhi: Vistaar Publications, 1999, p. 231.
47 Interview with E. Koepping, *Food, Friends and Funerals*, Munster: LIT, May 2008.
48 H. Gorringe, *Untouchable Citizens*, New Delhi: SAGE Publications, 2005, p. 233, this idea is recorded while discussing the status of women within the Dalit movement.
49 T. Pillai-Vetschera, *Ambedkar's Daughters: A Study of Mahar Women in Ahmednagar district of Maharashtra* in S. M. Michael (ed.), *Dalits in Modern India*, New Delhi: Vistaar Publications, 1999, p. 231.
50 It is important to note that Thulasigramam was declared to be a reserved constituency in 2001, this means that only members of the scheduled caste can stand for local elections. Until recently the Reddyars never permitted Paraiyars to participate in the elections.
51 Interestingly, Timothy Jenkins presents a similar aspect of reversal of 'ideals' among women in Kingswood, Bristol in southern England. T. Jenkins, *Religion in English Everyday Life: An Ethnographic Approach*, Oxford: Berghahn Books, 1999, p. 116ff.
52 F. Fanon, *The Wretched of the Earth*, London: Paladin, 1963, p. 170, see also H. K. Bhabha, *Location of Culture*, London: Routledge, 1994, pp. 44–5.
53 M. Mines, *Heterodox Lives: Agonistic Individuality and Agency in South Indian History*, in R. Guha (ed.), *Institutions and Inequalities*, New Delhi: Oxford Press, 1999, pp. 209–31.

Chapter 4

1 M. Azariah, interviewed on 30 January 2007 at 4 pm, Chennai, India.
2 T. Ingold, *The Perception of the Environment*, London: Routledge, 2000, p. 21.
3 By visible world I mean a tangible world and less visible world means, not necessarily tangible but part of the sensory perception and knowledge, which deeply impacts the tangible world. See also E. Koepping, *Food, Friends and Funerals*, Munster: LIT, 2008, p. 3.
4 E. Durkheim, *The Elementary Forms of Religious Life*, translated by K. E. Fields, New York: the Free Press, 1995, p. 44.

5 E. Durkheim, *On Morality and Society: Selected Writings*, Chicago, IL: University of Chicago Press, 1973. See the chapter on 'The Dualism of Human Nature and its Social Condition'.

6 B. Malinowski, *Magic, Science and Religion*, London: Souvenir Press Ltd., 1985, p. 59.

7 Ibid., p. 57.

8 C. Geertz, *Local Knowledge*, New York: Basic Books, 2000b, pp. 55–9.

9 C. Geertz, *Available Light*, Princeton, NJ: Princeton University Press, 2000a, p. 184.

10 J. D. Eller, *Introducing Anthropology of Religion*, London: Routledge, 2007, p. 28.

11 T. Asad, *Genealogies of Religion*, Baltimore, MD: The Johns Hopkins University Press, 1993, p. 29.

12 Ibid., p. 47.

13 A. Dawson, *Sociology of Religion*, London: SCM Press, 2011a, p. 31.

14 T. Ingold, *The Perception of the Environment*, London: Routledge, 2000, p. 168.

15 Ibid., p. 171.

16 P. Bourdieu, *Logic of Practice*, translated by R. Nice, Cambridge: Polity Press, 1999, p. 55.

17 S. Priest, *Merleau-Ponty*, London: Routledge, 1998, p. 230.

18 M. M. Langer, *Merleau-Ponty's Phenomenology of Perception*, London: Macmillan, 1989, p. 117.

19 T. Ingold, *The Perception of the Environment*, London: Routledge, 2000, pp. 54, 68.

20 T. Jenkins, *Religion in English Everyday Life: An Ethnographic Approach*, Oxford: Berghahn Books, 1999, p. 70.

21 D. K. Naugle, *Worldview: The History of a Concept*, Cambridge: William B. Eerdmans Publishing Company, 2002, p. 64. In this book Naugle provides an exhaustive account of the worldview concept from different academic disciplines.

22 C. Geertz, *The Interpretation of Culture*, New York: Basic Books, 1973, p. 127.

23 T. Asad, *Genealogies of Religion*, Baltimore, MD: the Johns Hopkins University Press, 1993, p. 52.

24 S. Clarke, *Dalits and Christianity*, Delhi: Oxford University Press, 1998, p. 71ff and K. S. Muthu, *Dalit Deities*, Madurai: Dalit Resource Centre, 2005.

25 It would be helpful to remember that Paraiyars consider Arunthathier as lower than themselves in caste hierarchy.

26 R. Deliege, 'Demonic Possession in Catholic South India', in *Indian Anthropologist*, 37(1): pp. 49–66, 2007. In this article, Deliege describes the construction of the spirit world in Paraiyar communities in Tamil Nadu, which applies to the Christian community in Thulasigramam as well.

27 F. Wilfred, *The Sling of Utopia*, Delhi: ISPCK, 2005, p. 141, also see S. Raj, 'The Santal Sacred Grove and Catholic Inculturation', *Journal of Ecumenical Studies*, Spring, 42(2): pp. 243–52, 2007.

28 A. Dawson (ed.), *Summoning the Spirits: Possession and Invocation in Contemporary Religion*, London: I. B. Tauris, 2011b. In this work one could follow the prevalence of spirit possession and their social impact across the globe.

29 E. Durkheim, *The Elementary Forms of Religious Life*, translated by K. E. Fields, New York: the Free Press, 1995, p. 284.

30 S. Priest, *Merleau-Ponty*, London: Routledge, 1998, p. 230 and M. M. Langer, *Merleau-Ponty's Phenomenology of Perception*, London: Macmillan, 1989, p. 117.

31 F. Wilfred, *The Sling of Utopia*, Delhi: ISPCK, 2005, p. 142.

32 S. Clarke, *Dalits and Christianity*, Delhi: Oxford University Press, 1998, p. 71ff and K. S. Muthu, *Dalit Deities*, Madurai: Dalit Resource Centre, 2005.

33 J. T. Appavoo, *Dalit Religion*, in J. Massy (ed.), *Indigenous People: Dalits*, New Delhi: ISPCK, 1994, p. 118.

Chapter 5

1 M. Foucault, *Power/Knowledge: Selected Interviews and Other Writings 1972–1977*, C. Gordon (ed.), Hemel Hempstead: Harvester Wheatsheaf, 1988, p. 98.

2 S. Lukes, *Power: A Radical View*, Hampshire: Palgrave, 2005, p. 83.

3 Ibid., p. 85.

4 Ibid., p. 118.

5 B. Russell, *Power*, London: Routledge, 2004, pp. 23–34.

6 G. Poggi, *Forms of Power*, Cambridge: Polity, 2001, p. 14.

7 S. Lukes, *Power: A Radical View*, Hampshire: Palgrave, 2005, pp. 132–3.

8 Ibid., pp. 94–5.

9 Ibid., pp. 132–3.

10 T. Parsons, *Power and the Social System*, in S. Lukes (ed.), *Power*, New York: New York University Press, 1986, p. 113.

11 M. Percy, *Power and the Church*, London: Cassell, 1998, pp. 6–16. Also see S. Sykes, *Power and Christian Theology*, London: Continuum, 2006.

12 E. Koepping, *Food, Friends and Funerals*, Munster: LIT, 2008, pp. 112–30, the discussion on the nature of sermons preached by the male Lutheran pastors in Australia resonate with the situation in Thulasigramam Christian community.

13 E. Koepping, *Food, Friends and Funerals*, Munster: LIT, 2008, p. 56.

14 G. Shiri, *Plight of Dalit Christians in Karnataka*, in V. Devasahayam (ed.), *Dalits & Women*, Chennai: Gurukul, 1992, p. 95.

15 D. Mosse, *The Politics of Religious Synthesis: Roman Catholicism and Hindu Village Society in Tamil Nadu, India*, in C. Stewart and R. Shaw (eds), *Syncretism/Anti-Syncretism: The Politics of Religious Synthesis*, London: Routledge, 1994, p. 86.

16 R. Pais, *Scheduled Castes, Employment and Social Mobility*, in S. M. Michael (ed.), *Dalits in Modern India*, New Delhi: Vistaar Publications, 1999, pp. 321–39. Here, Richard discusses all the possible avenues available for Dalit (Schedule Caste) communities for social mobility, which are denied for those who convert to Christianity.

17 L. Lobo, *Visions, Illusions and Dilemmas of Dalit Christian in India*, in G. Shah (ed.), *Dalit Identity and Politics*, New Delhi: SAGE Publications, 2001, p. 254.

18 Scheduled Caste is the legal category to designate all the backward Dalit communities in India, see R. Pais, *Scheduled Castes, Employment and Social Mobility*, in S. M. Michael (ed.), *Dalits in Modern India*, New Delhi: Vistaar Publications, 1999, pp. 321–39.

19 L. Lobo, *Visions, Illusions and Dilemmas of Dalit Christian in India*, in G. Shah (ed.), *Dalit Identity and Politics*, New Delhi: SAGE Publications, 2001, p. 254.

20 The intention for conducting a grander festival than the Hindu Reddyars will be discussed in the next chapter as a strategic move to negotiate their status. Obviously, there is no consensus on this issue.

21 D. Mosse, 'Idioms of Subordination and Styles of Protest among Christian and Hindu Harijan Castes in Tamil Nadu', *Contributions to Indian Sociology*, 28(1): 67–106, 1994.

22 M. Moffatt, *An Untouchable Community in South India: Structure and Consensus*, New Jersey: Princeton University Press, 1979. N. Sudhakar Rao also critically evaluates Moffatt's hypothesis in his article, *The Structure of South Indian Untouchable Castes: A View*, in G. Shah (ed.), *Dalit Identity and Politics*, New Delhi: SAGE Publications, 2001, pp. 74–96.

23 R. Deliege, 'Replication and Consensus: Untouchability, Caste and Ideology in India', pp. 155–73, even though he mentions that Hindu Paraiyars are graded 'lower' than the Catholic Paraiyars, he goes on to say that such ambiguous observations are insignificant, p. 164.

24 As discussed earlier in the chapter the nature of power by G. Poggi, *Forms of Power*, Cambridge: Polity, 2001, p. 14ff.

25 H. Gorringe, *Untouchable Citizens*, New Delhi: SAGE Publications, 2005, p. 118.

26 D. Mosse, *The Politics of Religious Synthesis: Roman Catholicism and Hindu Village Society in Tamil Nadu, India*, in C. Stewart and R. Shaw (eds), *Syncretism/Anti-Syncretism: The Politics of Religious Synthesis*, London: Routledge, 1994, p. 93ff.

27 D. Mosse, 'Idioms of Subordination and Styles of Protest among Christian and Hindu Harijan Castes in Tamil Nadu', *Contributions to Indian Sociology*, 28(1): 83–5, 1994 and L. Vincentnathan, 'Untouchable Concepts of Person and Society', *Contributions to Indian Sociology*, 27: 76, 1993.

28 A. M. A. Ayrookuzhiel, *Dalit Theology: A Movement of Counter Culture*, in J. Massy (ed.), *Indigenous People: Dalits*, New Delhi: ISPCK, 1994, p. 251. Reflecting on the collective Dalit situation Ayrookuzhiel says,

> The Dalit experience in one word can be described as dependency or powerlessness. Self-reliance in any sphere of their life such as economic, political, educational, legal, religio-cultural is impossible for them. A dependent people are not free people. Spiritual cultural growth is possible only when a people are proprietors to themselves, which is not the experience of Dalits.

Chapter 6

1 D. P. Mines, *Fierce Gods*, Indianapolis: Indiana University Press, 2005, p. 29.

2 A. P. Cohen, *The Symbolic Construction of Community*, London: Routledge, 1993, p. 14.

3 Ibid., p. 18.

4 C. Geertz, *The Interpretation of Cultures*, New York: Basic Books, 1973, p. 19f.

5 Ibid., p. 37.

6 Ibid., p. 127.

7 I. Pyysiainen, *How Religion Works: Towards a New Cognitive Science of Religion*, Boston, MA: Brill, 2003, p. 38f, even though I do not fully subscribe to the

view of cognitive approach to the study of religion, I feel it is important to understand the process of meaning construction of the religious symbols.

8 E. Leach, *Culture and Communication*, Cambridge: Cambridge University Press, 1976, p. 49.

9 C. Geertz, *The Interpretation of Cultures*, New York: Basic Books, 1973, pp. 127–30.

10 Ibid., p. 95.

11 Ibid., p. 167.

12 J. D. Eller, *Introducing Anthropology of Religion*, London: Routledge, 2007, p. 65.

13 V. Turner, *Dramas, Fields and Metaphors*, London: Cornell University Press, 1978, pp. 55, 236.

14 T. H. Eriksen, *Small Places, Large Issues*, London: Pluto Press, 2001, p. 226 and C. Bell, *Ritual: Perspectives and Dimensions*, Oxford: Oxford University Press, 1997, p. 160.

15 V. Turner, *Dramas, Fields and Metaphors*, London: Cornell University Press, 1978, p. 24 and also Dan Sperber demonstrates in his book the process of transforming old representations, symbols and rituals into new life by changing actors and universe, *Rethinking Symbolism*, Cambridge: Cambridge University Press, 1975.

16 Some of the community members claim that Rani is mentally unstable, since she believes in the plausibility of her experiences.

17 D. Morgan, *The Sacred Gaze*, London: University of California Press, 2005, p. 75ff.

18 J. D. Eller, *Introducing Anthropology of Religion*, London: Routledge, 2007, p. 68.

19 For a broad discussion on this subject see E. Arweck and W. J. F. Keenan (ed.), *Materializing Religion: Expression, Performance and Ritual*, Aldershot: Ashgate, 2006.

20 T. Jenkins describes a similar procession, but in a bigger scale at Kingswood Whit Walk, which provides space for various groups to express not just their religious identity but also socially and territorially significant messages. *Religion in English Everyday Life: an Ethnographic Approach*, Oxford: Berghahn Books, 1999, p. 100ff.

21 V. Turner, *Dramas, Fields and Metaphors*, London: Cornell University Press, 1978, p. 236.

22 L. S. Crumrine explains 'defecation' of a religious artefact as a potent symbolic action to express the community's feelings. *Mayo Santos: A Paradigmatic*

Analysis of a Sacred Symbol in R. F. Spencer (ed.), *Forms of Symbolic Action*, London: American Ethnological Society, 1969, pp. 134–50.

23 C. Geertz, *The Interpretation of Cultures*, New York: Basic Books, 1973, p. 116ff.

24 V. Turner, *Dramas, Fields and Metaphors*, London: Cornell university press, 1978, p. 260.

25 V. Turner, *The Ritual Process: Structure and Anti Structure*, Ithaca, NY: Cornell University Press, 1969, p. 184, see also B. C. Alexander, *Victor Turner Revisited*, Georgia: Scholars Press, 1991, pp. 46, 66.

26 C. Geertz, *The Interpretation of Cultures*, New York: Basic Books, 1973, p. 113; see also C. Bell, *Ritual: Perspectives and Dimensions*, Oxford: Oxford University Press, 1997, p. 160.

27 H. K. Bhabha, *The Location of Culture*, New York: Routledge, 1994, pp. 146–9 and also C. Geertz, *The Interpretation of Cultures*, New York: Basic Books, 1973, p. 17.

Chapter 7

1 S. Clarke, *Transformations of Caste and Tribe*, in R. Robinson and S. Clarke (eds), *Religious Conversions in India*, New Delhi: Oxford University Press, 2003b, p. 217.

2 The feminine understanding of Jesus, which existed in the Middle Ages, does not find reference in the contemporary teachings of CSI. See C. W. Bynum, *Jesus as Mother: Studies in the Spirituality of High Middle Ages*, Berkeley, CA: University of California press, 1982.

3 As such it would be comparable with the saint relationship within Roman Catholicism, which expects or at least hopes for, an exchange of favours. See A. M. Yel, *Appropriation of Sacredness at Fatima in Portugal*, in E. Arweck and W. J. F. Keenan (ed.), *Materializing Religion: Expression, Performance and Ritual*, Aldershot : Ashgate, 2006, pp. 221–35.

4 A. P. Cohen, *The Symbolic Construction of Community*, Routledge: London, 1993, p. 74.

5 C. Upadhya, *The Concept of Community in Indian Social Sciences: An Anthropological Perspective*, in S. S. Jodhka (ed.), *Community and Identities*, New Delhi: SAGE Publications, 2001, pp. 32–55.

6 As part of my fieldwork, I also travelled across 18 villages in various districts and Christian communities, where such reproduction of hierarchy was

encountered and the local church leader acted as the gatekeeper of the Christian community.

7 F. Barth, *Boundaries and Connections*, in A. P. Cohen (ed.), *Signifying Identities: Anthropological Perspectives on Boundaries and Contested Values*, London: Routledge, 2000, p. 31, where he discusses the various human activities towards reconstituting one's communal boundaries.

8 E. Koepping, *Food, Friends and Funerals*, Munster: LIT, 2008, p. 60ff.

9 Ibid., p. 72.

10 Ibid., p. 90.

11 Ibid., p. 140.

12 Ibid., p. 161.

13 Ibid., p. 170.

14 Ibid., p. 185.

15 T. Jenkins, *Religion in English Everyday Life*, Oxford: Berghahn Books, 1999, p. 43ff.

16 Ibid., p. 14.

17 Ibid., p. 44.

18 Ibid., p. 96ff.

19 Ibid., p. 101.

20 Ibid., p. 102.

21 Ibid., p. 102.

22 Ibid., p. 100ff.

23 Ibid., p. 219.

24 B. Okri, *The Famished Road*, London: Vintage, 2003.

25 Mabiala Justin-Robert Kenzo, 'Religion, Hybridity, and the Construction of Reality in Postcolonial Africa', *Exchange*, Brill Academic Publishers, 33(3): 244–68, 2004. Kenzo provides a good summary of the *Famished Road* in his paper.

26 M. J-R. Kenzo, 'Religion, Hybridity, and the Construction of Reality in Postcolonial Africa', *Exchange*, 33(3): 252, 2004.

27 Ibid., p. 257.

28 Ibid., p. 258.

29 Ibid., p. 258.

30 Ibid., p. 258.

31 Ibid., p. 261.

32 Ibid., p. 261.

33 Ibid., p. 262.

34 Ibid., p.267.

35 M. Foucault, *The Use of Pleasure: The History of Sexuality*, vol. 2. London: Penguin, 1992, p. 8.

36 E. Maroney, *Religious Syncretism*, London: SCM Press, 2006. This work provides a historical account of religious syncretism.

37 B. Meyer, *Beyond Syncretism: Translation and Diabolization in the Appropriation of Protestantism in Africa*, in C. Stewart and R. Shaw (eds), *Syncretism/Anti-Syncretism: The Politics of Religious Synthesis*, London: Routledge, 1994, pp. 45–68.

38 J. Keirnan, *Variation on a Christian Theme: The Healing Synthesis of Zulu Zionism*, in C. Stewart and R. Shaw (eds), *Syncretism/Anti-Syncretism: The Politics of Religious Synthesis*, London: Routledge, 1994, pp. 69–84.

39 D. Mosse, *The Politics of Religious Synthesis: Roman Catholicism and Hindu Village Society in Tamil Nadu, India*, in C. Stewart and R. Shaw (eds), *Syncretism/Anti-Syncretism: The Politics of Religious Synthesis*, London: Routledge, 1994, pp. 85–107.

40 Besides my observation, B. E. Schmidt also discusses the limitations of syncretism in her article, *The Creation of Afro-Caribbean Religions and their Incorporation of Christian Elements: A critique against Syncretism*, in D. E. Singh and B. C. Farr (eds), *Christianity and Cultures: Shaping Christian Thinking in Context*, Eugene, OR: Wipf & Stock, 2008, pp. 89–99.

41 D. Goh, 'Chinese Religion and the Challenge of Modernity in Malaysia and Singapore: Syncretism, Hybridisation and Transfiguration' *Asian Journal of Social Science*, 37: 107–37, 2009.

42 P. Kitiarsa, 'Beyond Syncretism: Hybridization of Popular Religion in Contemporary Thailand', *Journal of Southeast Asian Studies*, 36(3): 461–87, 2005.

43 R. J. C. Young, *Colonial Desire: Hybridity in Theory, Culture and Race*, London: Routledge, 1995, p. 20ff.

44 E. Shoat, *Notes on the Post-Colonial*, in F. A.-K and K. Seshadri-Crooks (eds), *The Pre-Occupation of Postcolonial Studies*, London: Duke University Press, 2000, p. 137.

45 S. Clarke, *Transformations of Caste and Tribe*, in R. Robinson and S. Clarke (eds), *Religious Conversions in India*, New Delhi: Oxford University Press, 2003b, p. 217.

46 Synergy. *Roget's 21st Century Thesaurus*, Third Edition. Philip Lief Group, 2009.

47 P. A. Corning, 'The Synergism Hypothesis: On the Concept of Synergy and Its Role in the Evolution of Complex Systems', *Journal of Social & Evolutionary Systems*, 21(2), 1998.

Bibliography

General bibliography

Abbinnett, R. (2003), *Culture & Identity: Critical Theories*, London: SAGE Publications.

Alcoff, L. M. (2006), *Visible Identities, Race, Gender, and the Self*, New York: Oxford University Press.

Alexander, B. C. (1991), *Victor Turner Revisited*, Georgia: Scholars Press.

Alexander, J. C. (ed.) (2006), *Social Performance: Symbolic Action, Cultural Pragmatics and Ritual*, Cambridge: Cambridge University Press.

Appavoo, J. T. (1994), *Dalit Religion*, in J. Massy (ed.), *Indigenous People: Dalits*, New Delhi: ISPCK.

— (1997), *Dalit Way of Theological Expression*, in V. Devasahayam (ed.), *Frontiers of Dalit Theology*, Delhi: ISPCK/Gurukul.

Arockiadoss, P. (1997), *The Significance of Dr. Ambedkar for Theologising in India*, in V. Devasahayam (ed.), *Frontiers of Dalit Theology*, Delhi: ISPCK/Gurukul.

Arulraja, M. (1997), *Some Reflections on a Dalit Reading of the Bible*, in V. Devasahayam (ed.), *Frontiers of Dalit Theology*, Delhi: ISPCK/Gurukul.

Arulraja, M. R. (1996), *Jesus the Dalit*, Hyderabad: Volunteer Centre.

Arweck, E. and Keenan, W. J. F. (eds) (2006), *Materializing Religion: Expression, Performance and Ritual*, Aldershot: Ashgate.

Asad, T. (1993), *Genealogies of Religion*, Baltimore, MD: The Johns Hopkins University Press.

Atkinson, P. (1990), *The Ethnographic Imagination: Textual Construction of Reality*, London: Routledge.

Ayrookuzhiel, A. M. A. (1994), *Dalit Theology: A Movement of Counter Culture*, in J. Massy (ed.), *Indigenous People: Dalits*, New Delhi: ISPCK.

— (2006), *Essays on Dalits, Religion and Liberation*, Bangalore: CISRS/ATC.

Azariah, M. (1985), *The Unchristian Side of the Indian Church*, Bangalore: Dalit Sahithya Academy.

— (1994), *The Churches Healing Ministry to the Dalits*, in J. Massy (ed.), *Indigenous People: Dalits*, New Delhi: ISPCK.

— (2000), *A Priests Search for Dalit Theology*, Delhi: ISCPK.

Ballhatchet, K. (1998), *Caste, Class and Catholicism in India 1789–1914*, Surrey: Curzon Press.

Barth, F. (2000), *Boundaries and Connections*, in A. P. Cohen (ed.), *Signifying Identities: Anthropological Perspectives on Boundaries and Contested Values*, London: Routledge.

Bell, C. (1997), *Ritual: Perspectives and Dimensions*, Oxford: Oxford University Press.

Beteille, A. (2002), *Caste, Class and Power*, New Delhi: Oxford.

Beyer, P. and Beaman, L. G. (eds) (2007), *Religion, Globalization and Culture*. Leiden: Brill.

Bhabha, H. K. (1990), *The Third Space*, in J. Rutherford (ed.), *Identity: Community, Culture and Difference*, London: Lawrence & Wishart.

— (1994), *The Location of Culture*, London: Routledge.

Bird, A. (2010), *Caste and Christianity since Gandhi and Ambedkar*, in Duncan B. Forrester (ed.), *Forrester on Christian Ethics and Practical Theology: Collected Writings on Christianity, India, and the Social Order*, Surrey: Ashgate.

Bourdieu, P. (1977), *Outline of a Theory of Practice*, translated by R. Nice, Cambridge: Cambridge University Press.

— (1999), *Logic of Practice*, translated by R. Nice, Cambridge: Polity Press.

— (2000), *The Biographical Illusion*, in P. du Gay (ed.), *Identity: A Reader*, London: SAGE Publications.

Bowie, F. (2000), *The Anthropology of Religion: An Introduction*, Oxford: Blackwell Publishers.

Brockington, J. L. (1981), *The Sacred Thread: Hinduism in its Continuity and Diversity*, Edinburgh: Edinburgh University Press.

Carr, D. (1994), *A Biblical Basis for Dalit Theology*, in J. Massey (ed.), *Indigenous People: Dalits*, New Delhi: ISPCK.

Carrette, J. R. (2000), *Foucault and Religion: Spiritual Corporality and Political Spirituality*, London: Routledge.

Chatterjee, P. (1993), *Caste and Subaltern Consciousness*, in P. Chatterjee (ed.), *Subaltern Studies VI*, Delhi: Oxford University Press.

— (ed.) (1993), *Subaltern Studies VII*, Delhi: Oxford University Press.

Chatterji, S. K. (1994), *Why Dalit Theology?*, in J. Massey (ed.), *Indigenous people: Dalits*, New Delhi: ISPCK.

Clarke, S. (1998), *Dalits and Christianity: Subaltern Religion and Liberation Theology in India*, Delhi: Oxford University Press.

— (2003a), *Conversions to Christianity in Tamil Nadu*, in R. Robinson and S. Clarke (eds), *Religious Conversions in India*, New Delhi; Oxford University Press.

— (2003b), *Transformations of Caste and Tribe*, in R. Robinson, and S. Clarke (eds), *Religious Conversions in India*, New Delhi: Oxford University Press.

— (2008), *Subalterns, Identity Politics and Christian Theology in India*, in S. C. H. Kim (ed.), *Christian Theology in Asia*, Cambridge: Cambridge University Press.

Cohen, A. P. (1993), *The Symbolic Construction of Community*, Routledge: London.

Cornille, C. (ed.) (2002), *ManyMansions?: Multiple Religious Belonging and Christian Identity*, New York: Orbis Books.

Cox, H. G. (1989), *Many Mansions: A Christian's Encounter with Other Faiths*, London: Collins.

Crumrine, L. S. (1969), *Mayo Santos: A Paradigmatic Analysis of a Sacred Symbol*, in R. F. Spencer (ed.), *Forms of Symbolic Action*, London: American Ethnological Society.

Davies, C. (1999), *AReflexive Ethnography*, London: Routledge.

Davies, D. (2002), *Anthropology and Theology*, Oxford: BERG.

Dawson, A. (2011a), *Sociology of Religion*, London: SCM Press.

— (2011b), *Summoning the Spirits*, London: I. B.Tauris.

Dayanandan, P. (2002), *Dalit Christians of Chengalpatu Area and the Church of Scotland*, in G. Oommen and J. C. Webster (eds), *Local Dalit Christian History*, Delhi: ISPCK.

Deliege, R. (1997), *The World of the 'Untouchables': Paraiyars of Tamil Nadu*, translated by D. Phillips, Delhi: Oxford University Press.

— (1999a), *Demonic Possession in Catholic South India*, in S. M. Michael (ed.), *Dalits in Modern India*, New Delhi: Vistaar Publications.

— (1999b), *The Untouchables of India*, Oxford: Berg.

Devanesan, C. (1982), *The Educational Ministry of the Church:Priorities for the Mission of the Church*, Madras: CSI.

Devasahayam, V. (1991), *Pollution, Poverty and Powerlessness: A Dalit Perspective*, in A. P. Nirmal (ed.), *A Reader in Dalit Theology*, Madras: Gurukul.

— (1992), *The Eucharist: A Sacrament of Liberation*, in V. Devasahayam (ed.), *Dalits and Women*, Chennai: Gurukul.

— (1997a), *Authentic Christianity*, in V. Devasahayam (ed.), *Frontiers in Dalit Theology*, Delhi: ISPCK/Gurukul.

— (1997b), *Doing Dalit Theology: Basic Assumptions*, in V. Devasahayam (ed.), *Frontiers of Dalit Theology*, Delhi: ISPCK/Gurukul.

— (1997c), *Formative Factors of Dalit Theology*, in V. Devasahayam (ed.), *Frontiers ofDalit Theology*, Delhi: ISPCK/Gurukul.

— (1997d), *The Goals of Dalit Theology*, in V. Devasahayam (ed.), *Frontiers of Dalit Theology*, Delhi: ISPCK/Gurukul.

— (1997e), *Identity in Theology*, in V. Devasahayam (ed.), *Frontiers of Dalit Theology*, Chennai: Gurukul.

— (1997f), *The Nature of Dalit Theology as a Counter Ideology*, in V. Devasahayam (ed.), *Frontiers of Dalit Theology*, Delhi: ISPCK/Gurukul.

— (1997g), *New Thrusts of Dalit Theology*, in V. Devasahayam (ed.), *Frontiers of Dalit Theology*, Delhi: ISPCK/Gurukul.

Durkheim, E. (1973), *On Morality and Society: Selected Writings*, Chicago, IL: University of Chicago Press.

— (1995), *The Elementary Forms of Religious Life*, translated by K. E. Fields, New York: The Free Press.

Dussel, E. (1988), *Ethics and Community*, Wellwood: Burns & Oates.

Eller, J. D. (2007), *Introducing Anthropology of Religion*, London: Routledge.

Eriksen, T. H. (2001), *Small Places, Large Issues*, London: Pluto Press.

Fanon, F. (1963), *The Wretched of the Earth*, London: Paladin.

Faustina, S. (1997), *From Exile to Exodus*, in V. Devasahayam (ed.), *Frontiers of Dalit Theology*, Delhi: ISPCK/Gurukul.

Forrester, D. B. (1980), *Caste and Christianity*, London: Curzon Press.

— (2000), *Truthful Action*, Edinburgh: T&T Clark.

Frykenberg, R. E. (2008), *Christianity in India: From Beginnings to the Present*, Oxford: Oxford University Press.

Gandhi, M. K. (1978), *Hindu Dharma*, New Delhi: Orient Paperbacks.

Gay, P. du. (ed.) (2000), *Identity: A Reader*, London: SAGE Publications.

— (2007), *Organizing Identity*, London: SAGE Publications.

Geertz, C. (1973), *The Interpretation of Cultures*, New York: Basic Books.

— (2000a), *Available Light*, Princeton, NJ: Princeton University Press.

— (2000b), *Local Knowledge*, New York: Basic Books.

George, V. A. (2001), *Self-Realization 'Brahmaanubhava': The Advaitic Perspective of Sankara*, Washington: The Council for Research in Values and Philosophy.

Gilroy, P. (1997), *Diaspora and the Detours of Identity*, in K. Woodward (ed.), *Identity and Difference*, London: SAGE Publications.

Gladstone, J. W. (1988), *Christian Missionaries and Caste in Kerala*, in M. E. Prabhakar (ed.), *Towards a Dalit Theology*, Delhi: ISPCK.

Gnanavaram, M. (1997), *Eschatology in Dalit Perspective*, in V. Devasahayam (ed.), *Frontiers of Dalit Theology*, Delhi: ISPCK/Gurukul.

Gorringe, H. (2005), *Untouchable Citizens*, New Delhi: SAGE Publications.

Graham, C. (1956), *The Church of South India: A Further Stage in Development*, Church of South India. Chennai: India.

Hackett, R. (ed.) (2008), *Proselytization Revisited: Rights Talk, Free Markets and Culture Wars*, London: Equinox Publishing Ltd.

Hall, S. (1990), *Cultural Identity and Diaspora*, in J. Rutherford (ed.), *Identity: Community, Culture and Difference*, London: Lawrence & Wishart.

Harrison, S. (2006), *Fracturing Resemblances*, Oxford: Berghahn Books.

Ilaiah, K. (1996), *Why I am not a Hindu: A Sudra Critique of Hindutva Philosophy, Culture, and Political Economy*, Calcutta: Samya.

Ingold, T. (2000), *The Perception of the Environment*, London: Routledge.

Jacobsen, K. A. (2008), *South Asian Religions on Display: Religious Processions in South Asia and in the Diaspora*, New York: Routledge.

Jacobsen, K. A. and Raj, S. J. (eds) (2008), *South Asian Christian Diaspora: Invisible Diaspora in Europe and North America*, Surrey: Ashgate.

Jenkins, R. (1996), *Social Identity*, London: Routledge.

Jenkins, T. (1999), *Religion in English Everyday Life: An Ethnographic Approach*, Oxford: Berghahn Books.

Jeremiah, A. (2006), *Meeting the Samaritan Woman: Encountering Jesus' Ecumenism for the Mission of Today's Church*, in J. George (ed.), *God of all Grace*, vol. 2, Bangalore: UTC and Asia Trading Corporation.

— (2010), *Exploring New Facets of Dalit Christology in Critical Interaction with John D Crossan's Portrayal of Historical Jesus*, in S. Clarke and D. Manchala (eds), *Dalit Theology in the 21st Century: Discordant Voices, Discerning Pathways*, New Delhi: Oxford University Press.

— (2012), *Localizing Christianity for Social Change: The Subversion of Caste in Rural South India*, in A. Adogame and S. Shankar (eds), *Religions on the Move*, Leiden, Netherlands: BRILL Academic Publishers.

Jodhka, S. S. (ed.) (2001), *Community and Identities*, New Delhi: SAGE Publications.

John, Sri. (2006), *Psychoanalysis of Myths in Dalit (Paraiyar) Culture*, in J. Massey and S. Lourdunathan (eds), *Breaking Theoretical Grounds for Dalit Studies*, New Delhi: Centre for Dalit/Subaltern Studies.

Juergensmeyer, M. (2001), *Terror in the Mind of God: The Global Rise of Religious Violence*. Berkeley, CA: University of California Press.

Kalu, O. U. (ed.) (2008), *Interpreting Contemporary Christianity: Global Processes and Local Identities*, Cambridge: William B. Eerdmans Publishing Company.

Kaur, R. (2005), *Performative Politics and the Cultures of Hinduism*, London: Anthem Press.

Kawashima, K. (1998), *Missionaries and A Hindu State*, New Delhi: Oxford University Press.

Kaye, J. W. (1859), *Christianity in India: An Historical Narrative*, London: Smith, Elder.

Keirnan, J. (1994), *Variation on a Christian theme: The Healing Synthesis of Zulu Zionism*, in C. Stewart and R. Shaw (eds), *Syncretism/Anti-Syncretism: The Politics of Religious Synthesis*, London: Routledge.

Khare, R. S. (ed.) (2006), *Caste, Hierarchy and Individualism: Indian Critiques of Louis Dumont's Contributions*, New Delhi: Oxford University Press.

King, R. (1999), *Indian Philosophy*, Washigton, DC: Georgetown University Press.

Koepping, E. (2008), *Food, Friends and Funerals*, Munster: LIT.

Koshey, N. (1968), *Caste in the Kerala Churches*, Bangalore: CISRS.

Langer, M. M. (1989), *Merleau-Ponty's Phenomenology of Perception*, London: Macmillan.

Leach, E. (1976), *Culture and Communication*, Cambridge: Cambridge University Press.

Lipner, J. (ed.) (1991), *The Writings of Brahmabandhab Upadhyaya*, vol. I, Bangalore: The United Theological College.

— (1994), *Hindus: Their Religious Beliefs and Practices*, London: Routledge.

Lobo, L. (1996), *Dalit Religious Movements and Dalit Identity*, in W. Fernandes (ed.), *The Emerging Dalit Identity*, New Delhi: ISI.

— (2001), *Visions, Illusions and Dilemmas of Dalit Christians in India*, in G. Shah (ed.), *Dalit Identity and Politics*, New Delhi: SAGE Publications.

Lukes, S. (2005), *Power: A Radical View*, Hampshire: Palgrave.

Madtha, W. (1994), *Dalit Theology: Voice of the Oppressed*, in J. Massy (ed.), *Indigenous People: Dalits*, New Delhi: ISPCK.

Malinowski, B. (1985), *Magic, Science and Religion*, London: Souvenir Press Ltd.

Manickam, S. (1992), *Mission Approaches to Caste*, in V. Devasahayam (ed.), *Dalits & Women*, Chennai: Gurukul.

Marak, K. C. and Jacob, P. S. (2000), *Conversion in A Pluralistic Context*, New Delhi: ISPCK.

Maroney, E. (2006), *Religious Syncretism*, London: SCM Press.

Massey, J. (1994), *Ingredients for a Dalit Theology*, in J. Massey (ed.), *Indigenous People: Dalits,* New Delhi: ISPCK.

— (ed.) (1995), *Dalit Solidarity*, Delhi: ISPCK.

— (1997a), *Down Trodden*, Geneva: WCC.

— (1997b), *History and Dalit Theology*, in V. Devasahayam (ed.), *Frontiers of Dalit Theology*, Delhi: ISPCK/Gurukul.

Massey, J. and Fernando, L. (eds) (2007), *Dalit World-Biblical World: An Encounter*, New Delhi: Centre for Dalit/Subaltern Studies.

Massey, J. and Lourdunathan, S. (eds) (2006), *Breaking Theoretical Grounds for Dalit Studies*, New Delhi: Centre for Dalit/Subaltern Studies.

Massey, J. and Prabhakar, S. (eds) (2005), *Frontiers in Dalit Hermeneutics*, New Delhi: Centre for Dalit/Subaltern Studies.

Massey, J. and Shimray, S. (eds) (2007), *Dalit-Tribal Theological Interface: Current Trends in Subaltern Theologies*, New Delhi: TSC/WSC.

Mayo, M. (2000), *Cultures, Communities, Identities*, New York: Palgrave.

Mendelsohn, O. and Vicziany, M. (1998), *The Untouchables: Subordination, Poverty and the State in Modern India*, Cambridge: Cambridge University Press.

Meyer, B. (1994), *Beyond Syncretism: Translation and Diabolization in the Appropriation of Protestantism in Africa*, in C. Stewart and R. Shaw (eds), *Syncretism/Anti-Syncretism: The Politics of Religious Synthesis*, London: Routledge.

Michael, S. M. (ed.) (1999), *Dalits in Modern India*, New Delhi: Vistaar Publications.

Milner, M. (1994), *Status and Sacredness: A general Theory of Status Relations and An Analysis of Indian Culture*, New York: Oxford University Press.

Mines, D. P. (2005), *Fierce Gods*, Indianapolis, IN: Indiana University Press.

Mines, M. (1999), *Heterodox Lives: Agonistic Individuality and Agency in South Indian History*, in R. Guha (ed.), *Institutions and Inequalities*, New Delhi: Oxford Press.

Mizushima, T. (1997), *The Untouchables and Economic Change in a Dry Village in South India*, in H. Kotani (ed.), *Caste System, Untouchability and the Depressed*, Delhi: Manohar.

Moffatt, M. (1979), *An Untouchable Community in South India: Structure and Consensus*, New Jersey: Princeton University Press.

Mohanty, J. N. (2000), *Classical Indian Philosophy*, Oxford: Rowman & Littlefield Publishers Inc.

Monikaraj, D. (1997), *Mission, Evangelism, and Conversion*, in V. Devasahayam (ed.), *Frontiers of Dalit Theology*, Delhi: ISPCK/Gurukul.

Moore, H. L. (ed.) (2006), *Anthropology in Theory: Issues in Epistemology*, Oxford: Blackwell.

Moraes, G. M. (1964), *A History of Christianity in India*, Bombay: Manaktalas.

Morgan, D. (2005), *The Sacred Gaze*, London: University of California Press.

Mosse, D. (1994), *The Politics of Religious Synthesis: Roman Catholicism and Hindu Village Society in Tamil Nadu, India*, in C. Stewart and R. Shaw (eds), *Syncretism/Anti-Syncretism: The Politics of Religious Synthesis*, London: Routledge.

Muthu, K. S. (2005), *Dalit Deities*, Madurai: the Dalit Resource Centre.

Nagaraj, D. R. (1993), *Flaming Feet*, Bangalore: South Forum Press.

Nath, R. (1993), *Why I Am Not a Hindu*, Patna: Bihar Rationalist Society.

Naugle, D. K. (2002), *Worldview: The History of A Concept*, Cambridge: William B. Eerdmans Publishing Company.

Neill, S. (1985), *A History of Christianity in India*, Cambridge: Cambridge University Press.

Newlands, G. (2006), *Christ and Human Rights*, Hampshire: ASHGATE.

Nirmal, A. P. (1991), *Heuristic Explorations*, Madras: CLS.

— (1994), *Towards a Christian Dalit Theology*, in R. S. Sugirtharajah (ed.), *Frontiers in Asian Christian Theology*, New York: Orbis Books.

O'Hanlon, R. (1985), *Caste, Conflict, and Ideology*, Cambridge: Cambridge University Press.

Okri, B. (2003), *The Famished Road*, London: Vintage.

Oommen, G. (2002), *Pulaya Christians of Kerala: A Community in Dilemma*, in G. Oommen and J. C. Webster (eds), *Local Dalit Christian History*, Delhi: ISPCK.

Osella, F. (ed.) (2000), *Social Mobility in Kerala: Modernity and Identity in Conflict*, London: Pluto Press.

Pais, R. (1999), *Scheduled Castes, Employment and Social Mobility*, in S. M. Michael (ed.), *Dalits in Modern India*, New Delhi: Vistaar Publications.

Parish, S. M. (1994), *Moral Knowing in a Hindu Sacred City*, New York: Columbia University Press.

— (1996), *Hierarchy and its Discontents*, Philadelphia: University of Pennsylvania Press.

Parsons, T. (1986), *Power and the Social System*, in S. Lukes (ed.), *Power*, New York: New York University Press.

Paswan, S. (ed.) (2002), *Encyclopaedia of Dalits in India; General Study*, vol. I, Delhi: Kalpaz Publications.

Patterson, S. J. (1998), *The God of Jesus*, Pennsylvania: Trinity Press International.

Percy, M. (1998), *Power and the Church*, London: Cassell.

Pillai-Vetschera, T. (1999), *Ambedkar's Daughters: A Study of Mahar Women Ahmednagar District of Maharastra*, in S. M. Michael (ed.), *Dalits in Modern India*, New Delhi: Vistaar Publications.

Poggi, G. (2001), *Forms of Power*, Cambridge: Polity.

Powell, M. A. (1998), *Jesus as a Figure in History*, Kentucky: John Knox Press.

Prabhakar, M. E. (1991), *The Search for a Dalit Theology*, in A. P. Nirmal (ed.), *Reader in Dalit Theology*, Madras: Gurukul.

— (1992), *Missions in a Dalit Perspective*, in V. Devasahayam (ed.), *Dalits and Women*, Chennai: Gurukul.

— (1994), *The Search for a Dalit Theology*, in J. Massey (ed.), *Indigenous People: Dalits*, New Delhi: ISPCK.

— (1997), *Christology in Dalit Perspective*, in V. Devasahayam (ed.), *Frontiers of Dalit Theology*, Delhi: ISPCK/Gurukul.

Priest, S. (1998), *Merleau-Ponty*, London: Routledge.

Pyysiainen, I. (2003), *How Religion Works: Towards a New Cognitive Science of Religion*, Boston, MA: Brill.

Raj Kumar, P. (2010), *Dalit Theology and Dalit Liberation: Problems, Paradigms and Possibilities*, Surrey: Ashgate.

Ramaiah, A. (1994), *The Dalit Issue: A Hindu Perspective*, in J. Massey (ed.), *Indigenous People: Dalits*, Delhi: ISPCK.

Ram-Prasad, C. (2001), *Knowledge and Liberation in Classical Indian Thought*, New York: Palgrave.

— (2002), *Advaita Epistemology and Metaphysics*, London: Routledge Curzon.

Rao, N. S. (2001), *The Structure of South Indian Untouchable Castes: A View*, in G. Shah (ed.), *Dalit Identity and Politics*, New Delhi: SAGE Publications.

Robinson, R. (2001), *Negotiating Boundaries and Identities: Christian 'Communities' in India*, in S. S. Jodhka (ed.), *Community and Identities*, New Delhi: SAGE Publications.

— (2003), *Sixteenth Century Conversions to Christianity in Goa*, in R. Robinson and S. Clarke (eds), *Religious Conversions in India*, New Delhi: Oxford University Press.

Robinson, R. and Clarke, S. (eds) (2003), *Religious Conversion in India: Modes, Motivations and Meanings*, edited by, New Delhi: Oxford University Press.

Robinson, R. and Kujur, J. M. (eds) (2010), *Margins of Faith: Dalit and Tribal Christianity in India*, New Delhi: SAGE Publications.

Rose, G. (1992), *The Broken Middle*, Oxford: Blackwell.

— (1995), *Love's Work: A Reckoning with Life*, New York: Schocken Books.

Rowland, C. (eds) (1989), *Liberating Exegesis: The Challenge of Liberation Theology to Biblical Studies*, Louisville, KY: Westminster/John Knox.

Russell, B. (2004), *Power*, London: Routledge.

Rutherford, J. (1990), *A Place Called Home: Identity and the Cultural Politics of Difference*, in J. Rutherford (ed.), *Identity: Community, Culture and Difference*, London: Lawrence & Wishart.

Schlee, G. (ed.) (2002), *Imagined Differences: Hatred and the Construction of Identity*, New York: Palgrave.

Schurer, E. (eds) (1979), *The History of the Jewish People in the Age of Jesus Christ*, Edinburgh: T&T Clark.

Shanks, A. (2008), *Against Innocence: Gillian Rose's Reception and Gift of Faith*, London: SCM Press.

Sharma, A. (2000), *Sankara's Life and Works as a Source for a Hermeneutics of Human Rights*, in B. J. Malkovsky (ed.), *New Perspectives on Advaita Vedanta*, Leiden: Brill.

Sharma, U. (1999), *Caste*, Buckingham: Open University Press.

Shiri, G. (1992), *Plight of Dalit Christians in Karnataka*, in V. Devasahayam (ed.), *Dalits & Women*, Chennai: Gurukul.

Shoat, E. (2000), *Notes on the Post-Colonial*, in F. Afzal-Khan, and K. Seshadri-Crooks (eds), *The Pre-Occupation of Postcolonial Studies*, London: Duke University Press.

Shriram, S. (1999), *The Fourfold Hierarchy*, in S. M. Michael (ed.), *Dalits in Modern India*, New Delhi: Vistaar Publications.

Silva, N. (2002), *The Hybrid Island*, London: Zed Books.

Singh, D. E. and Farr, B. C. (eds) (2008), *Christianity and Cultures: Shaping Christian Thinking in Context*, Eugene: Wipf & Stock.

Smart, N. (1983), *Worldviews: Crosscultural Explorations of Human Beliefs*, New York: Charles Scribner's Sons.

Sperber, D. (1995), *Rethinking Symbolism*, Cambridge: Cambridge University Press.

Srinivas, M. N. (1966), *Social Change in Modern India*, Madras: Allied Publishers.

Stewart, C. and Shaw, R. (eds) (1994), *Syncretism/Anti-Syncretism*, London: Routledge.

Sugirtharajah, R. S. (2003), *Postcolonial Reconfigurations*, London: SCM Press.

—(2005), *The Bible and Empire: Postcolonial Theory and Practice*, Cambridge: Cambridge University Press London.

—(ed.) (2006), *Voices from the Margin*, Maryknoll: Orbis Books.

Sykes, S. (2006), *Power and Christian Theology*, London: Continuum.

Thorat, S. (2009), *Dalits in India*, New Delhi: SAGE Publications.

Thorat, S. K. and Deshpande, R. S. (2001), *Caste System and Economic Inequality: Economic Theory and Evidence*, in G. Shah (ed.), *Dalit Identity and Politics*, New Delhi: SAGE Publications.

Thumma, A. (2000), *Dalit Liberation Theology*, Delhi: ISPCK.

—(2002), *Wisdom of the Weak*, Delhi: ISPCK.

Tillich, P. (1963), *Systematic Theology*, vol. II, Chicago, IL: University of Chicago Press.

Turner, V. (1969), *The Ritual Process: Structure and Anti Structure*, Ithaca, NY: Cornell University Press.

—(1978), *Dramas, Fields and Metaphors*, London: Cornell University Press.

Upadhya, C. (2001), *The Concept of Community in Indian Social Sciences: An Anthropological Perspective*, in S. S. Jodhka (ed.), *Community and Identities*, New Delhi: SAGE Publications.

Walcott, H. F. (2001), *Writing up Qualitative Research*, Thousand Oaks, CA: SAGE Publications.

Webster, J. (2005), *Prolegomena to Christology: Four Theses*, in S. R. Holmes and M. A. Rae (eds), *The Person of Christ*, London: T&T Clark International.

Webster, J. C. B. (1992),*The Dalit Christians: A History*, Delhi: ISPCK.

—(2002), *Religion and Dalit Liberation*, New Delhi: Manohar.

Weedon, C. (2004), *Identity and Culture*, Berkshire: Open University Press.

Weeks, J. (1990), *The Value of Difference*, in J. Rutherford (ed.), *Identity: Community, Culture and Difference*, London: Lawrence & Wishart.

Wilfred, F. (2005), *The Sling of Utopia*, Delhi: ISPCK.

William, K. (1994), *Dalit Theology: Voice of the Oppressed*, in J. Massey (ed.), *Indigenous People: Dalits*, New Delhi: ISPCK.

Williams, R. (2007), *Wrestling with Angels: Conversations in Modern Theology*, London: SCM Press.

Wilson, B. (1988), *Religion in Sociological Perspective*, Oxford: Oxford University Press.

Wilson, K. (1991), *Towards a Humane Culture*, in A. P. Nirmal (ed.), *A Reader in Dalit Theology*, Madras: Gurukul.

— (1994), *A Dalit Theology of Human Self-Development*, in J. Massy (ed.), *Indigenous People: Dalits*, New Delhi: ISPCK.

Witherington III, B. (1995), *The Jesus Quest*, Illinois: Inter Varsity Press.

Woodward, K. (ed.) (1997), *Identity and Difference*, London: SAGE Publications.

Yandell, K. E. and Paul, J. J. (eds) (2000), *Religion and Public Culture*, Surrey: Curzon Press.

Yel, A. M. (2006), *Appropriation of Sacredness at Fatima in Portugal*, in E. Arweck and W. J. F. Keenan (eds), *Materializing Religion: Expression, Performance and Ritual*, Aldershot: Ashgate.

Young, R. J. C. (1995), *Colonial Desire: Hybridity in Theory, Culture and Race*, London: Routledge, p. 20ff.

Journal articles

Ayres, L. (1995), 'Representation, Theology and Faith', *Modern Theology*, 11(1): 23–46.

Balachandran, A. (2000), 'Catholics in Protest: Lower-Caste Christianity in Early Colonial Madras', *Studies in History*, 16(2): 241–53.

Chatterji, S. K. (1989), 'Indigenous Christianity and Counter-Culture', *Religion and Society*, 36(4): 3–17.

Daniel, A. (1995), 'Approaches of Mission and Church Towards the Indian Caste System', *Religion and Society*, 42(2): 5–12.

Daube, D. (1950), 'Jesus and the Samaritan Woman', *Journal of Biblical Literature*, 69: 137–47.

Fernandes, L. (2011), 'Unsettled Territories: State, Civil Society, and the Politics of Religious Conversion in India', *Politics and Religion*, 4(1): 108–35.

Goh, D. (2009), 'Chinese Religion and the Challenge of Modernity in Malaysia and Singapore: Syncretism, Hybridisation and Transfiguration', *Asian Journal of Social Science*, 37: 107–37.

Jeremiah, A. (2005), 'Reclaiming 'Her' Right: Re-reading the Story of Tamar (Genesis 38:1–27) from Dalit Women Perspective', *Bangalore Theological Forum*, October, 183–98.

— (2007a), 'K.P. Aleaz and 'Inculturation': A Subaltern Critique of Indian Christian Vedanta', *Asia Theological Journal*, 21(2): 398–411.

— (2007b), 'Privatization of Water - A Theological Critique and Ensuing Challenges for the Church', *Reformed World*, 57(1): 3–16.

— (2011), 'Dalit Christians in India: Reflections from the Broken Middle', *Studies in World Christianity*, 17(part. 3): 258–74.

Kenzo, M. J.-R. (2004), 'Religion, Hybridity, and the Construction of Reality in Postcolonial Africa', *Exchange*, Brill Academic Publishers, 33(3): 244–68.

Kitiarsa, P. (2005), 'Beyond Syncretism: Hybridization of Popular Religion in Contemporary Thailand', *Journal of Southeast Asian Studies*, 36(3):461–87.

Kurian, S. G. (1995), 'Struggle for Survival-Experience of Christian Dalits in Kerala', *Religion and Society*, 42(2): 11–24.

— (1998), 'Kerala: the Christian Dalits Experience: A Case Study of the Palais Diocese', *Religion and Society*, 45(4): 69–80.

Lloyd, V. (2007), 'On the Use of Gillian Rose', *Heythrop Journal*, 48(5): 697–706.

Maliekal, J. D. (2001), 'Identity-Consciousness of the Christian Madigas Story of a People in Emergence', *Jeevadhara*, 31(181): 25–36.

Massey, J. (1990), 'Christian Dalits in India: An Analysis', *Religion and Society*, 37(3): 40–53.

Mosse, D. (1994), 'Idioms of Subordination and Styles of Protest among Christian and Hindu Harijan Castes in Tamil Nadu', *Contributions to Indian Sociology*, 28(1): 67–106.

Narayanan, K. R. (2000), 'The President Speaks', *National Council of Churches Review*, 243–55.

Oommen, G. (2002), 'Dalits' Socio-Religious Aspirations and Christianity', *Religion and Society*, 140–51).

Prabhakar, M. E. (1981), 'Caste-Class and Status in Andhra Churches and Implications for Mission Today: Some Reflections', *Religion and Society*, 28(3): 9–35.

Shiri, G. (1993), 'In Search of Roots: Christian Dalits in Karnataka and their Struggle for the Liberation', *Religion and Society*, 40(4): 28–35.

Still, C. (2009), 'Caste, Identity and Gender among Madigas in Coastal Andhra Pradesh', *Journal of South Asian Development*, 4(1): 7–23.

The Catholic News Review. (1992), *The Examiner*, Editorial, New Delhi, 143/3, 18 January 1992.

Vincentnathan, L. (1993), 'Untouchable Concepts of Person and Society', *Contributions to Indian Sociology*, 27: 53–82.

Webster, J. C. B. (2004), 'Exploring the 'Pastoral Theology' Dimensions of Dalit Liberation', *Religion and Society*, 49(2–3): 49–74.

Williams, R. (1995), 'Between Politics and Metaphysics: Reflections in the Wake of Gillian Rose', *Modern Theology*, 11(1): 3–22.
Yengoyan, A. A. (2009), 'Clifford Geertz, Cultural Portraits, and Southeast Asia', *The Journal of Asian Studies*, 68(4): 1215–30.

Other resources

Andrews, A. (1993), *The Problem of Caste in the Church: A Challenge to the Praxis of Theology of Liberation with Special Reference to the Church in Tamil Nadu*, Unpublished M.Th thesis, Edinburgh University.
Clarke, S. 'Paraiyars Ellaiyamman as an Iconic Symbol of Collective Resistance and Emancipatory Mythography', *Religion Online*, http://www.religion-online.org.
CMS Pamphlet. *Travancore: Then and Now*, The Center for the Study of World Christianity archives, New College, University of Edinburgh.
The Laws of Manu. (1886), translated by George Buhler, Oxford: Clarendon Press.
Narula, S. (1999), *Broken People*, New York: Human Rights Watch (Organization).

Index